John O´Connor

An Essay on the Rosary and Sodality of the most holy Name of Jesus

John O'Connor

An Essay on the Rosary and Sodality of the most holy Name of Jesus

ISBN/EAN: 9783742826664

Manufactured in Europe, USA, Canada, Australia, Japa

Cover: Foto ©Lupo / pixelio.de

Manufactured and distributed by brebook publishing software (www.brebook.com)

John O´Connor

An Essay on the Rosary and Sodality of the most holy Name of Jesus

AN ESSAY ON THE ROSARY AND SODALITY

Of the Most Holy NAME of

JESUS.

WHEREIN

The profound Respect due to this Adorable Name is ascertained: the execrable Vices of Blasphemy, Cursing, and profane Swearing, are inveighed against; and efficacious Remedies are prescribed.

TOGETHER WITH

An Account of the Rise and Progress of the said ROSARY and SODALITY: their Excellency, Privileges, Indulgences, &c.

To which are subjoined,

The ROSARIES of the NAME of *JESUS* and of the Blessed VIRGIN: with their respective Mysteries, Meditations and Collects, *correctly* set forth.

By the Rev. J——N O C——NN——R,

O. P. P. G. P. A.

These are written, that you may believe, that JESUS is the CHRIST *the Son of* GOD; *and that believing you may have Life in his Name.* John xx. 31.

═══════════════════

DUBLIN:

Printed for the AUTHOR, and sold at Mr. *Richard Cross*'s, Bookseller, *Bridge-street*, and at Mr. *James Fitzsimons*'s, *Clapel-Alley, Bridge-street*. M DCC LXXII.

PERMISSU SUPERIORUM.

TO

The R. R. Dr. *B——rke*.

My L——d,

BY inscribing to your L——p the following Sheets, I mean not to enumerate your Merits, to celebrate your Praises, or to harangue you with pompous Pages, the ordinary Subject of Dedications: It would not only exceed the Bounds I intend prescribing to myself, but appear unnecessary, as that profound and extensive Knowledge displayed in the many excellent and useful Works, so deservedly esteemed

abroad

DEDICATION.

abroad as well as at home, of which you are the worthy Parent, clearly evinces. These Productions* proclaim a Fund of Erudition and Talents, not concealed *under a Bushel*, but shining forth, with great Lustre, for the Good of Mankind. And while we view this eminent Knowledge united to the admirable Character of a faithful and vigilant Pastor, enforcing Instruction by good Example, it must indeed be confessed they form the most exalted Character, deservedly canonized by God himself, in the subsequent Words: *He that shall Perform and Teach, he shall be great in the Kingdom of Heaven* †.

I might, with great Justice, expatiate upon these, and other interesting Particulars,

---

* *Promptuarium Dogmatico-Canonico-Morale.—Officia Propria Sanctorum Hiberniæ, &c.—Historical Collections out of several Protestant Historians, &c.* to which is affixed an Appendix, *Setting forth, the Abbies, Priories, and other Religious Houses dissolved in Ireland, &c.—Hibernia Dominicana.* This excellent and extensive Work is remarkable for restoring to Light, many important Informations relative to our Isle, heretofore almost unknown, and which otherwise would, in all Probability, have been shortly buried in Oblivion.

† Matth. v. 19.

DEDICATION.

lars, which so eminently characterize You, and which shall endear and immortalize your Name, did I not perceive your Humility and Piety forbidding me to speak your Praises, whilst the Merits and Glory of the most sacred Name of JESUS our GOD, are evidently the Subject of the following Sheets: For as this most august Name is infinitely superior to those of the most perfect Creatures, so the Tongue ought to be silent, the Pen lie still, but to celebrate the Dignity and Sanctity of that most adorable Name, which indisputably claims every Effort, however feeble, to promote its Honour and revive the Veneration so justly due to it.

I mean therefore, only to express briefly my grateful Thanks for your indulgent Perusal of this Work, (though actually engaged in preparing, no doubt, a most useful Work for the Press) and deigning to declare repeatedly your Approbation of it: as also for the many useful Hints you have been pleased to suggest. All which justly claim this public Acknowledgment with Thanksgiving, as well as the Tribute of a Dedication of this *Essay*, which is humbly
offered

DEDICATION.

offered to you, as a small Proof of my Respect and Gratitude.

That God may long preserve your Life, so Necessary to the Public Good, Honourable to your Country, and Ornamental to Us: so conducive to the Advancement of useful Knowledge and solid Piety, especially of the ONE thing necessary—The Love of God and the Glory of his most sacred Name—shall be the constant Prayer of,

My L——d,

Your L——p's

most Obliged

and

most Obedient

humble Servant,

J—n O C-nn-r.

THE CONTENTS.

Chap.		Pag.
I.	Of the Names of God.	1
II.	The Meaning and Excellency of the Name of *Jesus*.	8
III.	The Efficacy of the Name of *Jesus*.	14
IV.	We are bound to praise the Name of *Jesus*.	21
V.	Of Swearing.	29
VI.	The first Condition necessary to render an Oath lawful; viz. Judgment.	36
VII.	The second Condition necessary to render an Oath lawful; viz. Justice.	43
	Sect. 1. The Principles of Roman Catholics grossly misrepresented by their Adversaries.	46
	Sect. 2. Oaths of Monopoly, Combination, and such like, unlawful.	63
	Sect. 3. Oaths sworn by Roman Catholics to those of a different Persuasion, equally binding as if sworn to those of their own Communion.	67
VIII.	The third Condition necessary to render an Oath lawful; viz. Truth.	72
IX.	Of Imprecations.	82
X.	Of Blasphemy.	94
XI.	How heinous to Blaspheme, Curse, or profanely Swear.	105
XII.	Apologies, to excuse or extenuate the Crimes of Blasphemy, Cursing, or profane Swearing, frivolous.	118
XIII.	The Means to amend.	126
XIV.	The Origin of the Sodality inscribed to the most holy Name of *Jesus*.	134
XV.	The Progress of the Sodality in Spain, &c.	143

CONTENTS.

CHAP.		Pag.
XVI.	Of the Rosary of the Name of Jesus; its Excellency.	149
XVII.	Motives to engage us to enter into the sacred Sodality, and to recite frequently the Rosary of the Name of Jesus.	158
XVIII.	The Indulgences and Privileges granted to the Members of the Sodality of the most holy Name of Jesus.	167
	Plenary Indulgences belonging to the Sodality.	177
	Particular Indulgences belonging to the Sodality.	178
	Privileges granted to the Sodality.	180
XIX.	The Conditions of the sacred Sodality.	181
	The Rules of the sacred Sodality.	184
XX.	An Observance of the Rules of the sacred Sodality, and a daily Recital of the celebrated Devotion of the Rosary of the most holy Name of Jesus, how meritorious.	187

A Prayer recommended to be repeated before the Rosary of Jesus. 203
The Rosary of the most holy Name of Jesus. 205
The Litany of the most holy Name of Jesus. 216
The Psalm and Hymn, sung at the Procession, on the second Sunday of the Month, in Latin and English. 220
The Hymn, Pange Lingua, sung at the Benediction, in Latin and English. 222
The Rosary of the Blessed Virgin. 229
The Litany of the Blessed Virgin. 245
The Canticle Magnificat, sung at the Procession on the first Sunday of every Month, in Latin and English. 250
The Hymns, Antiphons and Collects, sung at Complin, in Latin and English. 252

THE PREFACE.

AT a Time, when the infinite Majesty of the great God is impiously attacked by his Creatures, and his most holy Name shamefully profaned by their vile *Oaths, Imprecations,* and *Blasphemies.* At a Time, when the profound Respect and Veneration so justly due to the all-sacred Name of God, appear banished the Hearts of the Faithful, and the detestable Vices of Blasphemy, Cursing or profane Swearing, are so universally substituted in their place. Nay, at a Time, when some Members of the Christian Republic are become so abandoned, as to form themselves into *Clubs* or *Societies**, for the more effectual Propagation of those hellish Vices: it becomes the indispensible Duty of every Christian, to use their utmost endeavours to stem the dangerous Torrent, and to try every Preservative to guard against the spreading Impiety.

As this Duty more immediately concerns Ecclesiastics, 'tis, no doubt, their Obligation, to use every lawful Effort to effect a Reformation, and stop the dreadful Contagion. A Desire of forwarding so laudable a Work, will, as the Author hopes, plead a sufficient Apology for his undertaking to compile the following Sheets; who, though unequal to the Task, yet, as if unmindful of his Inabilities, chearfully offers his *Mite*, from

---

* Instituted in the Year 1770, to be mentioned in the Sequel of this *Essay.*

from a Desire of co-operating with the Public Good, as well as of gratifying some pious Christians, who are of Opinion, that something of this Kind, might prove the Means of eradicating those Vices from some, and of promoting a greater Respect to the most venerable Name of the Lord, in others.

For these Reasons, the Author attempts to shew the profound Veneration and Love due to God's most sacred Name: as also, the Danger and Heinousness of those epidemic Vices, Blasphemy, Cursing and profane Swearing, so contrary to the Sanctity of his awful Name. As all Oaths are not forbidden, the Conditions necessary to render an Oath lawful, are set forth and explained. Lastly, for so dangerous and universal a Malady, Remedies are prescribed, especially a most powerful, yet mild Specific, *viz.* An Entrance into the *Sodality*, inscribed to the most holy Name of *Jesus*, together with a strict Observance of its Rules; and a frequent Recital of the *Rosary*, also sacred to the most holy Name of *Jesus*.

These, so holy in themselves, shall appear most acceptable to Heaven and advantageous to us: highly extolled by the Church, and strenuously recommended to the Faithful, not only as an efficacious *Remedy* for the *profane* Swearer, but as a sure *Preservative* for the *devout* Christian.

A Devotion of this Kind, could not fail to attract the Attention and Veneration of such Persons, as have their Salvation at Heart: many of whom have warmly expressed a Desire of knowing the Origin and Progress of the *Sodality* and *Rosary*, sacred to the most holy Name of *Jesus*, which, the Author, though destitute of such Helps as would facilitate the Performance, and enable him to do more Justice to the Cause, endeavours to gratify, in a *plain* and *concise* Manner, as his Intention

PREFACE.

tion is not to tread the flowery Paths of Rhetoric, but to inculcate folid Truths, and promote as far as his weak Abilities will permit, a true, folid, and lafting Devotion to the moft holy Name of *Jefus*: Becaufe it is *a Name which is above every Name* †: *Neither is there any other Name under Heaven given to Men, whereby we muft be faved* ‡.

This *Effay*, though calculated for fo glorious an End, like every other Production of the Kind, muft expect to meet its Enemies, and undergo fuch Criticifms §, as perhaps Impiety or Ignorance may fuggeft: Some by barefacedly inveighing againft all fuch Works of Piety, with their baneful Tongues, which even the moft facred Truths of Religion do not efcape. Whilft others, a little more modeft, endeavour, by *Innuendo's*, and fuch like *conclufive* Arguments, to bring them into difrepute and difufe.

But, Chriftian Reader, do not permit yourfelf to be toffed to and fro, by every Wind of Doctrine: for all and every Chriftian, whether Learned or Ignorant, whether Rich or Poor, whether Noble or Ignoble, whether Young or Old, are indifpenfibly bound to decline the damnable Practice of Curfing, Swearing and Blafpheming; and are equally obligated to praife the Name of the Lord. How far the celebrated *Rofary* and *Sodality* will contribute to forward the important Work, fhall appear in the Sequel of this *Effay*.

The

† Philip. ii. 9.   ‡ Acts iv. 12.

§ *Pope*, in his Effay on Criticifm, fpecifies thofe who may affume the Office of a Critic, in the following Lines:
 " Let fuch teach others who themfelves excel,
 " And cenfure freely who have written well."

The Author only says, in his own Behalf, that he would not attempt to commit his Endeavours to the Press, without being first fully approved: and, as it is the first of the Kind published in any Language, as far as the Author can learn, (except by way of a brief Appendix confined to a single Sheet) he humbly hopes for the kind Indulgence of his Readers.

In short, the Importance of the Subject calls for the Perusal of this small Work: not its *Merits*. Receive it then, Christian Reader, such as it is; and if fortunately it shall prove the happy Means of banishing the execrable Vices of Blasphemy, Cursing, and profane Swearing from your Mouths; and of conveying a lasting Love and Veneration for the most amiable and august Name of *Jesus* to your Hearts; were the Author's Labours abundantly more, he shall think them infinitely compensated by so desirable a Change, and his Wishes fully gratified.

Our Help is in the Name of the Lord, who made Heaven and Earth. Psalm cxxiii. 8.

AN ESSAY ON THE ROSARY AND SODALITY.

CHAP. I.

Of the Names of GOD.

AS the great Creator and Lord of Heaven and Earth, Almighty God, is, in himself, a Being infinitely pure and perfect: He cannot be conceived by our weak minds as he really is, neither can we give him a Name expressive of his infinite Perfections, or adequate to his great and glorious Being *. Yet this great Being is, and has been known, served, and adored under sundry Names, as *Emanuel* (God with us); *Adonai* (Lord); the *Wonderful One*; the *Prince of Peace*, &c. The Names, however, that more properly denote the *Divine Nature*, says the Angelic Doctor St. *Thomas*, are first, the Name GOD †, as it conveys to our minds an idea of "a Being that is universally provident; for the "Deity is that Being, who sees all things with "a perfect Providence and Goodness:" so that the

* S. Tho. 1. p. q 13. a. 1.   † Ibid. a. 8.

the Name GOD signifies a Being infinitely good and provident, superior to all other Beings, and their first Cause. "This is what all men understand by the Name GOD*." The other Name is that which God gave to Himself, when thus asked by *Moses* (who was sent by the Lord to speak to the Children of *Israel*): *If they shall say to me*, says Moses, *what is his Name? what shall I say to them?* God said to Moses, *thus shalt thou say to the Children of Israel:* HE WHO IS *hath sent me to you* †. This Name of God, HE WHO IS, "is the most proper Name of God ‡," says the Angel of Schools, St. *Thomas*; as it signifies an unbounded and fathomless Ocean of Perfections. It speaks a Being self-existent and eternal, that knows not Beginning or End, and whose inexpressible Perfections are rather to be admired and adored, than expressed. In short, the Name HE WHO IS, denotes a Supreme Being, infinitely Great in every degree of Perfection, and the Source of every other Being.

This incomprehensible Being, GOD, or HE WHO IS, has also been revered under several other Names, as the Effects of his Power, Justice, Love, and other Attributes, have been experienced by His people. At one time, He is stiled the *strong God*, when fighting the battles and conquering the enemies of His chosen people. At another, He is called the *just God*, when punishing the wicked, or rewarding the righteous; and is frequently named the *patient God*, the *merciful God*, &c. from a wonderful forbearance, in not inflicting an immediate and exemplary punishment on sinners. These, and every other Name

---

* S. Tho. 1. p. q. 13. a. 8. ad 3. † Exod. iii.
‡ Ibid. a. 11.

Name, under which the Deity has been known, revered, and worshipped, tend to one and the same end: either to acknowledge Almighty God to be infinitely perfect and independent in Himself, or to confess him to be the First Cause and inexhaustible Source of every Blessing, whether spiritual or temporal, with regard to his creatures.

Among the various blessings conferred on mankind by Almighty God, the promise of sending the *Messiah* [*], to redeem the world, deservedly obtains the first place. Our first parent had scarcely transgressed, and entailed the guilt of original sin on his descendants, when the Lord resolved to send his only Son to cleanse *Adam*'s infected posterity; to satisfy for our sins, and cancel the hand-writing that stood against us. Hence, when the fulness of time approached; when the measure of the earth's iniquity had been filled up; when the critical moment arrived, which was to determine the fate of mankind; it was then, God's infinite mercy and truth moved him to fulfil his promise: and accordingly resolves to send the *Messiah, the long desired of Nations*, who, by the infinite Dignity of his Person, should superabundantly satisfy for the sins of the whole world.

This *Messiah* is no less than the second Person of the most adorable Trinity, and only begotten Son of the living God! It is he that chearfully accepts of the important commission, and resolves to assume human nature, that he might be susceptible of sufferings, and death itself for our sakes. He is to be born into the world, and *Mary*, a Virgin, whose humility and purity excelled that of Angels, is chosen to be

Mother

[*] Gen. ii.

Mother of the Man GOD; and accordingly, Gabriel the Archangel is dispatched from the Court of Heaven to her, with the glad tidings, that *by the overshadowing of the Holy Ghost, she should conceive and bring forth the Son of the Most High**. The humble Virgin, truly sensible of this extraordinary mark of the Divine favour, ascribes it to the goodness of his holy *Name: because He that is the mighty*; says she, *hath done great things to me and Holy is his Name*†.

Mary being thus appointed to bring forth the Redeemer of the World, continued in the practice of every Virtue; and at the expiration of the ninth month after the Annunciation, She brought forth the Saviour of Mankind in a Stable, at *Bethlehem*; where the Son of the eternal GOD, made Man, appears in a poor and abject state, trembling with cold, and abandoned by the ungrateful World He came to redeem. What a reception for the Infant, GOD! Or rather, what an amazing Condescension in him, whose Majesty the vast expanse of the Universe cannot contain; that He shall shiver with cold, and scarcely find a place wherein to recline his sacred Head! Yet so it was, that the Redeemer of the world, at his first appearance, was willing, by his example, to extinguish early in us, the fire of worldly vanity, to kindle in our hearts that of divine love. Notwithstanding his Humiliation upon earth, his Birth is celebrated by the whole Court of Heaven, amidst the greatest acclamations of Joy. Angels are dispatched from the throne of God, to announce his Nativity to the world; whilst the celestial Choristers most harmoniously sing, *Glory be to God on high*, and loudly proclaim the blessings of

---

* Luke i. 35.   † Ibid. 49.

of *Peace upon earth to men of good will.* The earth also joins in the general jubilee; the shepherds quit their flocks, to acknowledge the supreme Pastor of souls, *Jesus Christ*; and shortly after, the *Eastern* Kings, led by a star, hasten to adore the Divine Infant: by their homage and gifts they acknowledge his supreme Majesty, and confess him to be the anointed Saviour of the world.

As *Abraham* had received from the Lord *, at one time, his *Name*, and the *Law of Circumcision*, it became customary with the *Jews* to receive their Names at the time of Circumcision, " as " children do now at Baptism †:" the divine Infant conforms to the general custom, warranted by God's law, and resolves his adorable Name shall be proclaimed the eighth day after his birth; nay, though entirely free from the least tincture of sin, he subjects himself to Circumcision, as if he had been a sinner. The angelic Doctor assigns various reasons, why Christ permitted himself to be circumcised ‡: it was (says he) to confound the perfidy of future heretics, who would deny him to be true Man; as *Manicheus*, who impiously asserted the body of Christ to be only phantastic or imaginary: *Appolinarius*, who sustained the body of Christ was consubstantial with the Divinity; and *Valentinus* who said, that Christ descended from Heaven incarnate, or with a body, and did not assume it from a Virgin. All which he confuted by his Circumcision; whereby he manifestly shewed himself the son of *Abraham*, and effectually proved the verity of his human nature. Secondly, as the law of Circumcision

B 5 was

* Gen. xvii.
† S. Tho. 3. p. q. 37. art. 2. ad 3.   ‡ Ib. art. 1.

was in force at his coming, he shewed his humility and obedience in submitting to it: and also that by bearing the yoke of the law himself, we should, in future, be exempt from it. The Divine Infant, therefore, only waits till he receives his adorable Name, to give us an early sample of his unspeakable clemency. Oh Heavens! what Name shall be given to the Divine Infant, to the Son of the living God made man! shall his Name be called *Emanuel?* or shall he be called *Wonderful, Counsellor, God,* the *Mighty,* the *Father of the World to come,* the *Prince of Peace* *? No, but he shall be called by one Name, " which shall comprise or signify all those foretold by the Prophets †." A Name which has been from eternity appointed by his Almighty Father, it was announced to his Virgin Mother, by *Gabriel* the Archangel; and on the Day of his Circumcision it was proclaimed by the High Priest to the sons of *Adam,* to the inexpressible Joy of all Heaven and Earth: *His Name is called Jesus* §; *because he shall save his people from their sins* ‖. Oh adorable and most merciful Name! which implies nothing less than that our God is become our Redeemer, Mediator, and Saviour!

His sacred Name was scarcely proclaimed in the Temple, when he shewed himself sensible of our miseries, and ardently desires to begin the great work of our Redemption: though an Infant but eight days old, he gives an astonishing proof of his love. He who could have commanded legions of Angels to attend and adore him, submits to the law of Circumcision, nor does he wait for corporeal strength to bear the pain-

---

* Isaiah vii. ix.   † S. Tho. 3. p. q. 37. a. 2. ad 1.
§ Luke ii. 21.   ‖ Matth. i. 21.

painful operation; for he is no sooner called *Jesus*, than he resolves his precious blood shall begin to flow to expiate the sins of the world. Thus, when the eternal God resolved to extend his Mercies to the whole earth; when he determined to deliver mankind from the slavery of the Devil, under which it groaned for some thousands of years; when, in fine, he resolved to make us his adopted children, and heirs of Heaven; it was then he sent his only begotten Son, *Jesus*, upon earth; the Almighty Father resolving thereby to give the most signal and unheard-of proofs of his Mercy to us, by the ministry of his only begotten Son!

Admire, O Christian soul, the infinite Goodness of the Divine Infant! who though but eight days old, chearfully exposed his tender body to the circumcising knife; and shed his precious blood in drops, as an earnest of those streams, which afterwards so plentifully flowed on Mount *Calvary*, to expiate our sins, to reconcile us to his once displeased Father, to make us his adopted brethren, and heirs of his blessed kingdom. What inexpressible blessings have we not received; what may we not, in future, hope to enjoy, through the goodness of his all-gracious Name!

Yes, Christian reader, such are our unspeakable obligations to his adorable Name, that we can only silently admire the multitude of his tender mercies, and humbly confess, that we have reason abundantly to rejoice in the Salvation which he has so plentifully brought to us, in virtue of his all-saving Name; as was clearly foretold by the Royal Prophet, in the subsequent words: *We will (O Lord) rejoice in thy Salvation, and in the Name of our God shall we be exalted* [*].

ed *. Or rather more expresly in the words of the Prophet *Habacuc*, who, contemplating the future blessings mankind should enjoy, through the means of the most sacred Name *Jesus*, thus, in transports of joy, expresses himself: *I will rejoice in the Lord, and I will exult in God my Jesus* †.

CHAP. II.

The Meaning and Excellency of the Name of JESUS.

THE Name *Jesus*, when considered in a confined sense, signifies, a Deliverer or Saviour from any Evil or impending Danger; or from having obtained any *particular* or *temporary* safety for the people. Thus the son of *Nun*, who succeeded *Moses*, was called *Josue* or *Jesus*, because he led the *Israelites*, delivered by *Moses* from *Egyptian* bondage, into the Land of Promise. The son of *Josedech* the Priest, and the son of *Sirach*, bore also the same name, and were types of *Christ* our Saviour ‡.

But the Name *Jesus*, in its most enlarged sense, is *new*, and peculiar alone to the Son of the living God made man; because *Jesus* alone has brought to us a *spiritual* and *universal Salvation* §. The Name *Christ* is frequently added to that of *Jesus*, which declares him to be the *anointed* Saviour of mankind. Yes, Christian soul, it is *Jesus Christ* that has truly brought to us a spiritual and universal Salvation, by freeing us from the heaviest of all bondages, sin; and from the most formidable of all enemies, the devil. When wandering

---

* Psal. xix. 6. † Habac. iii. 18.
‡ Graveson de myst. & annis Christi, Dissert.
§ S. Tho. 3. p. q. 37. art. 2.

ing in the shadows of darkness, he called us into his admirable light; and when sinking into the jaws of perdition, he raised and gave us a title to the inheritance of his blessed kingdom. He strengthened our weakness by his power; and vanquished every enemy here, that could obstruct our entrance into the heavenly *Canaan* hereafter. It was this *Jesus*, that washed away the stain and guilt of sin, with his blood: He released us from the punishment due to it, by becoming our sacrifice, and suffering in our stead. The anger of God he appeased, and reconciled us to his once offended Father: the power of sin he has subdued by his grace: by the doctrines of his Gospel, he enlightens; and by the assistance of his Spirit, strengthens our minds. In short, he has used all wise methods *to save us from our sins*, and all in virtue of his adorable Name: * *but you are washed, but you are sanctified, but you are justified in the Name of our Lord Jesus Christ*. So, that the Name of *Jesus* imports, that the second Person of the most Holy Trinity and Son of the eternal God, has deigned to descend from Heaven, to assume our mortality, to suffer in our stead; thereby to become our Mediator, our Saviour, and effectually bring a spiritual and universal Salvation to mankind.

How justly then, does the Prince of Apostles, St. *Peter*, proclaim aloud, that there is no *other Name under Heaven given to men whereby we must be saved* †. And how highly does St. *Paul* admire its wonderful sanctity, when he affirms, ‡ *that no one can say Lord Jesus, but in the Holy Ghost*. No one can worthily pronounce that all-sacred Name

* 1 Cor. vi. 11. † Acts iv. 12.
‡ 1 Cor. xii. 3.

Name, unless with an heart cleansed from sin, and lips sanctified by the Divine Spirit. And does not the same Apostle of Nations as clearly assert its superior excellency, in the following words? * *Christ humbled himself becoming obedient to death, even to the death of the cross; for which cause, God also exalted him, and hath given him a Name which is above every Name: that in the Name of JESUS every knee should bend, of those who are in Heaven, on Earth, or in Hell. And every tongue should confess, that the Lord Jesus Christ is in the Glory of God the Father.* That every tongue should confess our Lord *Jesus* to be now, and to have been always in the glory of his Father, equal to him in substance and in all perfections. The blessed Angels of Paradise, who attend at the Throne of God, and see him face to face, most humbly prostrate and adore his august Name; the Saints also most gratefully concelebrate its praises with the other heavenly Hosts; whereby they have obtained admittance into the kingdom of God, and gloriously fill the vacated mansions of the apostate Angels. The Earth is called upon, by the Apostle, to adore the all-saving Name of *Jesus*; for when its inhabitants were drowned in impiety, and objects of God's wrath, *Jesus* came to relieve and save them. Nay, Hell itself is not exempt, but must revere the Name of the Lord, with fear and trembling: its accursed inhabitants must bend the knee to acknowledge *Jesus Christ* to be supreme Lord and Monarch of the universe, whom they impiously blasphemed whilst upon earth.

It may not be improper to remark here, that from *Christ*'s having brought to us a plentiful Redemption, in virtue of his adorable Name,

some

* Philip. ii.

some weak minds would fain conclude from thence, that they need not attend to the work of Salvation; it being, say they, already effected by the Son of God; and so yield themselves over to a fatal carelessness, which, in the end, must frustrate all our blessed Redeemer has done for them.

To remove this dangerous error, they should attentively reflect, that though *Jesus* has indeed brought us a plentiful Redemption, yet this great work is so tempered, as that the execution of it requires our concurrence, as free and rational creatures: for instance, though *Israel*'s temporal deliverance was effected by the conduct of *Joshua* (an eminent type of Christ our Saviour) and the wonderful blessing of God on his undertakings; yet the People were not indolent, they were to act their part also: that, by obeying his orders and fighting their own battles, they should be instrumental in their own deliverance.

In like manner, *Jesus* our Saviour, leads us out to war against our inveterate enemies, the World, the Devil, and the Flesh. He issues out to us his orders, and assigns to us our respective posts, or stations in life; and it is our duty to follow, to obey, to fight under him, to guard against our common foes: to arm ourselves with those invincible weapons, the holy sacraments, which he has mercifully provided for our defence and victory. In short, *Jesus* has done all that for us, which we could not do for ourselves: nay, *it is God that worketh in you, both to have a will, and to fulfil it through his good will**. But what we can do, is still left upon our hands; yet so left, that provided we use our endeavours, he will make us able

---

* Philip ii. 13.

able to do it. In a word, it is *Jesus* that saves his People from their sins; but still they are his *People* whom he saves: them that believe his sacred word: obey his precepts; devote themselves to his service: that worthily frequent the Sacraments, and praise his holy Name. In fine, he saves those, who endeavour to save themselves. Had *Jesus* done less than this, He would not have fulfilled the importance of his glorious Name; and more, would have defeated the design of it: for, to save those from punishment, who are still fond of guilt, would rather tend to encourage sin than to forbid it. A design highly unworthy of God, unprofitable to man, and by no means agreeable to the tenor of the Gospel.

It is not then, to the sinner that perseveres in sin, or neglects to work his Salvation by the performance of good works, that *Jesus* will be a Saviour: but it is to the penitent sinner, the devout worshipper; to the just and honest dealer; the bountiful alms-giver; to the meek and mortified Christian, who not only works his own, but becomes a zealous promoter of other men's Salvation, as far as in him lies: it is to these and such like, that *Jesus* will become a Saviour; to them his most excellent Name will administer unspeakable *comfort*, both here and hereafter; for, how can crosses really afflict the good Christian in this Life, whilst *Jesus* promises to comfort him? or how can adversity oppress, where he sustains? Temptation cannot overcome, where Christ defends; nor sin condemn, where he pardons. The Name of *Jesus* can sweeten the bitterest affliction, and remit more sin than we are able to commit. Neither shall the pangs of death or the horror of the Grave affright in the last moments of life; nor shall the terrors of Judgment drive the good Christian

tian to despair, whilst *Jesus*, who came to save the penitent Sinner, and is the Resurrection itself, has given his faithful Servants such inestimable pledges of his love, and earnests of everlasting life!

It is our duty then, to ask that we may receive; to labour and pray with all our might, that it may never be our unhappy lot to perish amidst such succours, or to refuse and neglect a Salvation that courts us to accept of it. In virtue of *Christ's* most excellent Name, we now have it in our power to work our Salvation, which before we had not. Wherefore, *whilst we have time, let us do good* * : for *Faith without good Works is dead* †.

We should not then, permit a day to pass without celebrating the praises of the most excellent Name, *Jesus*; we shall happily find it to be an impregnable *Tower*, under whose protection, we shall be secured from every evil: we shall find it a firm sheet *Anchor* in the tempestuous sea of this world, and a secure *Haven* of eternal repose in the next. The Name of *Jesus*, is a strong *Armory*, wherein we shall find invincible weapons to combat our most formidable Enemies, and subdue them. We shall find it an inexhaustible *Treasury* of comfort and relief, in time of affliction; of grace and mercy, for the penitent Sinner. In short, the most excellent Name of *Jesus*, is the divine source of every blessing, whether spiritual or temporal, conferred on us.

We may then, in truth affirm, that the Name, *Jesus*, is most holy and excellent, in virtue whereof, Christ has brought to us a *spiritual and universal Salvation*. O admirable Love! O unspeakable Clemency! O glorious and all-saving Name of
Jesus!

* Gal. vi. 10.   † James ii. 26.

Jesus! A foresight of the extraordinary blessings that were to be conferred on Mankind, in virtue of God's most holy Name, induced the Royal Psalmist to express himself in the following Words: *All the Nations thou hast made shall come and adore before thee, O Lord: and they shall glorify thy Name. For thou art great and dost wonderful things. I will praise thee O Lord my God, with my whole heart, and I will glorify thy Name for ever: for thy mercy is great towards me: and thou hast delivered my Soul out of the lower Hell*. This should be the language of every faithful heart: Thus should they express their grateful acknowledgments to their merciful Deliverer.

CHAP. III.

The Efficacy of the Name of JESUS.

WE may readily infer from the preceding chapter, that the Name of *Jesus*, which is above every Name, and through which we are to be saved, must be, *in itself*, efficacious beyond conception; nay even when duly and worthily invoked by Men. The many wonders wrought in consequence of that extensive Power, wherewith our blessed Redeemer was pleased to invest his Apostles and Disciples, are a glaring proof thereof. St. *Mark* informs us †, that *Christ* granted them a Power to perform Prodigies and Miracles in his Name: *In my Name,* says Jesus Christ, *they shall cast out Devils, they shall speak with new tongues, they shall take up serpents; and if they drink any thing mortiferous, it shall not hurt them: they shall lay their hands upon the Sick, and they shall be healed.*

In

---

* Psalm lxxxv.   † Mark xvi. 17, 18.

In virtue of these ample powers, the Apostles wrought many stupendous works in the Name of *Jesus:* witness that recorded in the third chapter of the *Acts*; that as *Peter* and *John* went up to the Temple to pray, a Man, who had been lame from his Mother's womb, lay at the Gate, begging an Alms from those who entered the Temple. Among others, he applied to the Apostles for relief: whereupon St. *Peter* looking stedfastly on him, answered: *Silver and gold I have none: but what I have, this I give thee. In the Name of Jesus Christ of Nazareth, rise up, and walk. And having taken him by the right hand, He lifted him up, and presently the plants and soles of his feet became firm. And leaping up, he stood and walked: and entered with them into the Temple, walking and leaping, and praising God.* The People, amazed, flock to the Temple to know the cause of this extraordinary cure! which St. *Peter* readily assigns: *that his Name* (Jesus), *through Faith in his Name,* says the Apostle, *hath made this Man sound.* The miraculous cure soon reached the ears of the Princes and Elders of *Jerusalem*, and as many as were of the priestly race, who assembled the next Day, cited the Apostles to appear before them: they were asked, by what Power or in what Name they had wrought that Work? *Peter, filled with the Holy Ghost, said to them: You Princes of the People, and Elders, hear: ......Be it known to you all, and to all the People of Israel; that in the Name of our Lord Jesus Christ of Nazareth, whom you crucified, and whom God raised from the Dead, even by him this Man stands sound before you: ......neither is there any other Name under Heaven given to Men, whereby we must be saved* *.

The

---

* Acts iv.

The Council perceiving the Constancy of *Peter*, and unable to deny the Miracle, were amazed and alarmed: they commanded the Apostles to withdraw, till they had resolved upon what was to be done: when unable to prove any thing criminal against the Apostles, and dreading the fury of the People, were they to persecute them without cause, the result of their conference was; that the Name of *Jesus should be no further divulged amongst the People*: and accordingly, charged the *Apostles not to speak at all, nor teach in the Name of Jesus*. To which the faithful and steady Ministers replied; *Judge you whether it be just in the sight of God, to hear you rather than God.* The Apostles being dismissed *with threats*, returned to their Brethren, when after relating what had passed, they jointly addressed the following prayer to Heaven. *Now, O Lord, look down on their threatnings, and grant to thy Servants with all confidence to preach thy word, in this, that thou stretch forth thy hand to cures and to wonders, and miracles to be done by the Name of thy holy Son Jesus.* And, far from being dismayed by the menaces of the Council, they continued to preach *Jesus* crucified, and rejoiced exceedingly, *because they were thought worthy to suffer reproach for the Name of Jesus.*

Though the Scriptures are replete with proofs of the Efficacy of God's most powerful Name, yet the instance now quoted may suffice to clearly shew its efficacy in the Infancy of Christianity. And if we have not as frequent Proofs of its power now, as in the first Ages of the Church, the reason is obvious: first, because they are not now so necessary, as the Christian Religion is fully established: and secondly, because God's sacred Name is not so frequently invoked in these later

later Ages, nor with the like spirit of piety and devotion, as formerly. Yet has Almighty God been graciously pleased to give us repeated Instances of it's efficacy, from time to time, to strengthen our faith and confidence in his Adorable Name, and convince us, that He is ever willing to impart blessings, to perform wonders in favour of those who devoutly and constantly invoke it.

I shall select one surprizing proof thereof, out of many, recorded in the life of the glorious Patriarch St. *Dominick*, Founder of the holy Order of Preachers, attested by Historians of undoubted veracity *. The Fact was this: Whilst the Patriarch St. *Dominick* resided in our Convent of St. *Sixtus* at *Rome*, he was frequently visited by the most respectable Prelates of that great Metropolis, who conceiving the highest opinion of his Sanctity and Learning, sought every opportunity to converse with him. Cardinal *Stephen*, who was among the Number of his Admirers, accompanied by two other Cardinals, went, one Morning, to visit the Saint; and whilst engaged in the most edifying conversations, they received an account, that a young Nobleman had been thrown from his horse, by its taking fright: that his head and limbs were most shockingly fractured, by his foot remaining in the stirrup; and when disengaged, was found stone dead. The Messenger also informed them, that the Corpse then lay stretched in the Oratory, an object of pity to all that beheld it.

Who is it that would not be affected at such a moving sight? But imagine to yourself, Christian Reader, the inexpressible grief of Cardinal *Stephen*, when advancing with the Saint and two

* S. Antonin. part. 3. tit. 23.—Theodoric. in vita, &c.—Fleury, Hist. Eccl. lib. 78. n. 32.

two Cardinals, to view the Corpse of the deceased Prince, he discovered it to be the shattered remains of his dearly beloved Nephew *Napoleon Ursini* *. The Cardinal, in a flood of tears, prostrates himself at the Saint's feet, beseeching him to petition Heaven for the revival of his Nephew, which the Saint, at first, through humility declined: But at length, moved, on the one hand, by the Cardinal's tears and intreaties; on the other, by the faithful promise of *Jesus Christ*: *If you ask the Father any thing in my Name, he will give it you* †.

Ani-

---

* Dr. *Burke*, in his *Hibernia Dominicana*, pag. 385. informs us, that *Napoleon Ursini* was one of the Ancestors, in a direct line, of Pope *Benedict* XIII. of happy Memory, who was assumed, out of the Order of Preachers, to govern the Universal Church in the Year 1724. The Sovereign Pontiff was heard, by Dr. *Burke* and other credible Witnesses, to declare; that *Napoleon Ursini*, who had been raised from the dead by the Patriarch St. *Dominick*, in the Oratory of St. *Sixtus*, was, under God, the cause of his Existence. Hence, in grateful memory of the extraordinary favour, he resolves upon and actually executed a thorough repair of the Church and Convent of St. *Sixtus*, which then was, and now is inhabited by the Children of St. *Dominick*, Natives of *Ireland*. The pious Pontiff frequently visited this Sanctuary, which he held in high Veneration; and for some time resided therein, performing a spiritual retreat, to the unspeakable comfort of the Religious, constantly exhibiting the strongest Proofs of profound Humility and solid Piety. This memorable fact is engraved on *Lapides* erected in the Oratory where the Miracle was wrought, (which the Author of this Essay had often the comfort of reading) as a perpetual Monument to the latest Posterity, of the surprising Miracle.

† John xvi. 23.

Animated then, with a strong and lively faith, he desires the Altar might be prepared for him to celebrate Mass. Whilst he offered the most holy sacrifice, with his accustomed devotion, at the Elevation of the *Host* and *Chalice*, he is raised a few Cubits from the Ground, in the presence of a numerous Congregation; a sure Presage of the desired Miracle. The Sacrifice being offered, full of Confidence in God, he approaches the Bier, on which the deceased Noble Youth lay stretched: he composes the fractured limbs, then raising his eyes and heart to Heaven, fervently implores the Father of Mercy, through the Merits of his only begotten Son, *Jesus*, to restore Life to the young Prince. Having finished his mental Prayer, He then with an audible Voice utters the following Words: *Napoleon, in the Name of* Jesus, *I command you to arise*. No sooner were the powerful words expressed, than Death obeys the command, and flies from the Corpse of the young Nobleman! His broken limbs knit and become stronger than before: He immediately rises, walks, and lives to have a numerous Progeny, to the unspeakable Joy of his afflicted Uncle, and admiration of the other Cardinals and Multitude present. This stupendous Miracle could not fail to increase the esteem and veneration of all that were present to the great St. *Dominick:* they sought occasions to testify their sense of his great merit and power, which he with humility declines, confessing himself no more than an unworthy Instrument; assuring them in the words of St. *Peter*, *That the Name of Jesus, through faith in his Name, hath made this Man sound* *. He then intreats them to join him in returning their most grateful thanks to Heaven

---

* Acts iii. 16.

ven for the signal favour, in the words of the royal prophet *: *Not to us, O Lord, not to us, but to thy Name be glory given.* This surprizing Miracle was wrought by St. *Dominick*, that great favourite of Heaven, at the hour of nine o'clock, on the 24th of *February*, in the year 1220 †. Thus, does the Efficacy of the Name of *Jesus* appear beyond contradiction, when duly and worthily invoked! Thus does the Son of the living God fulfil his Promise, to his faithful Servants, not only of the Apostolic, but also of succeeding Ages; that *whatsoever is asked of the Father in his Name, shall be granted.* Or, *if you ask me any thing in my Name*, says Jesus Christ, *I will do it* ‖. Every Supplicant then, who hopes to meet a favourable hearing, by invoking the Name of the Lord, should be mindful of the important Advice of St. *Paul* §, *Let every one*, says he, *depart from iniquity, who nameth the Name of the Lord.* To mention or invoke the most holy Name of the Lord with polluted Lips, defiled Hearts, or distracted Minds, is what renders our supplications ineffectual and abortive. Whilst, on the contrary, when the Soul is cleansed from Sin, and the petition made with the proper Conditions, it is then *whatever* we ask, through the merits of his gracious Name, we shall assuredly obtain, in due time: nay, to comprize all in a few words, the most important of all blessings, your Eternal Salvation, shall prove the sure reward of a devout Invocation of it: for, *whosoever shall invoke the Name of the Lord, shall be saved* §‖. "That " is," says the bright Luminary of the Church, St. *Thomas,*

---

* Psal cxiii. 9.
† Bremond, Annot. 1. in Bull. tom. 1. pag. 9.
‖ John xiv. 14.   § 2 Tim. ii. 19.   §‖ Rom. x. 13.

Thomas, " invoke the Name of the Lord worthily, " invoke it perseverantly, and your Salvation " will be secure *."

O wonderful Efficacy of the Name of *Jesus!* whilst we view a plentiful Salvation brought to the whole Earth, in virtue of it, how can we possibly refrain from crying out, in transports of Joy and Admiration, with the Psalmist: *O Lord, our Lord, how wonderful is thy Name in the whole Earth!* † The whole Earth abounds with the most distinguished marks of its efficacy, which, like unto a perpetual font, is ever pouring forth the Waters of Grace on the Sons of Men, unless we by our Impieties stem the sacred Torrent. *Let all the Earth* then *adore thee* (O God) *and sing to thee: let it say a psalm to thy Name* ‡.

CHAP. IV.

We are bound to praise the Name of JESUS.

IF we examine the inspired Writers on this head, we shall find them jointly and severally proclaiming the praises due to the most holy and august Name of God. They conceived a proper sense of its greatness: their writings are replete with encomiums on it, and the most persuasive arguments to engage us to praise it. The venerable Patriarchs and Prophets of the old Law, confessed themselves totally indebted to God's holy Name for every blessing they received: they clearly foresaw and foretold, that they, and future Generations, should be delivered from the slavery of the Devil, and saved from their sins, in virtue of the

most

* In Epist. ad Rom. † Psal. viii. 1.
‡ Psal. lxv. 4.

most holy Name of *Jesus*. And hence it was, that they frequently addressed him in the following words: * *Arise, O Lord, help us and redeem us for thy Name's sake.*

So conscious was the Royal Prophet of this truth, that he scarcely addressed a psalm to the Lord, wherein he did not expressly mention and glorify his holy *Name*, particularly in his 148th psalm, where he warmly invites all creatures to praise God's most sacred Name. He calls on the Heavens, the Angels, and all the heavenly Hosts; the Sun, Moon, and Stars, *to praise the Name of the Lord*. The sublunary Bodies are also called upon to celebrate the praises of his Name: Even, inanimate Creatures are not omitted; nor the Beasts of the field, nor the feathered Inhabitants of the Air! All are summoned to praise the Name of the Lord, but more especially the *Kings of the Earth and all People*; *Princes and all Judges of the Earth. Young Men and Maidens: let the Old with the Younger, praise the Name of the Lord: for his Name alone is exalted.*

If then, the Patriarchs and Prophets could not refrain from proclaiming the greatness of God's most adorable Name, and inviting all Nations to glorify it; with infinitely more reason we, Christians, should incessantly praise it: because, what they hoped for, we enjoy: in virtue of it, a plentiful Redemption has been brought to us; the Gates of Heaven are opened to us, nor can any thing exclude us from the perpetual Inheritance of its glorious Mansions, but to wilfully reject or neglect the grace and mercy, which the Name of *Jesus* has abundantly procured for us.

Hence,

---

* Psalm xliii. 26.

Hence, when we confider how much we are indebted to his All-gracious Name, it muſt appear evident beyond contradiction, that we can never ſufficiently admire and praiſe it! It was from a knowledge of the favours already beſtowed on Mankind, and a fore-knowledge of the unſpeakable bleſſings which were to be conferred on the Chriſtian World, that cauſed the Royal Prophet to call on all Creatures, to join him in celebrating the praiſes of God's moſt adorable Name: He invites the King, the Peaſant; the Rich, the Poor; the Healthy, the Sick; the Young and the Old, to praiſe the Name of the Lord: for, as Mankind of all ranks and degrees, of every age and condition, have or may experience the efficacy of his moſt powerful Name; ſo all Mankind are indiſputably bound by *Duty, Gratitude, Intereſt,* and *Neceſſity,* to praiſe his ever glorious Name.

Duty, becauſe it is the Tribute juſtly due to God's infinite Majeſty. *Gratitude,* in thankſ-giving for the favours already received, ſaying with *David: What ſhall I render to the Lord, for all the things he hath rendered to me? I will take the Chalice of Salvation, and I will call on the Name of the Lord**. Then gratefully thank him with the ſame Prophet, in the following words: *Bleſs, O my Soul! the Lord, and all that is within me, bleſs his holy Name, ... and never forget all his benefits*†. *Intereſt,* that you may merit a continuance of them: becauſe, 'tis from the Lord every real bleſſing muſt deſcend: for inſtance, if Afflictions or Croſſes preſs heavily upon you, and that you expect relief, your recourſe muſt be to the Name of the Lord, ſaying with holy *David*‡: *I have met with trouble and*

---

* Pſalm cxv. 3, 4. † Pſalm cii 2.
‡ Pſalm cxiv. 4.

and sorrow: and I called upon the Name of the Lord. Invoke the moſt holy Name of God worthily, and you ſhall derive the utmoſt comfort and conſolation from that ſweeteſt Name: like *David*, you ſhall obtain the deſired relief. You ſhall plainly diſcover, that your moſt earneſt endeavours to praiſe the amiable Name of the Lord, are totally inadequate to its goodneſs; and in raptures ſhall warmly invite all Creatures to celebrate jointly the moſt holy Name of God, in the words of the royal Pſalmiſt *: *Join with me to magnify our Lord, and let us all together celebrate his holy Name: I ſought the Lord, and he heard me; and he delivered me from all my troubles.*

Hence appears the neceſſity of Afflictions, from time to time, that we may know our own inſufficiency and be compelled to ſeek the Lord, agreeable to what *David* ſays: *Fill their faces with ſhame; and they ſhall ſeek thy Name, O Lord*†. If you deſire the remiſſion of your Sins, with an humble and contrite heart ſay, with the royal Penitent ‡: *For thy Name's ſake, O Lord, thou wilt pardon my ſin: for it is great:* and you ſhall obtain the forgiveneſs of them. Or with the *ten Lepers*, raiſe your voices, crying out, JESUS MASTER, *have mercy on us*; and you ſhall *be made clean* §. *For I write unto you,* ſays the Evangeliſt St. *John, that through his Name your Sins are forgiven you* ‖. If you are in want of any temporal Good, you muſt firſt, be reſigned to the wiſe diſpenſations of Providence: Then, like patient *Job*, proclaim the *Name of the Lord bleſſed,* and you ſhall aſſuredly obtain, in due time, a gracious

---

* Pſalm xxxiii. 4, 5.   † Pſalm lxxxii. 17.
‡ Pſalm xxiv. 11.   § Luke xvii. 13.
‖ 1 Ep. ii. 12.

cious return: your wants shall be supplied; and whatever you request, shall be granted: provided, what you ask tends to God's honour and your own welfare, agreeable to what the Psalmist says*: *Thou my God hast heard my prayer; Thou hast given an Inheritance to them that fear thy Name.*

In short a worthy Invocation of God's holy Name will intitle you effectually to the divine Protection, as he declares by his prophet *David: Because he hath hoped in me, I will deliver him: I will protect him, because he hath known my Name* †. What evils can affect the Soul, whilst under the Protection of its God? What Vice can stain the Soul, whilst under the Protection of *Sanctity* itself! The *Noon-day Devil*, with all his Emissaries, shall fly from the Man who praises the Name of his God: because, protected by *Omnipotence* itself. There shall no Evil come to him, for, *I will protect him,* says the Lord, and why? *Because he hath known my Name.* Ah, what an happiness to be under the *shadow of his Wings*, under *the protection of the God of Heaven!* What an unspeakable Comfort to a Christian Soul!

Lastly, *Necessity*; because we are not to be saved, but by praising the most holy Name of *Jesus:* For, there is no *other Name under Heaven given to Men, whereby we must be saved* ‡. Hence, if you have your Salvation at heart, you cannot accomplish the great Work sooner, or with greater certainty, than by praising the Name of the Lord: as he tells us by his Prophet *Isaiah* §, *Every one that calleth upon my Name,* says the Lord, *I have created him for my glory.* What powerful Inducements to praise the ineffable Name of the Lord!

If

---

* Psalm lx. 6.   † Psalm xc.
‡ Acts iv. 12.   § xliii. 7.

If these, so many and such sacred ties, shall not bind us to render Praise and Thanksgiving to the most holy Name of God, I know not what will! Perhaps, where love or gratitude cannot prevail, Fear may terrify us into our Duty. How frequently have Kingdoms, Provinces, Cities, Towns and Villages, been visited by the most dreadful Calamities of Famine, Plagues, War, Earthquakes, and a thousand other scourges, for the criminal neglect of not praising God's most sacred Name? How often has that shameful omission been productive of vexatious disappointments and failures in Trade, to teach Worldlings at their cost (since nothing else will convince them) that what they are incessantly labouring for, is uncertain and transitory; and that, without a faithful discharge of their Duty to God, they cannot expect any solid or lasting good in this life.

In short, those various misfortunes and disappointments that happen so frequently in the world, may, with the greatest justice, be ascribed to the omission of praising God's most venerable Name, or to a profanation of it. Nay, the royal Prophet prays, that such scourges and heavy judgments may befal those careless sinners that neglect to praise the Name of the Most High, and the impious miscreants that profane it. * *Pour out thy wrath,* says he to the Lord, *upon Nations that have not known thee; and upon kingdoms that have not called upon thy Name.*

Wherefore, if you mean to escape exemplary punishments on the one hand, or to reap unspeakable blessings, promised to those that glorify the Name of *Jesus,* on the other, you must be indefatigable in your addresses to his all-saving Name; and ever remember, that to love your God and glo-

---
* Psal. lxxviii. 6.

glorify his Name (notwithstanding the importance of your worldly avocations), must indispensibly be the principal object of your thoughts, the sole desire of your hearts, and the end of all your actions. *By him therefore let us offer the sacrifice of praise always to God, that is, the fruit of Lips confessing his Name* *.

There are various ways of giving Praise to God's most sacred Name. First, by the performance of good works: such as worthily frequenting the sacraments of *Penance* and the *Eucharist*; by alms-deeds; by fasting, praying, and thankfully receiving whatever the Divine Wisdom shall think proper to appoint for you, whether prosperous or adverse. In short, the Name of the Lord is glorified by every good work ordained to his Honour and Glory. Hence, St. *Paul* gives this salutary advice, † *Whatsoever you do in word or deed, do all things in the Name of our Lord* Jesus Christ.

Secondly, You glorify his Name, when you defend his Honour against Blasphemers, Cursers, or profane Swearers; when with a Christian courage, you check their insolence by a seasonable advice, or a prudent correction: for, by thus vindicating the cause of God upon earth, and publicly asserting the Honour due to his holy Name, you proclaim his *Name hallowed*, and will assuredly meet that blessed return, which *Christ* has faithfully promised, that he will own you before his *Father who is in Heaven* ‡.

Thirdly, We honour his Name by taking a *good* and *lawful* Oath. But it must be carefully remarked, that to constitute a *lawful* Oath, three Con-

---

* Heb. xiii. 15.   † Coloss. iii. 17.
‡ Matth. x. 32.

Conditions are expressly required by God himself: viz. *justice*, *truth*, and *judgment*, as he declares by his Prophet *Jeremy* *: *And thou shalt swear: as the Lord liveth, in truth, and in justice, and in judgment.* An Oath, when accompanied by these three conditions, will not be attended with any disrespect or irreverence to the most holy Name of God: on the contrary, it shall prove meritorious, and an act of Religion.

And lastly, Glory is given to the Name of the Lord, in a singular manner, by the *Rosary* and *Sodality* inscribed to the most holy Name of JESUS, wherein the praises of that all-gracious Name are distinctly set forth; and what he has done for us, in consequence of it, expressly commemorated, as we shall see more fully hereafter; only remarking at present, that there are some persons whose circumstances are so low, as not to be able to give praise to God by relieving their distressed fellow creature. Others perhaps, have neither power to correct, nor abilities to advise the profane swearer. But all and every Christian, whether Learned or Ignorant, whether Rich or Poor, may give Glory to the most holy Name of God, by learning and repeating that easy but powerful form of prayer, the ROSARY of JESUS: it will inform them briefly of the inestimable blessings they have received through it: it will remind them of what it cost *Jesus*, Son of the living God, to purchase those blessings for them; whilst a devout recital of the Rosary of the Name of *Jesus*, will prove a most acceptable return for the immense favours conferred, and merit a continuance of them to us.

In short, it will inspire you with the love of *Jesus*, and a desire of co-operating with his Goodness;

* iv. 2.

ness; it will animate you with an humble hope of fully enjoying one day or other, that happy eternity, which has been purchased for us, in virtue of the most holy Name of *Jesus*. Let us then *offer the sacrifice of praise always to God, that is, the fruit of Lips confessing his Name* *, by an humble, fervent, and constant recital of the Rosary of *Jesus*.

CHAP. V.

Of Swearing.

AS we are indispensibly bound to praise the Name of the Lord, we are equally obligated to avoid a Profanation of it, by declining *unlawful*, *rash*, or *false Oaths*, *Imprecations*, and *Blasphemies*. An Oath, as defined by Divines, is to call God to witness the truth of any thing we say or do: so that by an Oath, God is called upon as the first and infallible Truth, to ratify or vouch the truth of what we affirm.

An Oath is principally of three kinds: The first is an *assertory* Oath, whereby a man interposes the authority of God's Name, to assert a past or present truth; for instance, when a man swears that a matter *is* so, or *has* been so. The second is a *promissory* Oath, whereby the same Authority of God's most sacred Name is given as a pledge or surety for the performance of whatever you promise to do; for example, when you swear to give an alms, you pledge God's holy Name for the execution thereof. An *execratory* Oath is sworn, when a man not only calls upon God, as a Witness, but also as an Avenger of lies; for instance, when the swearer says, if what

I assert

* Heb. xiii. 15.

I assert be not true, or that what I promise, I will not perform, *that God may not be propitious to me, at the hour of death; that he may damn me; that the Earth may open and swallow me,* &c. which is the same as to say, If I swear a falshood, may God, the Author of truth, and Punisher of lies, reveal my perfidy to the whole world, by inflicting the heaviest and most exemplary punishments upon me, that his infinite Wisdom can devise, or his avenging Justice execute.

It is a matter of doubt among moral Divines, whether these expressions, *upon the word of an honest Man, on my Conscience, on the word of a Christian, on my Faith,* and such like, are to be accounted Oaths, some affirming, others denying. I shall only observe with a celebrated Author *, that if an Intention of swearing accompanies these words, they amount to the force of an Oath; but if they are uttered as mere Affirmations, alluding only to that truth or veracity of which every man may be supposed possessed, they are not to be deemed Oaths: yet such expressions ought to be industriously avoided, as they border upon an Oath; and a repetition of them, may readily lead to a frequency of swearing, in which there are many dangers.

To constitute an Oath, it is not necessary that the Name of GOD shall be *expressly* mentioned; as when you swear *by God, by Jesus, by the Holy Ghost, by Christ,* or *his sacred Wounds,* and such like: for a tacit and indirect invocation of God's holy Name is sufficient to form an Oath; as when you swear by any created being, calling upon it to witness the truth of what you affirm; for instance, when you swear by the *Bible, the Cross,*

our

---

* Billuart, tom. xii. dissert. 5. art. 2.

our Lady, &c. for, though these creatures, of themselves, give no strength or authority to an Oath, yet as the Majesty and Goodness of God really are, and appear in them, they have the same weight and authority. Hence, he that swears by the *Cross*, is understood to swear by the Son of God, who was crucified: He who swears by the *Bible*, swears by God, whose truth is contained and delivered therein: And he who swears by the *Mother of God (our Lady)* swears by him, whose Mother she is.

In short, as all created beings appertain to God, their Creator, and have a necessary relation to him, " and as the divine Truth shines forth in " them," says the Angelic Doctor; so they who swear by God's creatures, are always deemed to swear by God himself. Hence, our blessed Redeemer gives us the following important instruction: * *I say unto you*, says Jesus Christ, *do not swear at all, neither by Heaven, because it is the throne of God, nor by the Earth, because it is the footstool of his feet; nor by Hierusalem, because it is the City of the great King; neither shalt thou swear by thy head, because thou canst not make one hair white or black; but let your talk be, Yea, Yea, and No, No, and that which is over and above these, is of evil.*

By these words our divine Master teaches, that we are not to swear by any created being; because, as the Majesty and Power of God shine forth in them, of course, to swear by his creatures, is indirectly to swear by God himself. To prevent therefore, the custom of swearing by Himself or his creatures, he gives this general Command, *Do not swear at all*; whereby he means not to condemn all Oaths indiscriminately,

as

* Matth. v.

as some *heterodox* Believers would fain persuade us, but he intends only to forbid swearing by himself or his creatures, on trifling occasions, or to support and uphold falshoods; for Necessity and Truth alone, should impel us to swear. Thus, when *Necessity* obliges you to take an Oath, and that you swear the *Truth*, with Prudence and mature Deliberation, your Oaths are not to be condemned as unlawful; nay, they are meritorious, and an Act of Religion; for as the Angelic Doctor * teaches, an Oath in itself, when accompanied with the Conditions of *Justice*, *Truth*, and *Judgment*, is lawful and an Act of Religion, both as to its *Origin* and the *End* proposed by taking an Oath; for it originally proceeded from that faith or belief which men have, of God's being the first and infallible Truth, to whose infinite Knowledge the most hidden secrets are clearly revealed; and, as such, God is called upon as a Witness to the Truth of what we swear. An Oath is also lawful as to the *End* proposed by swearing, which is, to gain credit for the honest man, and to put an end to strifes and contentions, as St. *Paul* says: *for men swear by one greater than themselves; and the end of every Controversy among them, for confirmation, is an Oath* †.

But, though we confess God to be the first and infallible Truth, by means of a lawful Oath, and that our disputes become happily terminated thereby, yet an Oath is by no means a desirable good; because of the many dangers attending a frequency of swearing; for, when we consider, as St. *Thomas* ‡ remarks, that the custom of lawful swearing was introduced only as a *Remedy* to

gain

---

* 2. 2. q. 89. art. 4.   † Heb. vi. 16.
‡ Ibid. art. 5.

gain Credit for man, whose Veracity is often doubted of, even when he affirms a Truth; we must conclude, that as a *Drug* or *Medicine* is only to be taken when Necessity requires, lest it should lose its efficacy and become hurtful, so an Oath is to be taken only when Necessity obliges in Defence of Truth; lest by a frequency of swearing, even the truth, we should expose ourselves to profane the all-sacred Name of God, and thereby convert that salutary remedy into a mortal poison. *Do not,* says the Holy Ghost, *accustom yourselves to swearing, because there are many dangers in it* *: Hence, even a lawful Oath should be taken but very seldom, with great caution, and only when necessity requires it.

Such is the goodness of God, that lest we should err in so delicate a matter, the divine Wisdom has thought it meet to point out distinctly to us, by the prophet *Jeremy,* those conditions that must indispensibly accompany every Oath, to render it lawful: *And thou shalt swear: as the Lord liveth,* says he, *in Truth, and in Judgment, and in Justice* †. There can be no doubt of an Oath so taken, being lawful; it is warranted by the Example of God himself, who has frequently sworn, as the sacred Scripture informs us; *for God making a promise to Abraham,* says St. Paul, *because he had no one greater, by whom he might swear, swore by himself* ‡.

The Christian world do, and always did look upon Oaths, as the most sacred and binding Obligations upon Earth, between man and man; and it has ever been the custom, when man would give the best and most warrantable assurance for

the

---

* Eccl. xxiii. 9.   † iv. 2.
‡ Heb. vi. 16.

the truth of what he said, he called upon God, in a solemn manner, as a witness of the truth of what he affirmed or promised.

It should be ever most carefully remarked, that though the Lord is pleased to empower you to call upon his most holy and august Name, 'tis upon certain conditions, and under certain restrictions. He permits you to call upon him as a Witness, only when Necessity requires you to affirm a Truth, or as a Surety for the Performance of any lawful Action, which you promise to do.

In the taking of an Oath, you should have the fear of the Lord before your eyes: *You shall fear the Lord your God*, says he, *and you shall serve him alone; and you shall swear by his Name* *. Not upon every occasion, but *thou shalt swear*, says he, *in Judgment, and in Justice, and in Truth* †. As if he had said, Though I permit you to swear by my awful Name, you must be extremely careful, under the penalty of incurring my highest displeasure, not to swear by my Name, rashly, or on trifling occasions, but only when Necessity impels you to it. You must be also careful, not to call upon me, as a Surety or Witness, for the Performance of what is unlawful, or the Omission of what is lawful, to be done. Nor, in fine, shall you swear by my holy Name, to enforce an Untruth, or uphold a Falshood.

But, as a fuller knowledge of these Conditions seems necessary to the generality of Christians, who, when they approach the Tribunal of Confession, make no distinction between Oaths; nay, often comprehend *Imprecations* and *Blasphemies*, under the general appellation of an *Oath*, though widely

---

* Deut. vi. 13. † Jeremy iv.

widely different; one exceeding the other in Malice and Impiety: it, therefore, appears highly neceſſary to explain them more fully, in the following Chapters. But, it is proper firſt to remark with the Catechiſm of the Council of *Trent* *: "That the Name of God, that the Letters and Syllables of it, or the naked Word alone, of itſelf, is not here altogether to be regarded; but that we muſt ſeriouſly conſider what that word, which ſignifies the Almighty and Eternal Majeſty of the Tri-une Godhead, means. From hence it is eaſily gathered, that the Superſtition of ſome *Jews* was vain, who durſt not pronounce the Name of God, though they durſt write it; as though the Divine Power were in thoſe Letters, and not in the Thing." And though the Commandment be put in the ſingular number, *Thou ſhalt not take the* Name *of the Lord thy God in vain*, "this is not to be underſtood," ſays the ſame Catechiſm, "of any one Name, but all the Names which are uſed to be attributed to God; for there are many Names aſcribed to God, as, *Lord, Almighty, Lord of Hoſts, King of Kings, Strong*, and others of the like ſort, which we read in Scripture, all of which have the like and the ſame Veneration."

It is alſo to be remarked, that if an Oath be tendered by a Judge, Magiſtrate, or any other perſon legally qualified to tender an Oath: if the perſon to whom the Oath is thus tendered, forſwears himſelf, his crime is much aggravated; becauſe the formality and ſolemnity generally uſed upon ſuch occaſions, leave room for reflection and deliberation. And conſequently, the perſon ſo
ſwearing

* In 2. Decalog. Precept.

swearing a Falshood, becomes wilfully and premeditately guilty of Perjury, which is an heinous crime.

CHAP. VI.

The first Condition necessary to render an Oath lawful, viz. JUDGMENT.

"A Rash Oath wants Judgment," says St. *Thomas* *. By this Condition Almighty God requires, that we shall not swear rashly or inconsiderately, but discreetly, and only when Necessity impels us to it; maturely considering the matter we are about to swear, whether it be of that moment as to require an Oath. We are forbid to swear on trifling occasions, or even in weighty matters, when they can be proved without an Oath. In a word, the condition *Judgment*, forbids all rash, idle, and indiscreet Oaths, *though in the Truth.*

Great Caution and Circumspection then, should be used before you take an Oath, or swear at all. You should attentively consider the matter, with all its circumstances, whether it be of that importance as to require an Oath: you should also be cautious not to swear out of love, hatred, anger, fear, or any other disorderly passion; for these so bias and cloud the Judgment, that men but too often, on that account, take very indiscreet and imprudent Oaths: so much prudence and discretion is required in taking an Oath, that the *Canon* law will not allow Children, until arrived at the fourteenth year of their age, to take an Oath*;

---

* 2. 2. q. 89. a. 3.

Oath *; presuming, that before they have attained that age, they have not sufficient Judgment to swear with that respect and reverence so justly due to God's most venerable Name.

The primitive Christians were so averse to the taking of Oaths, that they shunned them like Perjury: if called upon to swear to-day, they put it off till to-morrow; when called upon to-morrow, they deferred it, if possible, till next day. Thus did they endeavour to guard against the Custom of Swearing, lest they should offer any Irreverence to God's most sacred Name. But, when Necessity obliged them to swear, upon any interesting occasion, they first retired into the Church, where, on bended knees, they craved the Assistance of Heaven, lest they should offer the smallest Irreverence to the most holy Name of God. Nay, St. *Cornelius*, Pope, required they should be fasting, when an Oath was to be taken, lest the Vapours that arise from a full stomach, should obscure the rational Faculties, and expose them to swear without due Respect to the most awful Name of the Lord. The *Jews* † held the Name of God in such high Veneration, that the Priests alone were empowered to mention it, and that only, when they solemnly blessed the people in the Temple: and except upon that occasion, whenever they met with the Name GOD, even in reading the Scriptures, they called him *Lord*; so awful and venerable did the adorable Name GOD, appear to them, that they thought themselves unworthy to mention it, even when reading the Prophets; and much more so, to call

upon

---

* Cat. Con. Triden. In 2. Decal. Precep.
† Segneri, Christ. Istruito Rag. 10.

upon him to witness every trivial occurrence in their common discourses.

Can Christians, unless bereaved of all sense of Religion, hear these Truths, and not blush with Shame and Confusion? when they recollect, that the adorable Names *God, Jesus, Holy Father, Holy Ghost,* &c. have been numberless times abused by them in their common Conversations, which are often low, trivial, and unlawful! Are Christians less indebted to God's most gracious Name, than the *Jews?* they, indeed, received temporal Blessings from God, but you have received both temporal and spiritual Blessings of the utmost Importance, in virtue of the most holy Name of *God,* or of *Jesus.* The gates of Heaven, which were shut against the *Jews,* are now opened to you, at no less an Expence than the Blood of *Jesus,* Son of the living God! Are you not bound then, by the strictest ties of Duty and Gratitude, not only to praise his adorable Name, but also to refrain, in future, from offering it the least Irreverence? You should carefully decline all Oaths whatever, though in the Truth and what is lawful, unless when Necessity impels you to it. There is, indeed, a strange Perverseness in human Nature; some persons are extremely alarmed when they are obliged to swear a lawful Oath before a Magistrate, though God's Honour, their own or their neighbour's Good requires it; and yet these very persons will not hesitate to take the Name of God in vain, and profane it a thousand times, where there is no Necessity at all!

How abominable then, the Custom that prevails now-a-days, among Christians of all Ranks and Degrees; of every Age and Sex; They can
scarcely

scarcely open their Mouths, without making the Name of the *Deity*, the subject of their senseless exclamations, by crying out O Jesus! O Lord! O God! at every Sentence they speak; thus presumptuously taking unwarrantable freedoms with the most holy Name of the Lord, without the least appearance of meaning or necessity. Whilst others irreverently call upon God to witness their Fooleries, at every trifling Occurrence. Nay, as St. *Augustin* complains, in his time, "they often swear "as many Oaths, as they express words."

If they relate any fact, though of a trivial nature, they must seal it with an Oath. If they buy or sell the most trifling article, the bargain is seldom closed without an *Oath* or *Execration*. How frequently do we find this to be the case in the public Markets, and other public Places of this City. Such abominable Oaths, Imprecations and Blasphemies are to be heard in the Fish and Meat Markets; at the Markethouse, Smithfield, public Stands, &c. as are sufficient to strike the Hearer with Horror on the one hand, and Amazement on the other, that the Vengeance of God does not instantly fall upon their guilty Souls, and plunge them into endless misery! If they follow Business, every Sentence they utter, every Assurance they give, must be upheld and enforced by an Oath; as if they could not vend their Wares, or transact their Business, without profaning God's holy Name, and selling their Souls to the Devil!

If we ascend a step higher, and take a view of of what is called the *polite* World, we shall hear God's sacred Name villified and abused by those who, from the advantages of Education, should tremble at the Impiety. Some *Bravo's* think they cannot manifest their courage and cleverness better,

than

than by sending forth a Volley of Oaths, or Imprecations! And think they cannot display a fertile Invention more, than in the coinage of new ones: Nay, some of these refined Geniuses have lately formed themselves into *Clubs* or *Societies* * for the Infernal Purpose! Others are of Opinion, they cannot shew to Advantage in Company; that their Conversations are languid and insipid, unless seasoned and enlivened with some vile Oath or Imprecation! Though in fact, every good Man must shudder at their Impieties, and is bound, at least, to fly their Company, to avoid the Infection, which such malignant Tongues spread to the scandal of every good or sensible Man that hears them. What they aim at, as a Commendation, is in fact, what should render them odious to Society, and contemptible in the eyes of every good and rational Man.

There are but few Persons however, so abandoned, who in their cooler moments will not allow the Custom of profane swearing, to be highly criminal and injurious to God: Yet, are they ready to assign various Excuses which they would fain persuade themselves, will sufficiently exculpate them, and apologize for the hateful practice. One will say, He was in a Passion. Another, that he swore without Thought, or through Custom. A third, that he would not be believed unless he swore. Though these appear to be the most feasible Excuses that can be alledged, they are however, insufficient to excuse or palliate the criminal Practice. As to the first, it is certainly the Duty of every Christian, to curb his disorderly Passions; and a Neglect thereof, subjects him to the sinful Consequences attending his uncontrouled Passions.

To

* In the Year 1770.

To swear without Thought, *is* also criminal, unless it be so sudden, as not to leave room for Reflection: But where there is time for Reflection, 'tis their duty to think seriously before they swear, or mention God's most venerable Name. Every momentous affair should be accompanied with Reflection: for instance, suppose you had any Matter of Importance to transact, and that a rash or inconsiderate Expression would frustrate your Designs, and render them abortive; would you not be extreamly cautious, lest an unguarded Word should give offence, and prevent the intended transaction taking place? Every rational Being would certainly act upon that cautious principle. If human prudence dictates so great circumspection in wordly affairs, how much more powerfully do the Laws of Reason and Grace require, that God's most awful Name shall not be mentioned impertinently, idly, or irreverently; that we shall not swear rashly, tho' in the truth: nor take his sacred Name (through which, we are to transact the important business of Salvation) in vain: As he declares: * *Thou shalt not take the Name of the Lord thy God in vain: for he shall not be unpunished that taketh his Name upon a vain thing.*

As to the other Excuse, *that People will not believe you unless you swear*, it is both frivolous and wicked: for, can you possibly imagine, that to gain the Assent of those to whom you speak, 'tis lawful to profane the Name of God, by rashly pledging his Honour, to secure your own? Besides, by a constant custom of swearing, you by no means gain the end proposed: You say, you will not be believed unless you swear. But surely, it

---

* Deut. v. 11.

it cannot be thought, that any rational Christian will believe a rash Swearer: for, what should give credit to our Assertions with every sensible Man, is a good life, and a constant Custom of telling Truth; and not the criminal Practice of frequent Swearing: And it may be looked upon as a certain Truth, that a Man who attempts to strip God of his Honour, by pledging his holy Name, upon every trifling occasion, will not be backward, if in his power, to impose upon his Neighbour, and rob him of his Property. It would therefore, highly tend to the discouragement of this Vice, if you would decline dealing or treating with such Persons, as are prone to take such unwarrantable freedoms with the most holy Name of God.

It would also prove highly meritorious, to decline a Custom, which too much prevails among Heads of Families and others, who force their Servants or Dependants, upon the least doubt arising of their Honesty, to swear to their Innocency; though they know full well, that Servants are weak enough to swear upon such trivial occasions, and will sooner forswear, than criminate themselves. St. *Chrysostom* exclaims against such uncharitable Monsters, in the following words: * " If thou knowest, " that he, from whom thou exactest an Oath, is a " good Man, why then art thou not contented " with his Word? But if he is not, why dost " thou force him to forswear himself?" If you have reason to suspect their Integrity, some other expedient should be thought of, without calling on the most awful Name of the Lord; you should advise, correct, or discharge them: for God's most holy Name should not be invoked or pledged as a surety,

except

---

* Homil. xv. ad Pop. Antioch.

except when *Necessity* and the vindication of *Truth* indispensibly require it.

In short, the rash and profane Swearer's Veracity is not at all ascertained by a frequency of Swearing: for it is universally believed, by every Man of sound Understanding, that he who swears upon all Occasions, would as soon swear a Falsehood as a Truth: for Custom begets, in time, such a facility and indifference, that Men care not what they swear, provided it be attended with a prospect of profit or pleasure.

Attend then, to the wholesome Advice which the Apostle St. *James* gives: * *Above all things, my Brethren, swear not, neither by Heaven, nor by Earth, nor by any other Oath whatsoever. But let your Speech be It is, It is, It is not, It is not, that you may not fall under Judgment.*

C H A P. VII.

The second Condition necessary to render an Oath lawful, viz. Justice.

" AN unlawful or wicked Oath wants Justice," says the Angelic Doctor †. An Oath becomes unlawful two ways: first, by swearing *to do what is unlawful to be done:* for instance, if you swear you will be revenged of your Enemies; that you will commit Robbery or Murder, &c. Such Oaths are unlawful and sinful, and the Swearer treats the holy Name of God with the highest Indignity, by calling upon him, as a Witness or Surety, for the Performance of what is improper or criminal to be done: for thereby the profligate Swearer endeavours, as far as

* Chap. v. 12.   † 2. 2. Q. 89. A. 3.

as in him lies, to engage God, the Source of all Sanctity, in his wickedness, by calling upon him as a Voucher for the Performance of what he is sure must offend him.

The heinousness of such Oaths will appear more glaring when you consider, that in the one sin, *viz.* of Swearing to do a criminal Action, the Malice of two is comprised: for instance, you swear you will do an Injury to your Neighbour: in this one, the Malice of two is included; first, the Desire of Revenge, contrary to God's express command, requiring we shall forgive our Enemies, and do good to those that hate and persecute us. The other is yet worse, which is to call God as a Witness or Surety for the Execution of what he has strictly forbidden. Imagine to yourself, a reputable Man, and fond Parent, forbids his Daughter to marry a certain Man of infamous Character: if she not only resolves to disobey the Paternal Command, but even invites her Parent to attend her wedding, does she not compleat the act of disobedience to the highest degree? In like manner, the promise of doing a bad Action, is doubtless sinful in itself, because forbidden by Almighty God; but to call upon the Father of all Sanctity and Goodness to witness it, and to give his holy Name, as a Surety for the performance of what he has forbidden, is treating the God of Heaven with the most glaring indignity and disobedience.

An Oath also becomes unlawful or wicked, when you swear *not to do what is lawful or proper to be done:* for example, that you will not give an Alms to the Poor; that you will not say your Prayers, frequent the Sacraments, forgive your Enemies, &c. This manner of Swearing is also
highly

highly offensive to Almighty God: because you pledge his holy Name for the Non-performance of what he either counsels, or commands you to do: And as the performance of good works is pleasing to God, of course, it must be wicked and injurious to him, to attempt binding yourselves, under Oath, to the Omission of them. Besides, the Swearer makes use of God's holy Name, as a Bar against the Inspirations of the Holy Ghost; which is, in fact, attempting to set the Divine Persons of the most Adorable Trinity at variance. Shocking Blasphemy!

There are many Persons who think, that if they have sworn to do a bad Action, they are, in consequence of their Oath, bound to commit it. But it is quite the reverse: for, " as they commit a " Sin, by swearing to do a sinful Action," says the Angelic Doctor, " so they redouble the Sin by " keeping it*." Hence, the wicked *Herod* is justly blamed and condemned, not only for the rash Oath he had taken, of granting to his Daughter whatever she should ask †, but he sinned much more in gratifying her Cruelty, with the Head of the glorious Precursor, St. *John* Baptist. The *Jews* also sinned by swearing, *they would neither eat nor drink, till they had killed Paul* ‡.

This rash and criminal resolution of the *Jews*, reminds me of some Charges, as frightful as they are unjust, that are made against us, Roman Catholics, by some of our uncharitable Adversaries, which ought not to pass unnoticed or unanswered. But as the refutation of them will extend this Chapter beyond the intended bounds, it shall

be

* 2 2. q. 89. a. 7 ad 2. † Mark vi. 23.
‡ Acts xxiii. 12.

be divided into the following Sections, which may not be unseasonable at this Time.

SECT. I.

The Principles of Roman Catholics grossly misrepresented by their Adversaries.

THE several Publications that appear, from time to time, most unjustly branding Roman Catholics with such base and criminal Principles, as they, in fact, utterly abhor and detest; with a view, no doubt, of exasperating those who seem inclined to listen to the dictates of humanity, or are willing to give proofs of Compassion towards their Catholic Fellow Subjects. To render such Christian Sentiments and Feelings fruitless and abortive, is manifestly the design of these uncharitable Productions: instead of applying Oil to our Sores, they would fain enlarge the wound: and when every argument seems to have deserted them, they are forced to adopt that anti-christian Maxim: *Calumniare fortiter, aliquid adhærebit,* (fling dirt, some of it will stick.) In this their main force consists.

The Roman Catholics are stigmatized in these anonymous Papers, "as mortal Enemies to those "of a different Persuasion: as Persons who be- "lieve it meritorious to murder those of a differ- "ent Religion: that those principles are instilled "into their minds and strongly inculcated by their "Priests; nay, that we imbibe those principles "at the breasts of our Nurses," &c. An heavy Charge indeed! had it the least glimmerings of Truth. Sure, no Person, acquainted with the better sort of Roman Catholics, can credit
such

such vile insinuations? They must be totally unacquainted with Catholics, and their Principles, whose Characteristic is Hospitality blended with Charity and Friendship: and are they not found to be, in proportion to their Circumstances, as friendly, charitable and hospitable, as any other People whatsoever? Such notorious Slanderers then, must be actuated by low and uncharitable Sentiments; who, unwilling to think favourably of others, are determined to criminate at any rate. However, lest some weak or uninformed minds should be led astray, and poisoned by their false and malicious Insinuations, it may not be improper here, to give a *brief* Answer to this uncharitable and false charge; lest a patient Silence be construed into conscious Guilt.

No People upon Earth can enforce the necessity of Christian Charity in stronger terms, than We Catholics do: The words of St. *Paul* * are echoed by the Priests, in the ears of their hearers: *If I speak with the Tongues of Men and Angels, and have not Charity, I am become as a sounding Brass, and a tinkling Cymbal. And if I had the gift of Prophecy, and knew all the Mysteries, and every Science: And if I had all Faith, so as to move Mountains, and have not Charity, I am nothing. And if I shall distribute all my Substance to feed the Poor, and if I deliver up my Body so as to be burnt, and have not Charity, it avails me nothing.* We are not unmindful, that this Virtue of Charity obliges us to *do good to all Men* †. And that ‡ *Charity is patient, is kind;* (let our Adversaries also remember it) *Charity envieth not, dealeth not perversely.*

These

---

* 1 Corin. xiii. 1, 2, 3.   † Gal. vi. 10.
‡ 1 Corin. xiii. 4.

These are briefly our Principles relative to Charity, which oblige us to love *all* Mankind. When these principles come to be reduced into practice, they appear more striking; for instance: A Penitent appears at the Priest's knee, accusing himself of having offended his Neighbour, of having had a desire of revenge, of having defrauded or wronged any Person whatever. The Confessor severely rebukes him for the want of Charity, and will impose a Penance upon him, in proportion to the evil done, or intended to be done to his Fellow Creatures. He must also sincerely repent, firmly purpose amendment, he must restore, as soon as possible, what he has unjustly acquired, and repair, to the utmost of his Power, any evil he has occasioned, before the Priest can (in God's Name) impart the benefit of Absolution, or the Penitent receive it. Are these not strong preservatives to Christian Charity? Are they to be found except among Catholics?

Nor can they, consequently, be admitted to the Altar to receive the most Adorable Sacrament of the *Eucharist*, until they first forgive every injury from their Hearts; and, as soon as possible, seek a reconciliation with their offended Brother: 'tis then, and only then, they are permitted to approach the Altar, and *offer their Gift**. Animosities and Enmities which reign, at times, even among Catholic Princes, Private Families or Individuals, could never be imputed to the Principles of their Religion, which teach quite the reverse; but to the frailty and perverseness of human Nature, to which all Mankind appear more or less subject.

No Persons whatever can detest the atrocious Sin of *Murder* more than Roman Catholics do, from

* Matth. v. 24.

from Principles of *Religion*, *Reason*, and *Humanity*. Are they ignorant of what our blessed Redeemer declared when asked by a certain Man, what good he should do *to obtain everlasting Life?* *Jesus* replied: * *keep the Commandments.* *He saith to him: Which? And Jesus said: Thou shalt not Murder: Thou shalt not commit Adultery: Thou shalt not Steal: Thou shalt not bear false Witness: Honour thy Father and Mother: and, thou shalt love thy Neighbour as thyself.* No Catholic I presume, can think it a tenet of his Religion, to commit such an atrocious Crime, as would not only exclude him from eternal Life, but also evidently expose him to a sudden and ignominious temporal Death!

Do not Children learn from their Catechism, so soon as they are capable of Instruction, that God expresly commands: *Thou shalt not kill: Thou shalt not Steal:?* Is not this enforced to them in their riper Years, from the Altar or Pulpit? These are facts notorious even to Children, as well as the Adult, and upon examination it will be found to be truly the case. If any shall unhappily swerve from the Instructions they have received, they are Catholics only by Name; they are abandoned and reprobate Wretches, whom no laws can govern. And, I am apt to think, other Sects and Persuasions do not want their share of such Profligates.

Reason and *Humanity* also forbid the crime of Murder, both which require, that we behave to others, as we would expect and hope to be treated ourselves. But it seems, as if neither our Declarations, our Principles, or our Actions are sufficient to silence their Tongues, or stem the Torrent of their gross Calumnies and Detraction. They carry,

* Matth. xix. 17, 18, 19.

carry, however, with them, their own confutation: for, how comes it, if Roman Catholics, "from their Nurses Arms, from Inclination, from the Principles of their Religion, from the Maxims inculcated by their Priests, believe it meritorious to murder those of a different Persuasion," as is basely and falsely asserted, how comes it, I say, that they have continued (even by Acknowledgment of their Adversaries) to demean themselves as good Subjects to the King, amenable to the Laws, respectful to Magistrates, &c. for upwards of Seventy Years, in direct Opposition, to the dictates sucked in with their Nurse's Milk: regardless of the Principles of their Religion; refractory to the Instructions of their Teachers? &c.

This charge, big with Absurdity and Falsehood, proves, if any thing, that the Catholic Religion has long since ceased to exist; for instance, in the City of *Dublin!* for, if it had any Members, they must, from the Principles imputed to them, "be seditious, Murderers of those of a different Persuasion, observing no Faith with those of another Religion," &c. whereas it must be confessed, by every man who has an atom of Sincerity and Truth, that there are many thousands in this City, who profess the Catholic Religion, and that there are no People more peaceable; none more charitable, in proportion to their Abilities; none more averse to the Shedding of Blood; none more observant of moral Honesty than those who are the most stedfast Catholics, and are best acquainted with the Principles of their Religion. If any, who profess Catholicity, act a dishonest part in their dealings, which may happen to a few, especially when Poverty and
Distress

Distress stare them in the face, and where thousands are engaged in business, not only those of a different Persuasion, but their own most sensibly feel the smart and suffer by their failures; which amounts to a proof, that the Catholic Religion, or the Religious Principles of its Members, have no concern in their Misconduct, as is obvious to the meanest capacity.

In short, to comprise all that has been said in a few words, from the Charge made against us on the one hand, and from the Demeanour of the Roman Catholics on the other, it will appear, that our Adversaries have slipped insensibly into a Dilemma, which must unavoidably involve them in a manifest Contradiction, from which even the most subtle Argumentation cannot extricate them, *viz.* That we *are* Roman Catholics, and, That we are *not* Roman Catholics, at the same time. That we *are* Roman Catholics (or Papists) our Adversaries themselves assert; that we are *not* Roman Catholics, or Papists, is equally evident from the Principles which they impute to Roman Catholics or Papists, which *we* neither profess nor practise. On the contrary, we disavow, abhor and detest them; and, consequently, we are no longer, in fact, Papists or Roman Catholics, according to our Adversaries, as we absolutely renounce those fictitious Principles, with which Roman Catholics are most unjustly and undeservedly charged.

Hence, our Adversaries must allow, either that we, who are called Roman Catholics, must have deserted and renounced the Catholic Religion during the period of Eighty Years past, and do now actually renounce it, whilst we *have* acted, and *continue* to act, in direct opposition to its Tenets and Principles, as stated by our Adversaries; and, consequently, according to them, *we are not Roman Catholics*; or, *if we are*, it evidently follows, that the Roman Catholic Religion, which we profess, upholds no such damnable Doctrine. The first is glaringly false and absurd; the latter is the Truth: for the Catholic Religion, in the most solemn manner, censures and condemns such vile and shocking Tenets *; and agreeable to its real and genuine Principles, we, its professors or members, have demeaned ourselves humbly, peaceably, and friendly; and as such, we have and do prove ourselves stanch Roman Catholics.

I conjure you then, O Catholic Reader, to continue the same laudable Conduct: you may, indeed, be aspersed or ridiculed by some, for adhering strictly to your Religious tenets; but remember the words which our Redeemer addresses to you: *You shall be odious to all men on account of my Name; but he that shall persevere to the End shall be saved* †. Let no Invectives, Misrepresentations, or Calumnies whatever, cause you to swerve from the Duties of Religion, or induce you to infringe, in the least, upon peace and good order; carefully shun the least encroachment on the darling Virtue of Charity, which requires, that we shall love, even our persecutors, and pray for them, as *Jesus* did for his, when expiring upon the Cross.

Remember also, since it is the Will of God, that others enjoy temporal Blessings which you do not, that you must, under pain of forfeiting the perpetual Enjoyment of heavenly Goods, infinitely preferable to those of a fleeting, inconstant

---

* To be seen more fully in chap. VIII.
† Matth. x. 22.

stant World, submit to the Will of Heaven, and comfort yourselves in the words of the Royal Psalmist: *Some trust in Chariots, and some in Horses; but we will call upon the Name of the Lord our God* *.—*Our help is in the Name of the Lord, who made Heaven and Earth* †.—*Many are the Afflictions of the Just; but out of them all will the Lord deliver them* ‡. Since, therefore, our *Inclination*, our *Religion*, our *Declarations*, and our *Conduct*, loudly proclaim the uncharitable Charge to be *false* and *groundless*; its Authors will not, 'tis hoped, in future, be so barefaced as to advance such notorious Falshoods, which, the smallest Child, who knows any thing of his Catechism, can in Truth contradict.

If all this will not satisfy them, let them consult even those who have renounced the Catholic Religion, from whom they may learn (if there be any Veracity left) that it is by no means a Principle of the Catholic Doctrine, " that it is lawful " or meritorious to murder those of a different " Religion;" and that such shocking Doctrine is neither publicly nor privately inculcated by their Priests, but quite the reverse; for, abstracting from the Laws of God, the laws of the Land, the laws of Reason and Humanity, to which they are subject, and which strictly forbid the heinous Crime, the *Canon* Law so severely censures any Ecclesiastics who are so unhappy as to be guilty of Murder, that they incur an *Irregularity*, whereby they are debarred from ever exercising any Ecclesiastical Function; nor can they, notwithstanding a sincere Repentance, be again restored but by a *Papal* Dispensation, which

---

* Psal. xix. 8.   † Psal. xxiii. 8.
‡ Psal. xxxiii. 20.

which is very seldom granted *. Thus to deter Ecclesiastics from being guilty themselves, or advising others to commit the atrocious Crime of Murder †.

These Calumnies are not only unjust and antichristian, but ungenerous also, by endeavouring to blacken an harmless People, with a view to render them still more odious, who are already galled to the quick by *penal* Laws. Their base and false insinuations tend (and perhaps are intended) to inflame the minds of those who are inclined to commiseration and lenity towards their fellow creatures; who are fond of making it our *Interest* as well as our *Inclination* and *Duty*, to love our Rulers; and, in short, render the Roman Catholics useful Members to Society.

It

---

* Wigant. Tract. XIV. Ex. 1. de Censuris.

† The pretended Misconduct of the Roman Catholic Clergy, during the troubles of *Ireland*, which began in the Year 1641, is the principal Calumny invented and urged by their Enemies to criminate them. The Charge, however, will appear false from the following Extract:

" That the *Popish Ecclesiastics*, far from encou-
" raging, did endeavour to prevent, early in this Re-
" bellion, all Acts of Cruelty and Injustice, by strictly
" forbidding them under the severest Penalties that
" they could inflict, is manifest from the Acts of the
" General Congregation of their Prelates at *Kilkenny*,
" in *May* 1642, extant in *B.riase*," (a Protestant Historian, in his Appendix to the History of the *Irish* Rebellion) " wherein, among many other Orders for that
" humane and christian Purpose, may be found the
" following:
We will and declare all those that murder, *dismember, or grievously strike; all Thieves, unlawful Spoilers, Robbers*

It is then humbly hoped, that they who are animated with the Godlike virtues of Compassion and Tenderness for the Distressed, and are actuated with a real Love for their Country, will not permit themselves to be deceived, or unduly influenced, by the false and groundless Suggestions of Calumny and Malice, *laying to our Charge many and weighty Accusations, which they cannot prove* *; as the *Jews* did against St. *Paul.*

I say, laying to our Charge what cannot be proved; for, is not the good behaviour of Roman Catholics notorious to the whole Kingdom? If a few have misbehaved, it is equally notorious, they are mean and ignorant, little acquainted with the Principles of their Religion, and much less observant of them; and, consequently, 'tis not
surprising

Robbers of any Goods, Extortioners, together with all such as favour, receive, or any ways assist them, to be excommunicated; *and so to remain, until they compleatly amend, and satisfy, no less than if they were* namely *proclaimed excommunicated.*

" It was also ordained by that Congregation, *That all and every such as, from the Beginning of the War, had invaded the Possession of Goods, as well moveable as immoveable,* spiritual *or* temporal, *of any* Irish *Protestant, not being an Adversary of this Cause, and did detain them, should be* excommunicated.

" Here is an authentic and unanswerable Proof of
" these Ecclesiastics just and humane Regards to the
" *Protestants* of *Ireland,* in that distracted and misera-
" ble Conjuncture." *Historical Memoirs of the Irish Rebellion in the Year* 1641, *extracted from Parliamentary Journals, State-Acts, and the most Eminent Protestant Historians,* p. 156. Printed in the Year 1758.

* Acts xxv. 7.

surprising they should, at times, prove refractory to the Laws of God and Man. It is not from the low bred ignorant Members of any Religion or Sect, we are to learn their respective Principles, but from their Teachers, and such as have had the Advantages of a liberal Education and Christian Instruction.

All those of the Catholic Religion who have had these Advantages, will unanimously declare, in all parts of the World, that they sincerely abhor and heartily detest the base and wicked Principles, with which they are as basely charged, by those, who are as uncharitable as they are ignorant. For, if our approved Authors are consulted *, they will be found to inveigh, in the strongest terms against those damnable Principles, with which they are so unjustly and cruelly branded.

If

---

* The present Sovereign Pontiff, Pope *Clement* XIV. who happily governs the Catholic Church, dispensing the blessings of Peace and Reconciliation to the most distant parts of the Earth, in his *circular Letter*, which begins, *Cum Summi Apostolatus*, addressed, on the 12th Day of *December*, in the Year 1769, to all the Catholic Bishops of the Universal Church, in all parts of the World, on Occasion of the late *Jubilee*, wherein he informs them, that " Scripture and Tradition are
" those Sources of Divine Wisdom, from which only
" we can draw every necessary Guidance either for
" our Belief or Conduct.

" For these are the two most valuable Instruments,
" wherein is comprised every Thing relating to religious Worship, moral Discipline, and a virtuous
" Conduct of Life. From them we acquire a Knowledge of the profound Mysteries of Religion, and
" of the Offices of Piety, Equity, Justice and Hu-
" manity.

If Individuals, who may be supposed to know any thing of their Belief or Tenets, are questioned concerning the absurd Doctrines of which they are accused, they will loudly proclaim their Abhorrence to them, and that such Principles never were inculcated to them by their Priests, either in public or private. If so, with what face can they be charged with professing and espousing such principles of Religion as they never before heard of! Is it not strange and unjust, that our Adversaries shall attempt to forge what Principles they please for us, and force us to adopt them, though we never so much as heard of them before, save from their uncharitable Misrepresentations!

It

" manity. From them we learn the Duties we owe
" to God, to the Church, to our Country, to our
" Fellow Citizens, and to the rest of Mankind. By
" them we clearly understand, that the Laws of true
" Religion, are the most solid and firm Support of
" our civil and social Rights; this is the Reason that
" there has scarce been ever a Person, who oppugned
" the sacred Institutions of Christ, who at the same
" time did not to the utmost of his Power disturb the
" Public Tranquility, renounce Allegiance to his So-
" vereign, and reduce every thing to a pernicious
" State of Anarchy and Confusion. For there is so
" close a Connexion between the Rights of Divine
" and Human Power, that all, who are conscious of
" the Power and Authority of Kings, being confirm-
" ed by a Sanction of the Christian Law, with chear-
" ful Minds pay Obedience to their Sovereigns, re-
" vere their Power, reverence and respect their Dig-
" nity.

" And really considering the Divine Institutions in
" this Point, to be equally interesting to the Preser-
" vation

It has been ever allowed, that the Proselytes or Professors of any Sect or Religion whatever, ought to be best acquainted with their own Tenets, whatever they may be. If imaginary Tenets only are framed and considered, at the Option of every Writer, how can the *real* Principles of the heterodox Believer be in fact confuted? To proceed regularly, their Principles should be known from the general Voice of the most Intelligent and Knowing of that Profession; which, when once properly avowed, they are then brought to the Touchstone of the Gospel, and thence must appear true or false. This small Indulgence is denied to Roman Catholics, who, though incontestably the greatest and most illustrious Society upon Earth, yet truly their Principles must not be, as they really are, and have been for seventeen hundred years and more; but such as an handful of Slanderers think proper to report them at an hour's warning! A shameful Absurdity! A base ungenerous proceeding!

When

" vation of the Public Tranquility, as to the Salva-
" tion of Souls, we are thereby induced earnestly to
" exhort you, venerable Brethren, that next after
" God and the sacred Rites of the Divine Worship
" established in the Church, you will turn all your
" Thoughts and Care to inspire the Minds of the
" People with a Spirit of Submission and Obedience
" to their Sovereign Princes. For they are placed in
" a more eminent Station above the rest of Mankind,
" as Guardians of the Public Weal, and to maintain
" the Laws of Equity among their Subjects *They*
" *are the Ministers of God unto good.* It is not *in vain*
" *they carry the Sword, being Avengers to execute*
" *Wrath upon him that doth Evil.*"

When Catholic Writers attempt to confute the Novelties of Sectaries, their opinions are fairly and candidly set forth, and quoted from the Learned of that Sect; but they never yet attempted to forge Principles for those they would mean to confute; and if such an unjust Attempt should be made, they would soon meet a proper Reply from those even of their *own* Persuasion, for their ungenerous and uncandid behaviour; who, as it is notorious, are as violent against each other, as against the declared Enemies of the Catholic Church, if they appear to swerve from the Truth, or at all misrepresent it. 'Tis to be hoped then, that our Adversaries will allow us the liberty of declaring our own Principles, and that they are such as we believe and profess them to be, and not what they think proper to invent and forge for us.

In fact, what man in his senses shall pretend to know the Principles of the Catholic Religion better than those learned Fathers and holy Doctors of the Church? Those brilliant Lights, those eminent Divines, those celebrated Writers, who appear so frequently in the Catholic Church, to the Admiration of the most learned of our Adversaries, throughout the whole Globe of the Earth! These bright Luminaries have taught, and do teach, in their Writings, from the Pulpit, and occasionally in Conversation, that it is highly *criminal* to consent, even by Thought, to such atrocious Actions as we are charged with, much more to reduce them into Practice. But to what resources must they not have recourse, who are determined to criminate and revile at any rate!

I know some persons will say, If Catholics were so peaceable as they are represented, how come

come so many Mobs, of which the Papists form, at least, a great part? As to the Northern Mobs, 'tis to be hoped the Papists (as they are pleased to call us) will not be charged as Principals, or perhaps at all, Accomplices. Mobs indeed have arisen in the Southern parts of the Kingdom, and I doubt not but some, nominally Catholics, have been seduced to join the Outrageous Assemblies, from Ignorance, or the Want of Employment, but by no means from the Principles of their Religion: Idleness is the Parent of Folly and Vice.

Not many years ago, there have been dangerous Mobs, computed at twenty or thirty thousand men, at a time, in the very City of *Naples*, the Seat of Government, who, from a want of Employment or Industry, could not, or would not, suffer any Additional Tax to be laid on the Necessaries of Life; and, therefore, to rid themselves of any threatened burthen, had recourse to the unlawful methods of illegal Associations and dangerous Insurrections, which they afterwards had reason sorely to repent. Yet their outrageous misconduct was never imputed to the Principles of their Religion. The King, Nobles, Clergy, &c. who all professed the Catholic Religion, perfectly well knew it taught quite the reverse. They clearly saw, that the want of Employment and Industry was the source of those *Lazaroni's* Misconduct; and, therefore, wisely resolved to employ them in Works profitable to themselves, and useful to their Country; by which means, the well-disposed became satisfied in themselves, and useful members to Society; whilst the turbulent and rebellious were deservedly kept in Awe by the Sword of Justice.

In

In short, our Adversaries in general, by their Conduct, manifestly counteract the Charge made against us; for if our Principles be such as they are represented, *viz.* " that we think it meritorious to " murder Protestants, or those of a different per- " suasion; and that Faith is not to be kept with " them;" how comes it that Protestants support a Neighbourhood, and seek Alliances with Catholics? that they have any dealings with them, or that they venture to dwell under one roof with them? It is evident, they keep a friendly correspondence with Roman Catholics both in City and Country; that their dealings together are very extensive; and that they frequently reside in one house with Catholics, as lodgers or guests. Hence it is plain, that Protestants apprehend no danger, either from the Inclination of Catholics or the Principles of their Religion.

Nay, do they not frequently make choice of Catholic servants, preferable to those of any other Persuasion, upon this principle: that if they cheat or rob their masters, to which servants in general are too much prone, they stand a better chance of having the injury repaired by them than by any others; " because," say they, " their " Priests will oblige them to Restitution."

In a word, do not Protestants of distinguished Characters frequently travel into Catholic Countries, and visit *Rome* itself, where they are convinced, from experience, that the Pope, Catholic Princes, Clergy, &c. treat Protestants with the same Charity and Politeness as they do those of their own Communion. Hence, many noble Personages have been happily disabused abroad of those Prejudices contracted at home; as they nobly and candidly confess. Thus do stubborn
Facts,

Facts, and the positive declarations, even of Protestants, evidently contradict the uncharitable Charge.

It must appear glaring then, to every man, if his mind be not seared to conviction and truth, that the misconduct of a Catholic is not to be imputed to the Principles of his Religion, but to some other cause, *viz.* the frailty of human Nature, the want of employment, encouragement, or industry.

These brief Remarks may suffice to remove from the minds of some, those unjust sparks of prejudice, which have been attempted to be fanned into a flame, by the envenomed, uncharitable and false productions of others, even in common News-papers; which formerly were intended for Amusement and Instruction, but are now become the vehicles of Calumny, Slander, and Falshood. And certain it is, let our Adversaries think as they may, that any Catholic who wounds the Reputation of his Neighbour, let his Religion be what it may, cannot be admitted to the *Sacraments*, till he has first made, or faithfully promises to make, a proper Reparation as soon as in his power; and also solemnly promises, in the presence of God, never more to be guilty of the like. If others were to make use of some such precautions, our ears would not be daily defiled with so many breaches of Christian Charity, nor should the Reader's mind be infected with such base and uncharitable Insinuations.

SECT.

SECT. II.

Oaths of Monopoly, Combination, and such like, unlawful.

IT has been already observed, that they who have unhappily sworn to do a *bad* action, sin grievously by taking such an Oath, and redouble the sin by keeping it. Hence, how wicked the *Combination* Oaths so frequently sworn by Journeymen, in the several branches of trade, to the manifest prejudice of their masters, and more especially the Public in general, though their wages are settled either by Law or Custom? How uncharitable also the Oaths of *Monopoly*, whereby some Tradesmen would fain engross a Manufacture to themselves, whilst they view their fellow-tradesmen and their families, though able and willing to labour, destitute of the common necessaries of life! Nay, some go so far as to assume the Authority of a Justice of the Peace, to tender Oaths to each other, whereby they mean to bind themselves mutually, not to work under such prices, as they think proper to appoint; threatning Death and Destruction, not unlike the menaces of the *Jews* to St. *Paul*, to such as will not coincide with them, and join in their unlawful Combinations; though the industrious honest man, satisfied with a *small* and *sober* pittance, is willing to *eat his bread in the sweat of his face*. Such proceedings are unlawful, their Oaths are iniquitous, they are null and void.

But what shall we think of those deluded people, who, under the specious pretence of an Oath perhaps taken over their cups, seduced inadvertently,

advertently, through malice, or no matter how, think themselves obliged to commit the most horrid crimes! destroying their Neighbour's goods, maiming their cattle, burning their houses, nay, sometimes burying the proprietors alive, or perhaps putting a more speedy period to their lives, and this under the pretence, either of having taken an Oath to that purpose, or as a remedy perhaps against pretended oppression. As to the first, the sacred Obligation of an Oath neither should nor can be the bond of iniquity, or an encouragement to crimes subversive of Laws divine and human, and perpetrated at the hazard of their lives; it is highly criminal to take such Oaths, and much more sinful to keep them.

As to the other, that such Outrages are a Remedy against Oppression: What more absurd than that every Individual shall arrogate to himself a Right to judge in such cases! Such a system would be evidently productive of Anarchy and Confusion; it would be subversive of all Law, Order, and Subordination; it would be, at once, to establish a Legislature of their own, and to act the part of Judge and Executioner! whereas they should *be subject*, as St. *Paul* says, * *to higher Powers; for there is no Power but from God; and the Powers that are, are ordained of God. Therefore he that resisteth Power, resisteth the ordinance of God. And they who resist bring Damnation to themselves. ..... Wherefore be you subject of Necessity; not only by reason of Wrath, but also for Conscience sake.* Besides, such unwarrantable Proceedings exasperate Government, and justly draw its frowns and punishments upon the Guilty. If they apprehend they are in any shape aggrieved,
let

---

* Rom. xiii. 1, 2, 5.

let them patiently submit to the wise dispensations of Providence: The trial is for their good, and the Tribulation only a just punishment due for their daily Offences. Let them pray to God, who can change the hearts of the great Ones of the Earth, for a Redress of their Complaints and Grievances, and in due time the Lord will graciously hear and relieve them. *Because he hath hoped in me, says the Lord, I will deliver him; I will protect him, because he hath known my Name. He shall cry to me and I will hear him: I am with him in his trouble: I will deliver him and I will glorify him**. What an unspeakable Comfort to a Christian, who bears his troubles and afflictions with resignation and patience!

But, to fly in the face of God's Law and that of the Land, for a redress of grievances or sufferings, is highly sinful, and by no means the method to obtain the desired Relief; and to attempt binding themselves by the sacred bond of an Oath to commit such Outrages and atrocious Crimes, is, to aggravate their Crimes beyond measure, and barring up every fair Avenue to Relief or Redress. They should devoutly call upon God's most sacred Name, that through its infinite Goodness, they may obtain grace to bear their trials with patience and resignation, saying with S. *Paul, For my part I am ready, not only to be bound, but also to die at Jerusalem for the Name of the Lord Jesus* †.

At the same time that the Poor are exhorted to bear their Crosses with Christian Patience, it is equally necessary to remind the Rich, to beware of grinding the face of the Poor, who plead they are often forced to unwarrantable steps by the hardness

---

* Psal. xc. 14, 15.   † Acts xxi. 13.

hardnefs of heart, inhumanity and infenfibility of the Rich : it is often remarked, that the Humane and Charitable feldom or never experience the leaft ingratitude from their indigent Neighbours; on the contrary, was it neceffary, they feem ready to fhed their blood for their generous and charitable Benefactor.

This Reflection muft infpire a noble mind with fentiments of charity and benevolence towards their diftreffed Brethren : But where they are infenfible to fuch feelings, let them remember, that the fupreme Lord of Heaven and Earth, is, the Father, the Protector of the Poor, he will not prove deaf to their Cries and Wants ; on the contrary, he is ever fteady to their caufe ; he who gave a Redundancy to the Rich, whereby they might have the merit of relieving their diftreffed fellow creature, may at once totally deprive them of their Riches, by calling them into another World, or perhaps may fpare their lives to feel the fmarts of Poverty, Hunger, and Indigence, in permitting them to fquander their fortunes in idlenefs and debauchery; whereas had they been attended with God's bleffing, they never would have known what diftrefs was, nor would they have denied to the Poor what was really their Due. The moft powerful means, therefore, to preferve life and the enjoyment of the goods of fortune, are, to feel the diftreffes of the Poor, to comfort and relieve them in their afflictions and wants.

S E C T.

SECT. III.

Oaths sworn by Roman Catholics to those of a different Persuasion, equally binding as if sworn to those of their own Commmunion.

WHEN it is carefully remarked, that an Oath derives its Force and Obligation, not from the Swearer, nor from the Person to whom he swears, but from God's most sacred *Name*, which is invoked and given as a Surety for the Truth of what is asserted or promised; it must appear evident, that a *lawful* Oath becomes obligatory, though given to a *Turk*, *Jew*, *Heretic*, or *Schismatic*. I say, a lawful Oath: for if the Oath be unlawful, it is not only meritorious but necessary to decline the Observance or Execution of it: as appears from the conduct of *David*, who though justly blamed for the wicked Oath he had sworn, to murder *Nabal*, yet he is celebrated in Holy Writ, for not keeping that rash and criminal Oath: for at the request of *Abigail*, *Nabal*'s Wife, he happily declined executing his rash and wicked Design[*].

It is evident then, that when you swear to do a bad action, or to omit a good one, you sin by taking such unlawful Oaths, and redouble the sin by keeping them. When therefore, Necessity impels you to swear, you should be extremely cautious to swear doing only, what is good and lawful to be done; and in that case, an Oath imposes a strict Obligation. And, if Circumstances do not change (for instance, you have promised upon Oath to give an Hundred Pounds to an Hospital, if by an unforeseen accident you lose the Money, the Obli-

[*] 1 Kings xxv. 34.

Obligation of the Oath ceases, unless it be afterwards recovered) you are in Conscience bound to fulfil your Oath, and that within the limited time, especially when the immediate Compliance tends to your Neighbour's Welfare, and the delay hurtful. Hence, if you promise upon Oath to do a Service to any Person, you are bound to keep it, and no diversity of Religion can excuse you from it. Though your Oath be given to a *Turk*, *Jew*, *Atheist*, or *Heretic*, it becomes obligatory, and you are equally bound to keep it, as if made to one of your own Communion.

Hence it appears, how unjustly the Roman Catholic Church is accused of supporting a Doctrine, which She in fact, detests, viz. *That Faith is not to be kept with Heretics: That a lawful Oath sworn to those of a different Persuasion, is not binding*, &c.

The Doctrine of the Catholic Church is quite averse to such Tenets, as may be fully seen in our Authors; and the Demeanour of the Roman Catholics of this Kingdom, daily proves the Charge to be false and groundless: for, if they believed, that it is not criminal to impose upon one of a different Persuasion, by a false Oath; or that a Promise made to Protestants, upon Oath, is not binding, why do they refuse taking them? If Roman Catholics believed, or could prevail on themselves to think, that they could with a safe Conscience, impose on their Neighbour, or any Person whatever, by a false Oath; or that lawful Oaths sworn to those of a different Persuasion, are not binding; surely they are not such Enemies to their Temporal Interest, as to refuse taking such Oaths, and frankly qualifying themselves for lucrative Places or honourable Employments!

The

The Truth is, we know the Catholic Church teaches, that Oaths are the most sacred and binding Obligations upon Earth, between Man and Man: That no Consideration whatsoever, should induce us to swear a false Oath; nor can any Authority whatever impower us to swear to do what is unjust or unlawful to be done. And every lawful Oath sworn to a *Turk, Jew, Atheist*, or *Heretic*, is obligatory; and a wilful breach of such Oaths is severely punished by Almighty God.

A terrible Proof of this Truth is recorded in the 25th Chapter of the 4th Book of *Kings*, where we read of the most frightful Judgment, that ever befel a King of *Israel*, being inflicted on *Sedecias*, for a Breach of Faith to the Infidel *Nebuchodonosor*, King of *Babylon*; who having subdued the Land of *Judea*, appointed his Uncle *Sedecias* to sway his Sceptre over that conquered Nation: first requiring from him an Oath of Fidelity or Allegiance, which *Sedecias* thought proper to break soon after. *Nebuchodonosor* being informed of the Perfidy of his Uncle, returns to *Judea*, dethrones *Sedecias* and makes him Prisoner: He then destroyed the City of *Jerusalem* by Fire, and the Temple itself did not escape the Flames: his two Sons were put to death in his Presence; when after beholding the affecting Scene, his Eyes are put out; and if his life was spared, it was only to prolong his Agony and Torments: for, by the express Command of *Nebuchodonosor*, *Sedecias* is bound with chains and led Captive to *Babylon*, there to end the small remainder of his painful Life in Misery and Bondage.

This exemplary Punishment was inflicted on the unhappy *Sedecias*, as the Prophet *Ezekiel* informs us, us, because *Sedecias disregarded his Oath**. It is to be observed, that though the Promise of Fidelity, sealed with an Oath, had been made to an *Idolater*, yet as God's Holy Name was called upon as a Witness or Surety for the Performance of what he had promised, so jealous is the Lord of the Honour due to his Adorable Name, that he favours even those who are his avowed Enemies, to punish the perjured Swearer, who presumes to mal-treat his most holy and terrible Name: for, says he, *thou shalt not forswear thyself, but shall keep thy Oaths to the Lord*†. And truly, we are not to be surprized, that the Lord should send such heavy Judgments on him that forswears himself: " for " the Lord, says St. *Chrysostom*, becomes almost " implacable, when Oaths are broken:" because, an Oath (as has been already remarked) derives its obligation, not from the Person's Merits or Religion, to whom we swear, but from God's most awful and venerable *Name*, which is given as a Surety. Hence, without any Distinction of Persons, you are obliged to keep your lawful *Oaths to the Lord*, together with Faith and Truth to your Fellow Creature. It appears evidently then, that the Roman Catholic Church is most unjustly accused of upholding a Doctrine, which She, in Fact, detests, viz. " that Faith is not to " be kept with those of a different Communion, " nor are Oaths sworn to them binding," and so forth: as we shall see more fully in the next Chapter.

Oaths extorted by Robbers from Persons robbed, for instance: that they shall not discover or prosecute

---

* xvii. 18. † Matth. v. 33.

cute them, are not binding: becaufe, as St. *Thomas* fays, fuch Oaths are againft " Public Juftice*."

It is fometimes the cafe, that Perfons call upon the Name of the Lord as a Witnefs or Surety, for the performance of what is, in itfelf, good and lawful to be done, with a view only, to accomplifh what is bafe and unlawful to be done. For inftance: how frequently are the moft folemn Oaths, of future Marriage, fworn by vile Deceivers to feduce the Innocent, and deftroy them? Thus are unfufpecting and unguarded Virgins fometimes deluded and deceived by fuch fpecious Promifes of Marriage, fealed with the facred bond of an Oath. Have they not found, from fatal Experience, that fo foon as their Undoers have accomplifhed their brutal Defigns, they difregard the Injury done, or the Engagements they are under, and leave the unhappy Victims of their Paffions, to lament their Folly and Credulity? Such a vile and impious Artifice cannot however remain unpunifhed, becaufe the Deceiver is guilty of an heinous Offence: firft, by reafon of the Injury done to his Fellow Creature. Secondly, by breaking his Oath. And thirdly, for making ufe of God's moft facred Name to cloak his bafe defigns.

It is true, fuch abandoned Profligates have and frequently do efcape the Rod of Civil Juftice, but they can never fly from God's avenging Juftice, which fhall perfecute the perjured Swearer to the very Gates of Hell. *Shall he*, fays the Lord, *who has broken his Promife efcape? No; for as I live, the Oath which he has broken, fhall be placed on his Forehead*†. As if to infinuate, that the breach of

E 2 a law-

---

* 2. 2. q. 89 art. 7. ad. 3. —— 3 Sent dift. 39. q. 1. art. 3. † Ezekiel xvii..19.

a lawful Oath, especially when attended with prejudice to our Neighbour, is of so heinous a nature, that it shall be fixed on the most conspicuous part of the Swearer's Body, his Forehead; for his greater Confusion and future Condemnation.

CHAP. VIII.

The Third Condition necessary to render an Oath lawful, viz. TRUTH.

"A FALSE Oath," says St. *Thomas*, "wants Truth," which is the third Condition necessary to render an Oath lawful: for, *thou shalt swear in Truth*, says the Lord*. By this Condition, says St. *Thomas*, we are required to swear nothing but the Truth, or what we judge to be really truth, after mature deliberation and reflection: for to call upon the Lord of all Truth to witness a falshood, is manifestly attempting to make him a Party to your wickedness, a Supporter and Defender of Lies; which must be highly injurious to the God of all Sanctity and Truth.

A false Oath is sworn, when a Man swears to a lie, that is, when he swears that to be true, which he knows or believes to be false, says a celebrated Author †. He is also perjured, who swears that which is really true, yet when he swears, he thinks it is false; because he swears to what he thinks is a lie. He also who promises any thing under Oath, and at the same Time does not intend to do it; or does not take the Pains he ought to do, to fulfil his Oath, (if what he has so promised be lawful and possible) is perjured: because he who calls upon God to witness, that he will do such a thing,

---

* Jeremy iv. 2.   † Natalis Alexander, Theol. Dog. & Moral. Tom. ii. Lib. 4, A. 7.

thing, and really intends not to do it, nor does he take proper pains to fulfil his Oath, in fact lies in his own Heart, and swears to the Lie. They also, are guilty of Perjury, who swear to do a thing that is not in their Power, nor likely to be at the limited Time. Thus Tradesmen often swear they will have their respective Manufactures ready at a certain Time, though in their hearts thoroughly convinced, it will not be in their Power. Thus Debtors promise upon Oath to discharge their Debts at an appointed Time, though persuaded in their minds it will be out of their power: nay, and perhaps are determined never to pay.

They are also guilty of Perjury who swear falsely, though their motive be charitable: for instance, to save others from blame or punishment: Thus Servants think it excusable to swear falsely, if they can thereby conceal their faults, and screen themselves or others from the Indignation of their Masters; it is however a damnable practice: for it is not lawful, for the preservation of the Universe, to swear a false Oath, much less to avoid blame or reproach. How lamentable, then, the misconduct of such Persons: for, though it appears to be the Will of Heaven, that they shall live in a state of servitude and drudgery; yet, it is also the Will of God, that such Servants as behave themselves *honestly*, *soberly*, and *piously*, shall be rewarded in the other life, with freedom and happiness, perhaps, superior to that of their Masters and Mistresses. If then, their Situation in Life deprives them of temporal happiness here, at least let them not by pilfering, cursing, swearing, &c. rob themselves of that eternal happiness, which God has mercifully prepared for them hereafter.

To call God to witness a lie or falshood, is treating him with the infamous Character of a Liar: which glaring irreverence must provoke him to wrath and indignation. 'Tis very offensive to Persons in high life to be branded with the injurious Title of a Liar. Every Man of Honour seems more offended with the Appellation of a *Liar*, than if he received a wound from the point of a Sword. If then, we may be allowed to compare small Matters with great, what shall we think of the injury offered to God's Honour, whilst the false, the perjured Swearer attempts to make his *God* uphold and patronize his Lies? Words cannot sufficiently express the heinousness of the Offence!

Nor does it diminish the Crime, that the falshood which you assert, is but of a trifling nature, and that you swear only in *Jest*: for instead of extenuating the Crime, this Circumstance serves rather to increase it: Because, as the Angelic Doctor says [*], " He that forswears himself in a
" Jest, does not avoid an Irreverence to God,
" but in some Manner increases it, and therefore
" is not to be excused from mortal Sin: because,
" without any Utility or Necessity, God is wan-
" tonly called upon to witness a falshood."
Hence Pope *Innocent* XI. in the Year 1679, condemned the following Proposition: *To call God to witness a small Lie, is not so great an Irreverence, that God can or will damn a Man for it* [†]. So that he who swears to a lie, though in a trivial Matter, by the irreverence offered to God's adorable Name, justly deserves everlasting Torments: for God's most sacred Name is not to be trifled with, nor is it to be invoked to give the least sanction or appearance of Truth to the smallest Lie.

There

---

[*] 2. 2. q 98. a. 3. ad. 2.   [†] Wigant, Tract. x. Exam. iv.

There are many Persons, who ignorantly persuade themselves to think, that they may with safety elude the force of an Oath by using Equivocations, Mental Reservations, or secret Evasions, whereby they swear *deceitfully* to their Neighbour, and impose upon him. For instance: By forming within themselves an Intention *not to swear*, though they actually *do swear:* Or by forming a different *Intention* or *Meaning* from that of the Person to whom they swear. Such a Method of Swearing is highly criminal, nor does it exempt them from the guilt of Perjury: because the Person that swears should use no deceit, but should swear according to the usual Meaning of the Words, and the Intention of the Person to whom he swears; or as the Scripture expresses it: *He that sweareth to his Neighbour, and deceiveth not* [*]. Hence St. *Thomas* teaches, " That when the In-
" tention of him that swears and of him to whom
" he swears, is not the same; if this be occasioned
" by fraud and deceit in him that swears, the
" Oath must be kept according to the usual
" Meaning of the Words, as he understands it
" to whom he swears [†]."

Hence, the two following Propositions were also *condemned* by Pope *Innocent* XI. *If any one, either alone, or before others, whether asked, or of his own accord, or for recreation's-sake, or any other end, swears, that he has not done a thing, which really he has done, understanding within himself something else than what he has done, or some other way from that whereby he did it, or some other additional Circumstance, does not lie, nor is he guilty of Perjury.* Therefore, according to the Doctrine of the Church, such a Swearer must be a Liar and perjured. The other Proposition is this: *Upon a rea-*

[*] Psal. xiv. 5.   [†] 2. 2. q. 89. a. 7. ad. 4.

reasonable Account it is lawful to swear without an Intention of swearing, whether the Thing sworn to, be little or great*. Thus, it clearly appears, by the Decisions of the Church, in what a detestable Light She holds all those, who when they swear, use Equivocations or Mental Reservations, whereby they mean to evade the Force and Obligation of an Oath, and deceive their Neighbour.

Though Perjury be a grievous Crime, even when you forswear yourself in a trivial Matter, yet it is much aggravated, when you swear to a lie, with a View to defraud or oppress the Innocent. It is a Sin of the deepest Dye, not unlike a Viper, which by feeding upon Scorpions becomes more envenomed and poisonous: because it includes a grievous Injury done to our Neighbour, grounded on the highest Disrespect that can be offered to Almighty God; nay such a Disrespect, as we would be ashamed to offer to our Fellow Creature.

Would you, O profane Swearer, have Courage enough to solicit a Gentleman of known probity and veracity, to swear, that such a Person, whose Life you mean to take, though innocent, is guilty of Robbery, Murder, or some such capital Crime? Would you, unless bereft of all Sense or Shame, attempt to ask a Man of Honour and Truth, to attest the false Accusation? I believe there are but very few Instances of such bare-faced Effrontry shewn, even to your Fellow Creature. Why then, will you presume to ask of God, what you dare not ask of Man? Or how can you have the Presumption to call upon the great God to witness your Lies, when you have not Courage to ask the like of an honest Man! Yet so it is, that the perjured Swearer takes much greater Liberties with his God, than he dares to take with his Fellow Creature! To

* Wigant. Tract. xvii. Append. Exam. iii.

To call God to witness a Falshood, is in Fact saying: that as the Swearer has not Veracity enough to intitle him to be believed, nor Power sufficient to execute his wicked Designs, he therefore, calls upon God to descend from Heaven, to supply his deficiency; that by the Interposition of his awful Name, he may be effectually enabled to accomplish his wicked Purposes. This is evidently making God, who is Sanctity itself, the Abettor and Warranter of Iniquity. Can any Thing equal these presumptuous Attempts, which are doubtless implied in the false Oath of every perjured Swearer!

Though Almighty God be infinitely merciful, it cannot however, be expected, that He shall remain insensible to such glaring Acts of Disrespect, as are Daily offered to his most venerable Name. He has often threatened, in the Holy Scriptures, to inflict the most severe Punishments on the perjured Swearer, and his avenging Justice has, from Time to Time, executed his Menaces in the most exemplary Manner. I shall relate one remarkable Instance thereof *.

There lived a certain Widow, of good repute, in the Island of *Corsica*, who had an only Daughter, to whom her Father bequeathed three hundred Crowns, as her Portion, when marriageable. The Mother not thinking the Money safe in her Possession, deposits it with her Neighbour, on whose Honesty and Integrity she relied so much, as not even to require an accountable Receipt. A few Years after, the Daughter being at Age, and her Marriage agreed upon, the Mother demands the 300 Crowns from her Trustee. But, how great was the Widow's Surprize, to find her supposed Friend,

* Segneri, Crist. Istruito. del Juramento.

Friend, in whom she had reposed so great a Confidence, denying positively, that he ever had received a Farthing from her! The distressed Mother could not pretend to contend the Matter at Law, not having any other Evidence than the Testimony of his Wife, who was the only Person present, when the Money was delivered to her Husband. She expostulated with the unhappy Couple on the Justness of her Demand; they, in return, declare themselves willing to swear before a Magistrate, and solemnly acquit themselves of the Charge.

The afflicted Widow hastens to the Chief Magistrate, and relates her Case: He consoles her, and promises every Thing in his Power to her Assistance: He cites the wicked Couple to Court, where a solemn Oath was tendered, which they took without Hesitation, declaring they knew nothing of the Money demanded. Not content with this vile Act of Perjury and Injustice, but, as if to render it more solemn, the perjured Couple add an execratory Oath: that, if they were not innocent, of what had been laid to their Charge, that God the Avenger of Lies and Perjury, should extend his Punishments not only to them, but also to their Children.

The Lord, whose all-seeing Eye clearly views the most hidden secrets of hearts, knowing full well they had called upon his most holy and awful Name to support that crying act of Injustice, becomes highly incensed against the wicked Couple, and his avenging Justice delays not to inflict the punishment which they so justly deserved, and so solemnly wished to themselves and their posterity.

The

The perjured Couple had three children; one of two months old, whom the mother, when going to Court, had left in a cradle; another of five years, and a third of twenty-five years old. The mother returning immediately from Court to her house, finds the cradle overturned, and the Infant smothered. Her guilty conscience quickly represents this catastrophe as a just judgment from the Almighty God, for the sin of Perjury which she committed; but instead of imploring forgiveness from the Throne of Mercy, and repairing the Evil she had done, inflamed with rage and despair, she, thinking the other child of five years had overturned the cradle, rushes on the harmless Babe, and stabs it to the very heart.

Nor did the tragedy end here; for, the Husband returning home about an hour after, with a conscience racking him for the sins of Injustice and Perjury he had committed, beholding one of his children smothered, another bleeding to death, and viewing the bloody weapon in his Wife's hand, without further enquiry, draws his sword and wounds her mortally. The Neighbours alarmed at the cries of the dying wife, rush into the house, and seeing the bloody instrument of death in the husband's hand, they drag him to the Court of Justice, which was then sitting, where he confessed himself guilty, and was condemned to immediate death.

You may, perhaps, think this a sufficient temporal Punishment for a false Oath; but the tragedy is not yet ended: for, whilst they sought, in vain, an hangman to execute the sentence, the elder Son returns home, and beholding his Mother a corpse on the floor, besmeared all over with blood, and understanding his father was the murderer,

derer, offers himself, without hesitation, to be the Executioner of his Father; that he might revenge the blood of his Mother, whom he tenderly loved. His rage now overcomes his shame; he mounts the ladder, and becomes his Father's Executioner!

The Divine Justice was not as yet satisfied; for a few days after, when the Son's passion had abated, he began to reflect on the infamy he had entailed on himself, by being his father's executioner, and unable to withstand the many afflicting thoughts that must have occured to his mind, on the melancholy occasion, at length plunges a dagger into his own breast, and so puts a period to his miserable life.

Thus did God's avenging Justice persecute the unhappy Couple for the sins of Perjury and Injustice. Their Posterity shared of the punishment; nay, the two innocent Babes had their part of the temporal Punishment, and fell victims to the Perjury of their wicked Parents. This exemplary punishment, frightful as it was, is only what might be reasonably expected in consequence of what the Lord has declared in the following words: * *A Malediction shall come,* says he, *into the House of him that swears falsely by my Name, and shall dwell in the midst of it, until it shall consume it, and its very Foundations.* A terrible Sentence fulminated against all those who forswear or perjure themselves! The punishment to be inflicted, shall fall, not only on the guilty head of the false swearer, but shall also reach the harmless Posterity! Beware then, O Parents, of so heinous a Crime! Let not the Love of Riches or Honours prompt you to acquire them by such criminal

* Zach. v. 4.

nal means: such Acquisitions are not to be counted upon; they are precarious, and never attended with a real Blessing.

You see the Lord has menaced Destruction to those that swear falsely: you also see the menace executed in the unhappy *Corsican* Family: what happened to them, may befal you, if you imitate their example: you cannot claim any special protection. Learn then, at their cost, to avoid the damnable crime in future; if you regard not yourselves, at least feel for your innocent Offspring, who are often punished for the crimes of their Parents.

Notwithstanding this hateful crime is so strictly forbidden, and so severely punished, does it not still rage amongst Christians to a shameful degree? How many swear to a Lie through Wantonness, without any apparent Necessity, and meerly for Amusement; whilst others, like the unhappy Couple already mentioned, swear falsely to oppress the Widow, and defraud the Orphan; or to rob their fellow creature of his property. Such acts of Injustice and Perjury must make every man, actuated by the least principle of Religion or Humanity, tremble; for, if the most exemplary Judgments do not visibly befal the perjured Miscreants, their Souls most certainly fall under the Divine Malediction: and, if the Punishments they so justly deserve, are for a time suspended, 'tis entirely due to God's infinite Mercy, that pleads time for their Repentance and Amendment, which, if neglected, they may expect to experience the Severity of his Justice, *who will render unto every one according to his Works.*

And,

And, truly, what Punishment can be really adequate to such an atrocious crime? What can be more injurious to the King of Glory, than for men to endeavour to make him palliate their Knavery, to engage his sacred Truth to patronize their Lies, and support their Falshoods! This is, indeed, to debase and defile his sacred Name to a shameful degree. Beware then, in future, of so heinous a Crime, and let the express Command of Almighty God be deeply imprinted on your Minds: * *Thou shalt not*, says the Lord, *forswear thyself in my Name, nor pollute the Name of thy God.*

CHAP. IX.

Of Imprecations.

AN Imprecation, Curse, or Malediction, is, to wish *Evil* to our Neighbour, ourselves, or any of God's Creatures. St. *Paul* most pressingly exhorts the *Romans* to decline so great a Sin, and informs them, that they are not to wish Evil even to their Enemies, who hate and persecute them: † *Bless them*, says he, *that persecute you: bless and curse not.* And to remove every Excuse that might be assigned to palliate so heinous a Crime, he further says, ‡ *Be not deceived: neither Fornicators, ... nor Railers, nor Extortioners shall possess the Kingdom of God.*

Though Christian Charity, which should ever animate our Actions, requires, that we shall not wish Evil to Ourselves or Fellow-creature, yet, does not daily Experience evince, that we cannot feel

---

* Levit. xix. 12.
† Rom xii. 14.   ‡ 1 Cor. vi. 9, 10.

feel the least Disappointment, without imprecating some Evil to ourselves, or some of God's Creatures. Strange Absurdity! to wish an Encrease of Evils to ourselves, which, in fact, every Man means and ought to shun.

If our Neighbour displeases us, even in trifling matters, nay, often without any Provocation at all, a peal of Curses is immediately thundered out against him. The innocent parts of Nature are often damned in the same manner, though the Disappointment resulting from them proceeds, too often, from our own Rashness and Imprudence. How often is God called upon to *damn them, the Devil to carry them away,* &c. Nay, are not the most dreadful Imprecations, at times, uttered even against your Domestics, Wife, or Children: and what, truly, would become of *either,* did not the amazing Goodness of God often refuse to grant such uncharitable wishes?

Many Persons are deceived by imagining, that if the Evil wished, does not befal them, there is no harm done. It is true, indeed, that if your evil Wishes have not their Effect, there is no harm done to your Neighbour, but not so to you, uncharitable Curser! for, if you wish the Evil from your heart, you commit as great a Sin, in the sight of God, as if the Evil which you ineffectually wish, had actually fallen upon him; because, Sin is committed by the interior Consent of the Will to a sinful Action, and the exterior Action in every Sin, * is only the Execution of what is already consented too and compleated in the Will; and just as it lies in the heart, so it is in the sight of God, who penetrates into the deepest Recesses of our Souls.

Hence,

* S. Tho. 1. 2. q 72. art. 7.

Hence, he who draws his sword with a Resolution to kill his Neighbour, is guilty of Murder in the sight of God, though he, by chance, parries the Thrust, and escapes the intended Evil; for, when you deliberately consent in your Mind to any Evil, you that moment become guilty of it in the sight of God; and the greater the Evil, the greater the Crime.

'Tis true, many Evils may befal your Neighbour from the actual Execution of a sinful Thought, which do not attend the Thought itself, so long as it is confined within the limits of your own Breast; for instance, you have formed a Design to rob your Neighbour, if you execute your evil Design, you entail Distress, and perhaps a thousand other Misfortunes upon him. But suppose you are prevented from executing your wicked Purpose; yet, as your determined Resolution was to commit Robbery, you stand guilty of Robbery in the sight of God; and though you shall appear innocent in the sight of Men, so long as you conceal your sinful designs, yet, so soon as you deliberately consent to perpetrate the evil Deed, you become guilty of it in the sight of God, the Searcher of Hearts. In like manner, though Almighty God does not always permit your evil Wishes to take effect, yet by your calling upon God, directly or indirectly, with your heart or mouth, to curse his Creatures, you become guilty of a grievous Crime in the sight of God, and the greater the Evil, the greater the Crime.

It is however a certain Truth, that those evil Wishes or Curses have sometimes, through God's Permission, the most dreadful Effects. If so, what will become of the uncharitable Curser?

If

If he be not as hardened and infenfible as a Rock, he muft be racked with the moft difmal Apprehenfions. Suppofe you call upon God to *damn your Fellow-creature: that the Devil may carry him away*, &c. If God fhould permit the Devil to carry away the Perfon you wifh to him, what horror would it not raife in your Breaft? To view your Fellow-creature hurried headlong into the Flames of Hell, in Confequence of your uncharitable Wifh! Sure, you would fcarcely enjoy a moment's Peace of Mind, when you would ferioufly reflect on the frightful Effects of your wicked Imprecation!

It is well known, that a Man who has committed Murder, though the horrid Crime remains concealed, feldom enjoys the leaft Tranquility of Mind; the Blood he has fhed, deeply ftains his Confcience: it diftracts him by Day, and haunts him by Night: it perfecutes him upon Earth, and cries to Heaven for Vengeance, which the Murderer hourly dreads falling on his guilty Head. How much greater the Crime of calling upon God to damn *Man*, whom he has formed according to his own Image and Likenefs, and whom he has redeemed at the Expence of his Blood! This is, indeed, to wifh eternal Death and Deftruction to both Body and Soul.

There is no Doubt, but that as Almighty God, who is Lord of his Creatures, can grant eternal Rewards to thofe that love and ferve him, fo he can inflict never-ending Punifhments on fuch as offend him: and as he can blefs, fo he can curfe at Pleafure; and one Word is fufficient to effect either: for, the Word of God is fo wonderfully powerful, that it produces whatever it expreffes, *God fpoke and it was done* [*], fays the Scripture:

nothing

[*] Gen. i.

nothing more is related for the Production of the Universe, nor was more necessary; because his Omnipotent Word, effects whatever it expresses. Not so with Man, whose Words are feeble, who often says and promises more, than perhaps he is able or willing to perform.

Notwithstanding, it has often been the Will of God, that Imprecations or Curses uttered by Man, shall have their Effect; as appears in the Prophet *Eliseus* *, who going up to *Bethel*, was mocked and insulted by a Multitude of Boys; whereupon, the venerable Prophet, looking back, cursed them in the *Name of the Lord*; scarcely had he expressed the Words, when the Curse alighted upon them; two Bears rushed furiously out of an adjacent Forest, and tore two and forty of them to pieces. Thus was God willing, the Curse should alight on the gibing Boys, as a Lesson to future Generations, to respect God in the Person of his Ministers and Servants.

This Judgment, in putting a Period to their Lives, put an End to the growing Impiety; and though the Punishment proved hurtful to the Body, yet it proved serviceable to the Soul, as St. *Paul* says of the incestuous *Corinthian*, whom he delivered *over to Satan for the Destruction of the Flesh, that his Spirit may be saved* †. And such is the Church's Motive for anathematizing or cursing its disobedient and scandalous Members.

Almighty God grants Efficacy, from time to time, also to the Curses of the Poor, of Orphans and Widows, as a Defence or Protection against the cruel and inhuman Oppressions of the imperious Rich; that they may dread oppressing the latter, or despising the former, on account of their

* 4 Kings ii.   † 1 Cor. v. 5.

their Poverty: *Provoke not,* says the Holy Ghost, *the Poor in his Want ..... for the Prayer of him that curseth thee, in the bitterness of his soul, shall be heard* *.

But, as the Curse of a Parent to a Child, is frequently attended with the most dreadful Consequences, the Danger and Enormity of so great a Vice, too common to Parents upon every trifling Fault committed by their Children, ought to be more fully exposed, to deter Parents from committing so unnatural a Crime. It is a Vice so contrary to the Light of Reason, that the very *Gentiles* themselves held it in Abomination. *Plato,* in his Code of Laws, forbids Parents cursing their Children, upon any Account whatsoever; because, their Imprecations are often attended with greater Evils, than the Parents themselves would really wish.

Various Reasons might be assigned, why the Curse of a Parent has, in general, so terrible an Effect on the Child; because, God means thereby to support the Dignity and Authority of a Parent, too often infringed upon and abused, by disorderly and disobedient Children; to the End, that the Dread of the Parent's Curse, should restrain the Child within the Bounds of his Duty; for, Parents hold the Place of God upon Earth, with regard to their Offspring, and should therefore be respected, honoured and obeyed. And, if in case of a wilful Disobedience in the Child, the injured Parent curses him, God frequently ratifies the Imprecation, as a just Punishment due to the disobedient Child: for, as *the Father's Blessing,* says the Holy Ghost, *establishes the House of the Children,* so *the Mother's Curse rooteth up the foundation* †.

To

* Eccl. iv. 2, 6.   † Eccl. iii. 11.

To disobey a parental Command, when it enforces what is lawful, is highly offensive to Almighty God, as he declares in the following Words: *If a Man has a stubborn and unruly Son, who will not hear the Commands of his Father or Mother, and being corrected, contemns to obey—the People of the City shall stone him.*

If to disobey a Parent be so heinous, how much more so to wish Evil or Death to them, who under God, have given them Life! *He that curseth his Father, or Mother, dying let him die* †. Can you read this Sentence pronounced against you, O disobedient Children! without trembling? Or can you hesitate a Moment, to use every Effort to repair the Evil you have done? Delay not to beg Pardon of Almighty God, whose Commands you have transgressed, by dishonouring your Parents, from whom also, you should beg Forgiveness; and shew, by an humble and filial Demeanour, the Sincerity of your Repentance and Respect. Remember, 'tis One of God's Commands, *to honour your Father and Mother*. Nay, Nature, and your very Existence demand it from you: and for your greater Encouragement, your prompt Compliance will be attended with the most signal Blessings, both here and hereafter, as Almighty God repeatedly promises.

Another Reason, why the Curses of Parents pronounced against their Children, are attended with the most frightful Consequences, is, often in Punishment of the Parent's own Impiety, Rashness, and Impatience. Hence, as the antient *Tertullian* remarks, ‡ God knowing full well the natural

---

* Deut. xxi. 18, 21.   † Levit. xx. 9.
‡ Con. Marc.

natural Propensity of Parents to study and labour for the Prosperity of their Offspring, are generally more affected at any Disaster happening to their Children through their Faults, than if the Evil actually befel themselves. And therefore, to restrain Parents from offending God, they are threatened with having their Sins punished, in the Persons of their Children, to *the Third and Fourth Generation* *.

This leads me, Christian Reader, to unfold briefly, a Difficulty, which may occur from the foregoing Doctrine, *viz.* How Children, who are Innocent, and by Reason of their infant State, are incapable of giving Offence to God or Man, shall be punished for the Crimes of their guilty Parents, as appears from the Scriptures, they are?

The knotty Difficulty has been abundantly cleared by the angelic Pen of the great St. *Thomas*, who informs us, † That there are two Kinds of Punishments; the one *spiritual*, which regards the Soul; the other *corporeal*, which regards the Body. Children are not punished with a spiritual Punishment, unless they have been, in some measure, Accomplices; which cannot be supposed the Case with Infants, who are incapable of *actual* Sin. And in this Sense the Prophet says, ‡ *The Son shall not bear the Iniquity of the Father.* But as to *corporeal* Punishment, Children are frequently punished by Almighty God for the Transgressions of their Parents: Thus the spurious Fruit of *David*'s Adultery, was not permitted to live, in Punishment of the Murder and Adultery he committed. Nay, as a just Judgment

---

* Exod. xx. 5.   † 1. 2. q. 81. a. 2.
‡ Ezech. xviii. 20.

ment on Parents, their Sins are punished to the *third and fourth Generations*, to infinuate, that finful Parents, even, when bending towards their Mother, Earth, shall become forrowful Spectators of *their* Crimes being punished in their Offspring, even at so great a Distance: and with Justice; for, as God is infinitely liberal in rewarding the Virtuous, he is also strict in persecuting the Wicked.

And, if he Threatens to punish the Crimes of Parents to the Fourth Generation, he promises to crown their good Deeds for a thousand Generations: *I am the Lord thy God*, says he, *mighty, jealous, visiting the Iniquity of the Fathers upon the Children, unto the Third and Fourth Generation of them that Hate me: And shewing Mercy unto Thousands, to them that Love me, and keep my Commandments* *. Admire, pious Reader, how much God's Mercy and Goodness exceed the Severity of his Justice!

Whilst Children should be extremely cautious, not to deserve the Parent's Curse; Parents should be equally careful to refrain from cursing their Children. Yet do not Fathers and Mothers often rashly and unnaturally Curse their Offspring, without perhaps waiting the Commission of a second Fault, and sometimes, at the most trifling Provocation, they pray, *that God may shorten their Days: that the Devil may break their Necks: that they may never prosper*, and such like impious and unnatural Imprecations! Whereas, were Parents to reflect on the dismal Consequences attending such Curses, they would certainly refrain from them. Their Curses may alight on their Children in their Youth, Manhood, or Old Age: the

Effects

---

* Exod. xx 5. 6.

Effects of a Curse are not confined to Time or Place.

Wherefore, let Parents beware of cursing their Children, and bear patiently with their Faults: Correct them with Prudence and Moderation; beware of striking them, as some Parents unguardedly do, with the same Violence, as a Smith does his Anvil. Correction should be given with Moderation; by good Instructions endeavour to work a Reformation, and enforce them by good Example. But above all, recommend them to God, who by his efficacious Grace, can effectually change their Hearts. In short, *Bless them*, as St. *Paul* says, *and do not Curse*.

You plead, that as your Children are disobedient and wicked, you cannot avoid cursing them. For that very Reason, you should not Curse them: because their Wickedness disposes them to receive the dire Effects of your Curse sooner; not unlike Tow, the drier it is, the sooner it catches the Flame.

It is strictly forbidden then, to Curse your Wife, Children or any of God's Creatures, whether animate or inanimate, that *Evil* should befal them. Nay it is not lawful to Curse the worst of God's Creatures, no not even the *Devil* himself: for *while the Ungodly curseth the Devil, he curseth his own Soul**, which St. *Thomas* thus explains †:

If a Sinner curses the Devil on Account of his *Wickedness*, by the same Rule he judges the Devil, he condemns himself. If on the other Hand, we consider the Devil, as to his *Nature*, it is not lawful to curse him: because he is an Angel, though by Rebellion, he is become an Angel of Darkness; besides, that he is appointed, by Divine

---

* Eccl. xxi. 30.   † 2. 2. q. 76. a. 1. ad 3.

vine Juſtice, the Executioner of reprobate Souls. Judge you then, if it be unlawful to Curſe the Devil, though God's great Enemy, and moſt deteſtable of his Creatures, how heinous it muſt be to Curſe thoſe Souls, which *Jeſus* has redeemed at the Expence of his Blood: or thoſe innocent Parts of Nature, your Lands, Cattle, Houſes, &c. which God's all-powerful Arm has formed for, and ſubjected to the Uſe and Dominion of Man.

In fine, reflect, Chriſtian Reader, that when you call upon God *to damn your Fellow Creature; to ſtrike him dead*, &c. You aſſume the Character of a *Judge*, and appoint your God the *Executioner!* for, a Judge does not put the Criminal to death; the Judge pronounces Sentence (ſuppoſe in the Caſe of Murder) and the Tops-Man executes it. Hence, as often as you call upon God to inflict any Evil on his Creatures, you act the Part of a Judge, and call upon your God to be the Executioner, or "Torturer," as S. *Auguſtin*[*] expreſſes it. Is this not treating the ſupreme Being with the higheſt Indignity and Diſreſpect! Is it not to diſhonour the Judge of the Living and the Dead, to a ſhameful Degree! Is it not to call upon the Lord *to ſerve you, even in your ſins?* as he juſtly complains by the Prophet *Iſaiah*.

Let all thoſe then, who have been unhappily addicted to this Crime, repent timely and ſincerely for the grievous Offence offered to God's infinite Majeſty: let them endeavour to repair the Injuries done to God's Creatures, by imploring his Bleſſing upon them: And for the Indignity offered to the Lord's moſt ſacred Name, never ceaſe to praiſe it: Reſolve to avoid, in Future, the deteſtable Practice of Curſing; and ever remember, that
a Curſe

[*] Serm. 4. de S. Steph.

a Curse uttered without Cause shall come upon a Man, says the Holy Ghost *. If your Imprecations, through God's Goodness, do not alight on the Person to whom you wish the Evil, they will certainly revert, and fall on the guilty Head of the uncharitable Curser. Let those then, who curse others, tremble, at least, for themselves, and beware in Time, lest they be numbered among those, of whom the Prophet complains, who passed by without saying, *the Blessing of the Lord be upon you*: *We have blessed you in the Name of the Lord* †.

How widely does this Mode of Salutation, recommended by the Prophet, differ from that practised by Christians now-a-days: the one is Christian-like; the other addresses him with an Oath or Execration, under the specious Pretence of Friendship and Esteem. When a Man meets his Friend or Acquaintance, he immediately accosts him with that uncivil, as well as unchristian Salutation: *By G—d, I am glad to see you*, as if, in Truth, you could possibly rejoice to see your Acquaintance well, whilst you abuse the Name of God, who gave him Existence and preserves it. Another says, *God d—n you, how do you do?* To call thus upon God to damn your Friend, and then ask him how he does, is absurd and impious: as if you could reasonably expect to find him well, whilst you wish Hell to be his Abode! A third says, *God d—n me, I am glad to see you.* A strange Compliment indeed, to Self, and Friend! first, to wish Damnation to yourself, and then assure your Friend you are glad to see him, as if you would wish him to share of your Torments!

---

* Proverbs xxvi. 2.   † Psalm cxxviii. 8.

Custom may indeed have made such Modes of Address fashionable, but not excusable. You say, such Expressions stand meerly for *Cyphers*; that they are intended only to express your Friendship more warmly; but that in Fact, you mean not to offend God, or that the least Evil should befal your Neighbour. Such Pleadings will not excuse you: for though the Person to whom you wish the Evil, receives no Harm from your uncharitable Imprecations, not so with you, who utters the Imprecation: because, you instantly become guilty in the Sight of God, by calling upon him to curse his Creatures, for which you must be accountable before the Tribunal of his Justice.

Though such Expressions may be looked upon by you, as *harmless*, as meer *Cyphers*, they are highly offensive to Almighty God; because you take unwarrantable Freedoms with his Holy Name. Such daring Irreverences offered to the Name of the most High, must not be looked upon as harmless. You say, the Words were expressed only in *Jest*: but remember, that to jest with the Name of God, is to sin in *earnest*.

CHAP. X.

Of Blasphemy.

TO blaspheme, is to speak Evil of God or his Saints, to treat him or them with Contumely or Reproach. It is a most grievous Sin, contrary to the Virtue of Religion, and the Praise due to God's most sacred Name.

Though the Sin of Blasphemy is generally committed by reproachful Expressions against God, yet as God can be praised by Thought, Word, or Deed,

Deed, says the angelic Doctor, so he can be blasphemed by either. Blasphemy is of two Kinds: the first is called *heretical*, when some Error against Faith is contained in the contumelious Language uttered against God: as when you *deny* to God what really belongs to him, for instance, *Patience, Justice, Sanctity, Providence, Goodness*, &c. Or when you attribute to God what does not appertain to him, for Example, *Sin*. Thus Heretics blaspheme, by making God the Author of *Sin*.

How frequently do abandoned Gamesters blaspheme, when at an unlucky Cast of a Die, or the Turn of a Card, they appear in Convulsions, and raise their Eyes to Heaven, in a reproachful Manner, as if to stare the Almighty in the Face, and bring him in guilty of Intelligence with the Adversary! But, if the Set or Game be lost, and his personal or perhaps real Estate also, the Property of his rising Offspring, 'tis then he sends up a Volley of Curses to the Throne of God, and blasphemes the Name of the Lord without reserve. Unhappy Creatures, who by Gaming, fool away their Money; and by Blasphemy, their Souls!

This heinous Vice of Blasphemy rages also, among the lower Class of People, who, dissatisfied with their Poverty, affirm, that God has not done right, in giving too much Riches to some, too little to others. Thus presuming to dictate to the Lord, when, how, and to whom he should dispense his Favours, and the Manner in which he ought to govern the Universe: not unlike the proud *Alphonsus* King of *Arragon*, who was accustomed to say, that had he been at the Creation of the World, he would have suggested to God a better Method to order and regulate the Affairs of the Universe.* Detestable Presumption! That

proud,

proud, ignorant Man shall pretend to dictate to the infinite Wisdom of the King of Kings!

God is also blasphemed when, through Flattery, we attribute to Creatures what belongs to God alone: for Instance, to call them *Gods*, to say they are *divine, omnipotent*, &c. "for whatever is peculiar to God, (says St. *Thomas*) is God himself*."

He is also blasphemed, when you wish there was no God; when you speak of him or to him, with Contempt or Reproach, as the Jews did when they thus spoke to the Son of God: †*Vah! Thou that destroyest the Temple of God and in three Days rebuildest it up again, save thyself if thou canst!* And lastly, God is blasphemed by speaking scornfully and reproachfully of his Saints: for, as God is praised in his Saints, because of the Works he wrought in them, so he is blasphemed in speaking contumeliously of them ‡. Hence, *Ecclesiasticus* says: § *Let not the Name of God be usual in thy Mouth, and meddle not with the Names of the Saints, for thou shalt not escape free from them.*

There is another Kind of Blasphemy called *simple* Blasphemy, because it contains not any Error against Faith, but only that Malice or Impiety which is ever inseparable from an Abuse or Contempt of God: for Instance, when in a contemptible Manner, you name *God's Blood, his Wounds, his Death,* &c. for, though *Jesus*, Son of the living God, retains both Body and Blood, which he mercifully assumed for our Sakes, yet they are not to be scornfully and disrespectfully mentioned by the sacrilegious Tongues of vile Sinners.

* 2. 2. q. 13. a. 1. ad 3.   † Matth. xxvii. 40.
‡ S. Tho. 2. 2. q. 13. a. 1.   § Eccl. xxiii. 10.

Sinners. And certain it is, that if such Expressions, though proceeding from Anger or Passion, are intended to contemn or reproach God, they are blasphemous.

Nay, though the Anger which prompts you to the impious Expression, be not conceived against God, but some one of his Creatures, yet the opprobrious and scornful Language favours too strongly of Blasphemy, to be excused from it [*]: For, where is the Christian (if not bereaved of every Sense of Religion) who does not shudder and feel his very Blood chilling in his Veins, when he hears the Saviour of the World, who by his *Wounds* and *Death*, brought an *universal Salvation* to Mankind, treated with Reproach and Contempt.

An explicit or express Intention of reproaching and dishonouring God, is not required to constitute a blasphemous act; a virtual and implicit Intention is sufficient, *viz.* when, by the Words, or Manner of pronouncing them, God, according to the general Notion of Mankind, is contemned and scorned.

Blasphemy is a Sin of so heinous and detestable a Nature, that the very naming of it is sufficient to strike a Christian Soul with Horror. Arguments would seem unnecessary to dissuade Christians from committing so grievous an Offence, did we not see it reigning among them, to the great Disgrace of Christianity. Blasphemy is the genuine Offspring of a corrupt, malignant and malicious Heart: it strikes directly at God himself, and strives to rob him of his divine Attributes and Perfections. Hence St. *Jerom*, quoted by St. Tho-

---

[*] Billuart, Art. de Blasphemia.

Thomas *, assures us, " that there is nothing so
" frightful as Blasphemy: every other Sin com-
" pared to it, is light." Because the Blasphemer
directly or indirectly attacks God in his own Person: Nor can the Malice of Man, great as it is,
soar higher.

If you desire to know, who is the presumptuous
Wretch who dares to abuse the Sovereign Lord of
Heaven and Earth? 'Tis vile Man, Dust and
Ashes, a despicable Worm of the Earth, who has
been distinguished, through God's Goodness, by
the most signal Favours and Blessings! It is he
that impiously and ungratefully revolts and flies in
the Face of God, his Creator, his Redeemer, his
bountiful Benefactor and future Judge! Well
may our Blessed Redeemer reproach the impious
Blasphemer, as he has already done the *Jews*:
Many good Works have I shewn to you, says Jesus
Christ; *for which of those Works are you for stoning
me* † ? For which of those unparalleled Favours,
which I have so plentifully bestowed on you, Oh
ungrateful Man! do you fling your Curses at me?
Is this the return I deserve for creating you, and
redeeming you at the Expence of my Blood! For
making you my Brethren, and Heirs of my heavenly Kingdom! Oh vile Blasphemer! what Excuse shall you be able to plead, when arraigned at
the awful Tribunal of his Justice? Not any, except
that already assigned by the incredulous *Jews*: that
you believed *Jesus Christ* to be Man only, and not
God. A desperate Expedient!

You cannot plead the least Glimmerings of
Profit or Pleasure, which sometimes prompt to the
Commission of other Sins, because, you wantonly
insult

* 2. 2. q. 13. a. 3. † John x. 32.

insult the Source of every solid Joy and Good. I say wantonly, for, without the least Appearance of Offence, you curse or otherwise maltreat the best of Benefactors, an all-gracious God, who, by Reason of his infinite Goodness and Clemency, is incapable of doing any or the least Injury to his Creatures; on the contrary, is ever heaping Blessings upon them. To treat a God of so much Goodness with Scorn, Derision or Contempt, is a Sin of the deepest dye, and of so heinous a Nature, as rather to require Tears to bewail and deplore it, than Words to express it.

I shall however give one Instance of the heinousness of this Crime, recorded in the Book of *Leviticus* *, where we read: that a certain Man, having had a Dispute with another, blasphemed the *Name* of God; upon which he was conducted to *Moses*, who ordered him to Prison, until the Will of God should be known on the Occasion; when the Sentence pronounced by Almighty God was, as follows: *He that blasphemeth the Name of the Lord, dying, let him die: all the Multitude shall stone him, whether he be a Native or a Stranger.* Here is a terrible Sentence pronounced, by God himself, against the vile Blasphemer! The Judgment is absolute, without Reserve, without Appeal. There is no Distinction of Persons hinted at: for Young or Old, Noble or Ignoble, Rich or Poor, Native or Stranger, that Blaspheme the Name of the Lord, must, by the Divine Decree, submit to be stoned to Death.

If not only the *Gentile*, but the *Jew* was to be thus treated for blaspheming the Name of God, who received only the *Figures* of what the Christian People now enjoy, what shall we think of those

* Levit. xxiv.

those who have been blessed with the *Reality*, who have had the Son of the living God himself, in Person, not only to promulgate the Law of Grace, but to satisfy for our Sins, and effectually expiate them, by dying on the Wood of the Cross; surely, it would not be in the least amazing, if the very Stones of the Street should become sensible, and rise of themselves, to revenge the Injury offered to their Creator, by crushing their Bodies to Death, and their sinful Souls into the fathomless Pit of Hell! We all know, the Veil of the Temple was rent assunder, the Earth quaked, the Rocks split, when the Redeemer of Mankind was mocked and crucified; with much more Reason should all Nature conspire against Sinners, to resent the Injury we offer him, whom we all believe and confess to be our God!

It is to be observed, that though God could have commanded, that the Blasphemer should die by the Hands of a common Executioner, yet this will not satisfy the injured Deity; for, he requires that the Multitude should unite in stoning the Blasphemer to Death; as if to insinuate, that every Hand should be employed in the Extirpation of such blasphemous Wretches: and not only Citizens, but Strangers and Travellers that blasphemed the Name of the Lord, by God's express Command, were to undergo the like Punishment, of being stoned to Death.

Were the atrocious Sin of Blasphemy to be expiated by such a temporal Punishment, it might afford some Comfort to the Sinner, but that is not the Case; for, *the Man*, says the Lord, *that curseth his God, shall bear his Sin* [*]. O Lord! whither must he bear it? He must carry it into the

---
[*] Levit. xxiv. 15.

the other World, unless cancelled by a sincere Repentance in this, where he must ever wear the Brand of his sacrilegious Impiety, in the dreadful Regions of the Damned; in an Abyss of everlasting Horror and Torments. This is not a meer Surmise, it is warranted by God's sacred Word: * *For such as bless him shall inherit the land; but such as curse him, shall perish.* So sure as those who bless and glorify the Name of the Lord, with Perseverance, shall inherit eternally the Kingdom of God, with its unspeakable Joys; so they who curse or blaspheme him, shall be doomed to neverending Torments.

Hell, however terrible it is, must be their perpetual Abode, and their Language bespeaks it to be the only Place of their future Residence. Blasphemy is the Language of the Damned; and so long as you imitate them, you proclaim yourself to be of their Number; as *Job* says, *Thou imitatest the tongue of Blasphemers; thy own mouth shall condemn thee* †. Your blasphemous Expressions will plainly discover, that you no longer appertain to God; that you have forfeited the glorious Title of his being adopted Children, to become Slaves to the Devil, and Heirs of endless Misery. Dreadful Change! Words are insufficient to express it.

The monstrous Evils, arising from the damnable Sin of Blasphemy, do not end here; for the Sinner, by his Blasphemy, propagates the odious Vice, and spreads a most dangerous Contagion.

Children and Servants often think themselves justified in following the Example of the blasphemous Parent or Master; and thus, by their Example, the heinous Vice gradually spreads to the

great

* Psalm xxxvi. 22.   † Job xv. 5, 6.

great Dishonour of God's most sacred Name, and the eternal Ruin of their own, and the Souls of others. Ah! Christian Reader, reflect, what an heavy Charge shall be brought against the horrid Blasphemer, on the Day of Judgment! 'tis already drawn by the Apostle St. *Paul:* * *By you the Name of God is blasphemed.* And not content with having blasphemed the Name of the Lord yourselves, for which you must render a most rigorous Account; but also, your being the Cause of teaching it to others, will form a separate Article in the Indictment, which shall be brought against you at his dreadful Tribunal, and will aggravate your Crimes beyond Measure.

There is no Punishment can thoroughly equal this heinous Sin: nothing less than the eternal and most excruciating Pains of Hell, can appear adequate to the detestable Offence given to the Deity. *Let Blasphemy,* then says St. *Paul, be taken away from you, together with all Malice* †. Let the detestable Vice, in future, be banished your Hearts and Mouths: every Christian should exert himself to banish the hateful Crime; for as all are obliged to glorify the Name of the Lord, so all should unite in the Destruction of the hideous Monster, Blasphemy: The Prince, by his Edicts; Prelates, by their Censures; Preachers, by their Sermons; Confessors, by their Instructions at the Tribunal of Confession; Heads of Families, by their Example, their Rebukes or Chastisements.

In a Word, all who have Power or Influence, should heartily exert themselves to exterminate the damnable Vice, which is so highly offensive to the Sovereign Lord of the Universe, and so dis-

---

* Rom. ii. 24. † Ephes. iv. 31.

disgraceful to the Christian Name. *Let Blasphemy then be taken away from you, with all Malice.* Let the grievous Crime be never more admitted into your Hearts, Mouths or Actions; and ever remember the Words of *Tobias,* thus speaking to the Lord: * *They shall be cursed that shall despise thee: and they shall be condemned that shall blaspheme thee.* There is no Alternative left for the Blasphemer, but either eternal Damnation, or an unfeigned Repentance. As I suppose you cannot hesitate in your Choice, defer not your Repentance a Moment; in such important Matters, Delays are dangerous, and the Evils attending final Impenitence are irreparable.

With Hearts then, overflowing with Sorrow, prostrate yourselves before the Throne of Mercy, and with Tears of Compunction labour to wash away the Stain of your sacrilegious Impieties. If the Searcher of Hearts finds you truly and sincerely contrite, he will not despise or reject you: his Clemency will move him to give Ear to your Supplications: his Grace will not be wanting to forward the glorious Conversion: and when in the Spirit of true Penitence you shall repeatedly address the Lord, in the following Words, you shall assuredly obtain Forgiveness and Mercy. *Remember not* (O Lord) *our former Iniquities: let thy Mercies speedily prevent us, for we are become exceeding poor. Help us, O God, our Saviour, and for the Glory of thy Name, O Lord, deliver us, and forgive us our Sins for thy Name's Sake* †.

We have, O Lord, spoken the Language of the damned: we have debased our Nature: we have forfeited our Title to thy blessed Kingdom,

by

---

* Chap. xii. 16. † Psalm lxxviii. 8, 9.

by our repeated Treasons: but above all, we have treated thee, our Creator, our Redeemer, and future Judge, with Reproach and Contempt! So grievous then, are our Sins, that we should not presume to approach the Throne of Mercy, did not thy Clemency most pressingly invite us. As then, thy Mercies are above all thy Works, grant to us, O God, our Saviour, for the Glory of thy most holy Name, *Jesus*, a sincere and hearty Sorrow for our past Offences: and in future, to hold the terrible Vice of Blasphemy in the utmost Abhorrence and Detestation: that we may repair the Evils we have unhappily seminated in others: and that the Remainder of our Lives may be sacred to the Praises of thy awful and most merciful *Name*.

The *Sodality* and *Rosary* of the Name of *Jesus*, cannot be too often recommended, which are so powerfully conducive to effect the desired Reformation; they will prove efficacious to draw down the Mercy of God upon you; they will serve to reform and bridle that dangerous Member, the Tongue; and cause it to become the Instrument of Praise and Thanksgiving to God's adorable Name, which before proved the fatal Cause of a Profanation of it: *The Tongue* (of a profane Swearer, Curser or Blasphemer) *is a Fire, a World of Iniquity. The Tongue is placed among our Members, which defileth the whole Body, and inflameth the Course of our Lives, being set on Fire by Hell* *. Endeavour then to purify and sanctify it, by a devout and constant Recital of the *Rosary*, sacred to the Praises of God's most gracious Name.

C H A P.

* St. James iii. 6.

CHAP. XI.

How heinous to Blaspheme, Curse, or profanely Swear.

THE Custom of Swearing, says St. *Chrysostom*, quoted in the Catechism of the Council of *Trent* [*], took its Rise, "not at the Beginning of the World, but when it began to grow old, and when Wickedness had far and wide spread itself over the whole Earth; and when nothing contained itself in its own Place and Order, but all Things being jumbled together and troubled, were tumbled upside down, and brought into utter Confusion; then, at last, after a long Time, that Custom of Swearing broke in upon Men: for, when Men's Perfidiousness and Wickedness were grown to that Pass, that they could not easily be brought to believe one another, then did they call God as a Witness."

Hence, St. *Augustin* has expressed his Sentiments on Swearing, in a clear and concise Manner, when speaking of the Decollation of St. *John*, the Baptist, he tells us, "That a false Oath is damnable, a true Oath is dangerous, nor is any Oath thoroughly safe." A true Oath is *dangerous*, because a Frequency of Swearing becomes too often the Effect of it, *in which there are many Dangers*. Nor is any Oath thoroughly *safe*, because Men are frequently induced to swear through Envy, Prejudice, Malice, or some other disorderly Passion, which prompts them to swear, at least *rashly*, which is criminal. But to swear *falsely,*

---
[*] Par. 3 in 2. Decalogi Precept.

falsely, which is, to call upon God to witness a Falshood, is evidently damnable; because it places the Soul on the very Brink of Perdition.

The Enormity of a Sin is known from the Greatness of the Command that forbids it. Hence, the Sin of Infidelity is accounted the greatest of all Sins, because forbidden by the *first* Commandment. The Sin of Perjury approaches next to that of Infidelity, and is therefore strictly forbidden by the *second*: whereby we are commanded, not even to take the Name of the Lord our God *in vain*, much less to call him down from Heaven to witness a Falshood.

The Heinousness of Perjury arises principally from hence, that it strikes immediately at the Honour due to God's most adorable Name, which must render it more grievous, in his Sight, than that of Murder; because Murder is a Sin committed immediately against our Fellow Creature, and mediately against God, who thus speaks in the *fifth* Commandment: *Thou shalt not kill*. Whereas, the Sin of Perjury, strikes immediately and directly at God himself, and consequently more sinful and odious. Yet some People imagine Murder to be more heinous in the Sight of God than Perjury; because the former is punished by the Civil Law, with greater Rigour than the latter. But though Murder is punished with greater Severity than Perjury, it follows not from thence, that Murder is more hateful in the Sight of God; because the Civil Power has just Reasons to apprehend, that if Murder was not punished capitally, in the most exemplary Manner, it would be more frequently committed, by reason of those predominant Passions of Malice, Envy, Revenge, and a thousand other Causes, which
usually

usually prompt bad Men to commit the horrid Crime, perhaps on very trifling Occasions.

It was therefore neceffary to reftrain and deter them from committing the atrocious Crime, by a Dread of capital Punifhments. Whereas, on the other hand, it could fcarcely be fuppofed (did not Experience evince the contrary) that Men could be fo vile and prefumptuous as to profane the Name of the Lord their God; or that they could be fo abandoned and perfidious as to call him from Heaven, who is Truth itfelf, to witnefs their Lies!

Men frequently, through a Want of Charity, offend and abufe each other, perhaps fometimes not without Provocation: but, that Man fhall become fo fhamefully profligate, as to abufe his God, his Creator, his Saviour, his kind Benefactor and future Judge, without the leaft Glimmerings of Provocation, would appear almoft incredible, did not the falfe Oaths, dreadful Imprecations, and fhocking Blafphemies, prove the Exiftence of the deteftable Impiety!

The Sin of Perjury is held in the utmoft Deteftation, and is rigoroufly punifhed by almoft every Nation of the Earth. It was held in fuch an abominable Light by the ancient *Romans*, that they punifhed it, by throwing the Offender headlong from the *Tarpeian* Precipice. This Penalty they afterwards altered, upon a Suppofition, that the Gods would vindicate their own Honour, by fome remarkable Judgment on the Offender. The *Greeks* fet a Mark of Infamy upon them; and after the Empire became Chriftian, if any one fwore falfely upon the Gofpels, he was to have his Tongue cut out. The *Jews* punifhed this Crime, and that of Blafphemy, in the moft exemplary

emplary Manner, as has been already mentioned. Nay, even among the *Turks*, a Perſon convicted of Perjury, is led through the City, in his Shirt, riding on an Aſs, with his Face to the Tail, which they hold in their Hands, having their Faces daubed, and on their Shoulders a Parcel of Guts and other Garbage, they are burned on the Cheek and Forehead, and for ever made incapable of being Witneſſes in any Cauſe whatever.

Laws are enacted againſt Perjury in all Chriſtian Countries: Here *, if any one ſhall profanely ſwear or curſe, he may be fined one Shilling. If the Offender be above ſixteen Years old, he is liable to be fined one Shilling, and to be confined in the Stocks for three whole Hours; if under that Age, he is to be whipped by the Parent, or Conſtable, in the Parent's Preſence. If an Offender be proved guilty of corrupt and wilful *Perjury*, or is proved the Cauſe of another's committing it, he is liable to forfeit forty Pounds: if not able to pay, to ſuffer ſix Months Impriſonment, without Bail; to ſtand in the Pillory one Hour where the Offence was committed: and to be for ever after diſabled to give Teſtimony in any Court of Record. The Judge may alſo ſend them to the Houſe of Correction, or tranſport them; their Ears may be nailed, &c. *Wilt thou then,* (O profane Swearer) *not be in Apprehenſion of Power?—If thou do'ſt Evil, be afraid, for he beareth not the Sword in vain* †.

The Sin of Perjury is, and always was held by the Catholic Church as a damnable Sin. In the primitive Ages of Chriſtianity, if any Chriſtian unhappily

---

* Lee's Statute Law of Ireland, Page 312.
† Rom. xiii 3, 4.

unhappily committed the Sin of Perjury, or induced others to commit it, it was enacted by the sacred *Canons*, that the Offender should fast *forty Days* on Bread and Water, and do Penance for *seven Years* *.

It is true, our tender Mother the Church, from the Circumstances of Times and Persons, has been obliged to mitigate the Rigour of her Discipline, and change these severe Penances into others much less severe. She however effectually supplies any Deficiency, by the Interposition of *Indulgences*, or in other Words, she applies the Treasures of the Church, that is, the superabundant Satisfactions and Merits of Christ and his Saints, as a Satisfaction for the temporal Punishment due to our Crimes. Yet the Mercy of God, thus dispensed to us by his Church, is also abused by profane and perjured Swearers, who, instead of availing themselves of this Act of Clemency, make no other Return, than to shamefully persevere in their Sins; nay, and sometimes make a *Profession* of swearing any Falshood they are required, provided they are bribed with the Price of their Iniquity. Determined Impiety! Shocking Presumption!

Let such perjured Profligates reflect, if they have any Thoughts at all about Salvation, that though the Throne of Mercy is now accessible, it may To-morrow be barred against them for ever. Every Delay to amend their Lives increases their Danger, and *he who loves Danger shall perish in it*, says the Holy Ghost †.

They sometimes lay great Stress on the Prayers of others; that though they do not themselves deserve Forgiveness, yet hope, through the Mediation

---

* Wigant, de Indulg.   † Eccles. iii. 27.

ation of the Saints or pious Christians, to obtain it. St. *Gregory* relates a memorable Fact relative to this vain Confidence: "That in his Time, the Sick resorted to the Tombs of the Martyrs, and were cured: Demoniacs also resorted thither, and the evil Spirit was instantly put to Flight. But, when the perjured Swearer approached, instead of being relieved, he was sorely tormented by the Devil [*]." By this Narrative, the holy Doctor insinuates, that the faithful, in his Days, visited the Tombs of the Martyrs, they venerated their Relics, as having been once the living Temples of the Holy Ghost, and requested their Intercession, whereby they happily obtained the desired Relief, and were freed from their respective Complaints.

Not any were precluded the general Relief but perjured Swearers, Cursers, and Blasphemers: for no sooner they approached the sacred Shrines, than their Pains were redoubled, or to speak the Language of the Saint, "they were sorely tormented by the Devil:" As if to insinuate that the Martyrs would not intercede for such vile Offenders, such declared Enemies of the most High, as dared, by their detestable Impieties, to insult the King of Heaven, to whom they are indebted for every Blessing, whether temporal or spiritual; nay, for their very Existence and Preservation.

And truly, it is no Wonder, that the Martyrs, and every other Inhabitant of the blessed Regions, should jointly, as Friends zealous for God's Honour, refuse to plead for such Miscreants, and leave them to be eternal Objects of his Wrath, and Victims of his Justice!

In

---

[*] Homil. 32. in Evang.

In short, the Lord holds the Sin of profane Swearing and Perjury in such Abomination, as to assure us, that * *the Speech that sweareth much, shall make the Hair of the Head stand upright, and its Irreverence shall make one stop his Ears.* He also says, *thou shalt not forswear thyself, but shall keep thy Oaths to the Lord* †. Oh Swearers, can the Almighty use Words more forcible or expressive of the Enormity of this Crime!

It is not less criminal to call upon God's all-saving Name to curse yourselves, your Fellow Creature, or any of God's Creatures; for, it is contrary to Charity, which obliges us to wish good to ourselves and Fellow Creatures: it is contrary to all that the Scripture prescribes, *of forgiving Injuries, doing good for Evil, praying for our Persecutors*, &c. It is contrary to that Brotherly Love so strongly recommended and enforced by *Jesus Christ*; it is flying in the Face of God's Goodness, and endeavouring to undermine the great Work of our Redemption; it is labouring to render his cruel Sufferings and ignominious Death fruitless and ineffectual! What can be more injurious to the Redeemer of the World, than that Man shall presume to curse and damn those Souls, for whose Salvation, the Son of the living God, *Jesus Christ*, laid down his precious Life!

This uncharitable Vice of Cursing, is scarcely to be exceeded except by the shocking Sin of Blasphemy, whereby God is immediately attacked in his proper Person. How dreadful to hear Men, vile Worms of the Earth, abusing the God of Heaven! To see them attempting to rob him of his Glory! To hear them crucifying the Son of God

---

* Eccl. xxvii. 15.   † Matth. v. 33.

God again, and tearing his sacred Body to Pieces, by their blasphemous Expressions; and those vomited forth by the very Wretches, whom *Jesus* has mercifully redeemed, by dying himself!

Such vile Offenders, such hateful Monsters, are more culpable than the very *Jews*, who nailed *Jesus Christ* to the Cross: for *they knew not what they did:* But you, Oh blasphemous Sinner! not only attempt to crucify *Jesus*, but also attempt to *dissect* him, whom you believe and confess to be your *God*, by such abominable Oaths, Imprecations, and Blasphemies, as would foul entire Pages to recite!

Nay, your Guilt exceeds that of the damned, and reaches beyond Hell itself: for if the damned blaspheme the Name of the Lord, it is while God exercises the Severity of his Justice over them, as the beloved Evangelist declares in his Book of *Revelations*, * *And they blasphemed the God of Heaven*, says St. *John*, *because of their Pains and Wounds*. But, that you, Oh Sinners, shall, without the least Provocation, wantonly blaspheme the Name of the Lord; nay, whilst you are receiving the strongest Proofs of his Love, is a Sin of the deepest Die, and not to be paralleled! It calls loudly to Heaven for the most dreadful Punishments, that the avenging Justice of an all-powerful God can inflict.

To Forswear, Curse or Blaspheme are, no Doubt, extremely sinful: but that Men shall professedly swear, curse or blaspheme meerly for the Sake of propagating those Vices, is an unparalleled Piece of Presumption. Yet so it is, that a
Club

* Chap. xvi. 11.

Club or *Society* has been lately formed * for the more effectual Propagation of those hellish Vices. The *Hell-fire Club* has been lately revived under the Title of *Holy Fathers*, who, it is said, are guilty of such horrid Impieties, Execrations, and Blasphemies, as must make any one's Ears, who professes Christianity, to tingle: Or to use the Scripture Phrase, it must *make the Hair of the Head to stand upright*, to hear the Deity attacked and insulted by such vile Oaths, Imprecations and Blasphemies, as would foul, if possible, even Hell itself!

Who can be silent, whilst the Honour of God, the Welfare of Christianity, and the Salvation of Souls, become so sensibly attacked by some giddy, profligate Youths, who so freely presume to insult and reproach a God, who mercifully died upon a Cross to give them Life? What can be more impious or absurd, than to abuse their Creator, their Redeemer, and future Judge by their shocking Oaths, Imprecations or Blasphemies! The Conduct of Sinners, with Regard to these Vices, seems wholly unaccountable: we can, indeed, in some Measure account for Covetousness; we may guess the Causes of Lust: we may assign the Incentives that urge to Revenge; and unfold the Motives that impel to Ambition, &c. but that Men shall delight in so great Profanation of God's most adorable Name, whereby the highest Indignity is offered to God, and neither real Profit or Pleasure can possibly accrue to themselves, is more than amazing!

It

---

* In the Year 1770 in the Centre of the Kingdom, not far from the *Shannon*; as if to spread its baneful Influence more rapidly to every Part of the Nation.

It is perhaps, becaufe they think, that Oaths, Imprecations or Blafphemies may fet off their Paffion better, and make it more terrible and impreffive? Or, that they fancy their Words and Sentences have not their due Cadence, without them: or, that they believe their Mirth and Jollity cannot be modifh enough, unlefs accompanied with fome Oath, Execration or Blafphemy: or in fine, whether it be to fupply a Deficiency of Difcourfe, or to render it more grateful to their Hearers, I fhall not pretend to determine: but certain it is, that let their Inducements or Motives to commit thefe Sins, be as they may, they are moft heinous in the Sight of God: and the formal Inftitution or Formation of a *Club* for the Propagation of thefe damnable Vices, at once proves it to be the genuine Offspring of an anti-chriftian, abandoned, and corrupt Heart.

I conjure fuch thoughtlefs Chriftians, to take a View of the Precipice of Eternity, of the dreadful Abyfs, on whofe brink they are madly fporting; and to recollect, that there is an *Hell*, wherein the Worm never dieth, nor are its Flames ever quenched: that this Hell is too open already for Sinners; they need not wantonly pray to be admitted.

I know thefe Geniufes have ftruck out an expeditious Method to rid themfelves at once of all Fears and Apprehenfions, *viz.* to deny peremptorily "that there is an Hell."—Though there fhould be no Hell, where is the Harm of declining thofe Vices? What Advantages can refult from them? But fuppofe there fhould be an Hell, for the Punifhment of the Enemies of God, as the facred Scriptures loudly proclaim; nay, the very Laws of Juftice and Reafon require a Punifhment adequate or proportioned to the Crime, as the greateft

and

and wisest Men have believed, and the most rational and enlightened Minds, even of the present Age, do believe: What will become of those *Bloods* who curse, swear, blaspheme, (not to mention other Crimes) and mould Religion, if any they have, according to their Caprice, notwithstanding the constant Stings and Rebukes of that silent Monitor, Conscience, which they endeavour to stifle and suppress? Let them beware timely of that terrible Sentence, which, if they persevere in their Sins, will most certainly be pronounced against them: *Depart from me ye cursed into everlasting Fire, which was prepared for the Devil and his Angels* *.

An higher Affront surely could not be invented, than Blasphemy, to provoke an infinite Power to with-hold all Mercy and Forgiveness from those, who are constantly defying and provoking its Justice. The Royal Prophet has beautifully expressed his Surprise at the Sinner's audacious Temerity, and God's amazing Patience, in the following Words †: *How long, O God, shall the Enemy reproach? Is the Adversary to provoke thy Name for ever? .... The Enemy hath reproached the Lord; and a foolish People hath provoked thy Name.*

What Punishment then, shall be inflicted on those, who profane the Name of the Lord? The Lord assures us, that *He shall not be unpunished that taketh his Name upon a vain Thing* ‡. To those who swear falsely he speaks, when he says §, *a Malediction shall come to the House of Him that sweareth falsely by my Name: and shall dwell in the Midst of it, until it shall consume it, and its very Foundations.* To those who call on his Name to curse

---

* Matth. xxv. 41.   † Psal. lxxiii. 10, 18.
‡ Deut. v. 11.   § Zach. v. 4.

curse his Creatures, he says; *Railers, ... shall not possess the Kingdom of God* *. And of the Blasphemer, *Tobias* speaks thus to the Lord: † *They shall be cursed that shall despise Thee: and they shall be condemned that shall blaspheme Thee.*

If the Terrors of the next World are not sufficient to bring profane Swearers, Cursers, or Blasphemers to Reflection and a Sense of their Duty, let them consider for a Moment, how odious and contemptible they are in the Eyes of all rational People: and, what may probably have more Weight with them, that in the End they will be cast off by all truly polite Company. Bad as the World is, with regard to Dissipation and Vice, it is to be hoped, very few, in Future, will be found silly enough to inlist under the Devil's Banner, through the Persuasions of such recruiting Officers, such *holy Fathers*, as they *ironically* stile themselves.

Let such Persons, then, as have happily escaped the diabolical Snare, hold such anti-christian Assemblies in the utmost Abhorrence: and, let all those who have been miserably seduced into the vile Association, abjure it timely, and prostrate themselves before the Throne of Mercy, which is yet accessible to them, though the most profligate and ungrateful of God's Creatures: let them reflect on the unwarrantable Freedoms they have taken with the most holy Name of God: let them consider seriously, that it is not a Creature they abuse by their Blasphemies, but it is their Creator, their Redeemer and future Judge they insult, whose infinite Power enables him, and whose avenging Justice requires him, to vindicate the Honour of his injured Name.

God

* 1 Cor. vi. 10.   † Tob. xiii. 16.

God now mercifully forbears with Sinners, most patiently waiting their Amendment: nor truly, can there be a stronger Proof of his wonderful Patience given, than that he shall wait the Sinner's Conversion, and readily crown his unfeigned Repentance with Mercy and Pardon, though guilty of High Treason against his Sovereign Majesty. Beware then Sinners, of abusing any longer the Goodness and Mercies of your God, lest you provoke him to cut you off suddenly in your Sins, and leave you to bewail your unhappy Fate, during a tedious Eternity; amidst unquenchable Flames, without the least Hopes of a Mitigation of your Torments, for ever deprived of the Sight and Enjoyment of God, his blessed Angels and Saints, in the Regions of Bliss and Glory.

Rouse then, O profane Cursers, Swearers and Blasphemers from your fatal Lethargy! Do not permit yourselves to be lulled into so dangerous an Insensibility: Hearken no longer to the Suggestions of the evil Serpent: Repent timely, lest God's avenging Justice lays hold on you: The Multitude of his tender Mercies now pressingly call and invite you to Repentance, promising the Remission of your Sins here, and everlasting Joys hereafter. Who can be so great an Enemy to himself, so enamoured with Torments or so averse to Happiness, as to hesitate a Moment at the Choice? Or, who can be hardy enough to defer his Conversion for a Moment, when he reflects on the dreadful Punishments that have befallen Blasphemers?

Every one that blasphemed the Name of the Lord, was, by his express Command, *to be stoned* *. In Punishment of the Sin of Blasphemy, an Angel

---

* Levit. xxiv.

Angel of the Lord, in one Night, *flew in the Camp of the Assyrians an Hundred and Eighty Five Thousand**. And *Holofernes*, for his Blasphemy, recited in *Judith* †, though General of a great Army, was beheaded by a Woman, in the midst of his Guards †. Who is it then, that can be obdurate enough not to tremble at the shocking Sin; or so totally abandoned as to defy, by it, the avenging Justice of God's all-powerful Arm. Let then, the Blasphemer, Curser, and profane Swearer frequently and fervently address the Lord, in the following Words: *Set a Watch, O Lord, before my Mouth: and a Door round about my Lips* ‡; to protect me from the dangerous Vices, so hateful to Thee, and fatal to Man.

CHAP. XII.

Apologies, to excuse or extenuate the Crimes of Blasphemy, Cursing, or profane Swearing, frivolous.

AS the Apologies or Excuses which Sinners generally make, to exculpate themselves from the Guilt of Blasphemy, Cursing, or profane Swearing, have been already briefly spoken of, when treating of those Vices in their respective Chapters, we shall, therefore, be the more concise in this.

All the Apologies made by Cursers, Swearers and Blasphemers will appear frivolous and trifling, when they reflect, that had they the *Love* and *Fear* of God in their Hearts (which they ought to have) they

---

* 4 Kings xix. 35.   † Judith vi.—xiii.
‡ Psal. cxl. 3.

they would not, by any Means, take such unwarrantable Freedoms with the Name of the most High: for, a Restraint proceeding from a real Love or Fear of the Lord, would in Time, effectually curb the horrid Vices, and at Length remove them. But the Case is quite different: for Men, in general, have not really the Love and Fear of God in their Hearts: they know, he does not now govern his People, as he formerly did the *Jews*, by the Law of *Fear*, but by the Law of *Love*; by giving the strongest Proofs of his unspeakable Clemency, to engage us chearfully to adore and sanctify his holy Name. They are not however, to think, that the all-powerful Arm of the Lord is disabled from inflicting the most dreadful Punishments on such, in the other Life, as have refused his Love and Kindness in this. Nay, he has often punished, in the most exemplary Manner, those obdurate Sinners, even in this Life, who presumed to abuse his wonderful Patience: the many frightful Examples he has made, clearly evince it, as we have shewn in the foregoing Chapters.

It appears however, from the Frequency of Swearing, &c. which now so universally prevails, that neither Favours nor Menaces are sufficient to curb the profane Wretch, or keep him within the Bounds of his Duty: for, not to dwell on that shameful Neglect of loving God, and thanking him for his innumerable Favours, which is plainly to be discovered in the Swearer or Blasphemer; it appears manifestly, he has not the least Apprehension or Dread of God's just Judgments falling on his guilty Head.

The Want of this holy Fear is the principal Source, from whence the hateful and abominable

Custom of profane Swearing & Blaspheming springs: for we see, that when a temporal Prince enacts a Law, his Subjects, either through Love or Fear, pay Obedience to it: Yet, when the King of Kings solemnly forbids the Profanation of his sacred Name, by the *second* Commandment, neither Love nor Fear can restrain the abandoned Swearer. If a Multiplicity of unspeakable Favours are insufficient to engage the Sinner to revere the most holy Name of God; at least let him dread a God, *who hath Power to cast into Hell. Yes I say to you, fear Him**.

When the Curser, Swearer or Blasphemer is rebuked for taking such Freedoms with the most holy Name of God, he readily pleads an Excuse for the atrocious Crime, alledging, that he has often endeavoured to wean himself from the execrable Vices, but to no Purpose; the *Habit* or *Custom* he has contracted, being of so long a Duration, that it cannot be overcome.

This is a trifling Excuse: for though some Difficulty will attend the Removal of any habitual Vice, yet, as God's Grace is ever ready to assist, and forward your Amendment, provided you use your Endeavours, of course, those Difficulties must speedily subside, and the dangerous Custom gradually decline. To plead Custom, as an Apology for Swearing, &c. is as impious, as it would be ridiculous for a Robber, arraigned at the *Bar*, to plead, that being so long accustomed to pilfer and rob, he could not refrain from it: his pleading Custom, as an Excuse, would aggravate his Crime in the Eyes of both Judge and Jury: And instead of obtaining Pardon by this Plea, or a Mitigation of his Sentence, it would rather prove a Means

---

* Luke xii. 5.

a Means of increasing his Torments, and hastening his Execution.

A true Fear of incurring the Indignation of the most High, would undoubtedly remove the hateful Custom: "For there is no Custom whatever, (says S. *Chrysostom*) which will not yield to fear truly such[*]. For Instance, you are accustomed daily to take Air and Exercise, to Eat and Drink plentifully: yet, if an eminent Physician tells you, you are feverish, you will readily break through these Customs; you will abstain from Food and submit to Confinement. From whence proceeds this ready Compliance? but from a Dread of increasing your Disorder and endangering your Life! If the Sinner had a like Fear of endangering or losing his Soul, he would readily break through the damnable Habit of Cursing, Swearing and Blaspheming. "You see, then (says the holy Doctor) that where there is a real Fear, it will easily curb, and at length remove any Custom, though ever so inveterate."

And truly, do we not daily see Children and Servants, who, though addicted to Swearing, &c. yet, when in the Presence of their Parents or Masters, can readily refrain from it? Nay, if the most abandoned Swearer, Blasphemer, or Curser, appears in a Court of Justice to give Testimony, though his Depositions shall continue perhaps for Hours, he will not be heard to utter an Oath or Imprecation? because, he is over-awed by the Presence of the Judge, and dreads incurring the Censure of the Court.

How frivolous then, the Excuses assigned by profane Swearers, &c. that they cannot break through the abominable Custom? They cannot only,

---

[*] Homil. 14. ad Popul.

only, because they will not: For, do not numberless Examples prove, that they can readily refrain from the odious Vices, when in the Presence of those invested with Power to rebuke or punish them. Truly, because the Lord is not *visibly* present, they dread not his Justice, but profane his adorable Name without reserve. But, O vile Cursers, Swearers, and Blasphemers know, that even the least Irreverence offered to his most sacred Name shall not escape his watchful Ear, nor the avenging Justice of his all-powerful Arm!

It is not however to be denied, that if a Sinner, who had been accustomed to Swear, Curse, or Blaspheme, sincerely repents, and uses every proper Method to overcome it, but, that in some Cases, Passion may so blind him, or the Effects of a bad Habit may so far get the better of him, that he may chance to swear an Oath, Curse, &c. without committing a mortal Sin, as an involuntary and indeliberate Act, agreeable to what *Ecclesiasticus* says*, *There is one that slippeth with the Tongue, but not from his Heart*. But, if instead of using your utmost Efforts, and applying the proper and proportioned Means to root out the evil Practice, you reinforce the damnable Habit with repeated Oaths, Imprecations, &c. it must highly aggravate your crime: " for to sin through Habit, (says " the angelic Doctor) is to sin more intensely †," and consequently more grievously.

Others there are, who plead *Passion* or *Anger* as an Excuse. What Folly! To think, that Passion shall excuse those Irreverences offered to the Lord, which is deemed insufficient to excuse an Affront offered to yourselves! If a Man, in a Passion strikes or otherwise abuses you, will

you

* Chap. xix. 16.   † 2. 2. q. 156. a. 3.

you not resent the Insult? Will his being in a Passion be accepted of as a sufficient Apology? 'Tis more than probable, that a Blow on the Face, or a Challenge to the Field, would be judged (though wickedly) the only suitable Return you could, in Honour, make for the Affront received. And yet you would have it, that Anger should excuse the most glaring Acts of Irreverence and Contempt offered to the infinite Majesty of God, who is incapable of giving the least Offence!

You say, you do not speak in that Manner, either to reproach God, or treat him disrespectfully: 'tis only perhaps to frighten those you are speaking to, or to give Weight to your Assertions: but in Fact, have no Intention of offending Almighty God by your Oaths, &c. But, is it possible, that Christians speak seriously, who mean thus to excuse themselves! Can they possibly think, that to intimidate those to whom they are speaking, or to gain their Assent, 'tis excusable to abuse God's most sacred Name, and treat it with Contempt. If a Sinner must vent his Passion, is he so very much at a Loss in Speech, as not to find any Words to explain himself, but such as manifestly tend to the Dishonour and Abuse of God's most holy and terrible Name!

Others in fine, say, they cannot at least refrain from cursing those, who curse them. This Method of reasoning is condemned by the Gospel Maxims, requiring us *to forgive our Enemies: to bless, and not to curse them,* &c.—*Not returning Evil for Evil,* says the Prince of Apostles, St. *Peter, nor Railing for Railing, but on the contrary Blessing: for this you are called, that by Inheritance you may possess a Blessing. For he that will love Life, and see good Days, let him refrain his Tongue from Evil,* *and his Lips that they speak no Guile**. So little do Christians attend to this Advice of the Apostle, that St. *Gregory Nasianzen* had Reason to complain, that Man is not afraid or ashamed to treat the venerable Name of God with disrespect and contumely, though the very Devils themselves tremble at it †! Which caused St. *Chrysostom* to exclaim against profane Swearers, Cursers, and Blasphemers, in the following Words: " You know not " what God is, or how he ought to be invoked ‡." From a want of this necessary Reflection, proceed those shameful Irreverences offered to the Lord's most sacred Name.

St. *Ambrose* remarks, that the *Jews* who blasphemed *Jesus*, whilst hanging on the Cross, blasphemed, indeed, with great readiness: and why? says the holy Doctor: Because they insulted him, as they suddenly passed by, without allowing themselves Time to reflect: for, had they remained to consider, that He, who was then nailed to the Cross, was the Son of the Living God, who gave Existence to every Creature, and on the Day of his Sufferings withdrew Light from the Sun, and threw all Nature into Convulsions: Had they stayed to consider these and other Prodigies attentively, they would not have blasphemed his tremendous Majesty, but would have struck their Breasts and confessed *Jesus*, then expiring for the Salvation of Man, to be the Son of the Living God: They would earnestly beg forgiveness and mercy, for the glaring Insults offered to their bleeding Saviour.

In a Word, there is no Apology can be made or admitted to justify or excuse the hateful Custom of Cursing, Swearing or Blaspheming, whereby so great

---
* 1 Pet. iii. 9, 10. † Orat. xxi. ‡ Homil. xxvi. ad Popul.

great an Irreverence is offered to the Omnipotent *Creator* and *Conservator* of all things: whereby so great an Indignity is offered to the *Divine Spirit*, who is ever willing to make his Abode in our Souls and sanctify them; and which also argues the highest Contempt of the *Saviour* of Mankind, who shed his precious Blood to redeem them. Did Men but reflect, that *Jesus*, whose Name they impiously revile, must judge those Irreverences offered to him, and that they know not the Day nor the Hour they shall be cited to the Bar of his Justice, to receive the Sentence of eternal Reprobation, the just Punishment of their vile Oaths, Imprecations and Blasphemies, they would certainly be more cautious in future.

At his dreadful Tribunal, the Sinner will plainly perceive, but too late, how much he has been deluded by frivolous Excuses, which shall be rejected by the just Judge as soon as alledged; the damnable Vices shall then appear in their natural Deformity, which must inevitably fill the Criminals with the most dreadful Apprehensions, and clearly expose to their View, the Eternity of Torments that awaits them.

The Neglect of making these, and such like Christian Reflections, is what exposes Mankind to those execrable Vices here, and shall make them smart under the Rod of God's avenging Justice hereafter. The present, is the Time to guard against those Punishments that are justly to be dreaded from the injured Deity. Repent then timely, and cease not, in future, to praise, honour and glorify God's most adorable Name.

The Sinner seems to have no other Plea left, but a false Confidence in the Mercies of the Lord, saying; " God's goodness is so unbounded, that He
" will

"will not permit us to be damned, though our
"Crimes are enormous, &c." I shall briefly answer
such presumptuous Sinners in the Words of *Ecclesiasticus*: † *Say not, the Mercy of the Lord is great, he will have Mercy on the Multitude of my Sins: For Mercy and Wrath quickly come from him, and his Wrath looketh upon Sinners: Delay not to be converted to the Lord, and defer it not from Day to Day: for his Wrath shall come on a sudden, and in the Time of Vengeance he will destroy thee.*

Hear this Sentence, and let it be deeply impressed on your Minds, Oh vile Cursers, Swearers and Blasphemers! who obstinately persevere in your Sins, and yet presumptuously hope for Mercy and Happiness. It is a false and deceitful Hope: For they only, who sincerely repent, *and call upon his Name, are created for his Glory.* *

CHAP. XIII.

The Means to Amend.

IT is, no doubt, the indispensable Duty of every profane Curser, Swearer or Blasphemer, that hopes for Salvation, to use his utmost Endeavours to amend his Life, to repair the Evils he has done, and wash away the Stain of his Crimes, with Tears of a sincere Repentance.

Some Means, however, ought to be prescribed in particular, whereby the repenting Sinner may be helped to accomplish the desired Amendment: I know not any more powerful to reclaim the Blasphemer, Curser or profane Swearer, than an Imitation of our great Original, *Jesus Christ*, when curing

---

† Chap. v.   * Isaiah xliii. 7.

ring the *dumb Man*, as is recorded in the Seventh Chapter of St. *Mark*.

Before our blessed Redeemer restored Speech to the dumb Man, *he looked up to Heaven:* whereby he teaches, that we are to raise our Eyes and Hearts to Heaven, praying from thence the Cure of our infected Tongues: "For if Man," says St. *Augustin*, " cannot govern his Tongue, let him have " recourse to the Lord, by Prayer, who with his " all-powerful Arm will effectually subdue and " tame it." *

This divine Glance, which the Lord gave towards Heaven, discovers to the profane Swearer and Blasphemer the Method he is to pursue for the Amendment of his Tongue; not tied as the dumb Man's was, but too loose in profaning the Name of its Creator: for, by raising your Eyes and Hearts from all earthly Beings, (which too often blind the former and captivate the latter) to contemplate the glorious Majesty of that God, whom you offend by your vile Oaths, Imprecations or Blasphemies, 'tis then the Impiety of the Sinner will appear in its proper Deformity, and may prove an effectual Means to excite in him, an unfeigned Repentance.

It will represent to the Sinner, in the most lively manner, how presumptuously Man, who is but a vile Worm of the Earth, dares to take such Freedoms with the Name of the most august and tremendous Monarch, perhaps to establish an Untruth, to curse his Creatures, or to blaspheme his most venerable Name, while, at the very same Time, all the Angels of Heaven, prostrate on their Faces, before the Throne of God, incessantly sing the ravishing Song which the beloved Evangelist heard, in

---

* Serm. 3. de verb. Dom.

in these Words: *Benediction and Glory, and Wisdom, and Thanksgiving, Honour and Power, and Strength unto our God for ever and ever, Amen.

The first Thing then, a Sinner is to do, who means to amend his Life, is to reflect seriously on his own baseness, and the infinite Majesty and Sanctity of God whom he offends: He must also raise his Heart to the Father of Mercy, imploring his Goodness to grant the necessary Assistance for his Amendment; after which, he should (as is related of our blessed Redeemer) *sigh*; that is, bitterly lament the grievous Offence given to the most High, by his execrable Oaths, Imprecations or Blasphemies.

The want of a true Sorrow, is the real Cause, why the Cure of our distempered Tongues is so seldom effected: Nay, do not Sinners, instead of exciting Sorrow in their Breasts, endeavour to stifle the Rebukes of Conscience, by assigning some frivolous Excuse, which often rather aggravates the Crime, than extenuates or excuses it: Every Apology tending to silence Conscience or to palliate the hateful Vices, representing them as harmless and inoffensive, must be totally inadmissible and highly Criminal.

Hence the Sinner, who means to amend his Life, should not only raise his Heart to Heaven, but also endeavour to expiate his atrocious Crimes by Tears of a sincere Repentance. His unfeigned Sorrow should be accompanied with other good Works to secure his Conversion and prevent a Relapse: for instance, let the Swearer impose upon himself, or cause to be imposed by his Confessor, the Performance of such Works as may effectually tend to curb and remove the sinful Passion. For Example, to form this Resolution: that so often as he profanes the Name of the Lord, he shall give

* Apoc. vii. 12.

an Alms to some distressed Fellow-creature, according to his Abilities; that he shall Fast, Pray, or humble himself to kiss the Ground, &c. Such Acts of Charity and Humiliation are highly pleasing to Almighty God, and have proved the happy Means of averting his Indignation from Sinners.

It is related of a Soldier, who was accustomed to profane the Name of the Lord upon every trifling Occasion, that being prevailed upon to go to Confession, he received, as Penance, a Charge, that so often as he transgressed in that way, he should form, with his Tongue, the Sign of the Cross on the Ground. His Compliance proved the Safety of both Soul and Body; for shortly after being in Company with a Number of his Brethren, Soldiers, he begins, according to Custom, to profane the Name of God. No sooner had he reflected on the Crime, into which he relapsed, than he immediately bends to the Earth, and whilst he had been making the Sign of the Cross, as directed by his Confessor, a loaded Musket was discharged; the Ball only grazing his Loins, without doing any other Damage than carrying away Part of his Coat and Shirt.

Here is a signal Stroke of the divine Protection, in favour of the penitent Soldier, who, upon the first Recollection of his Crime, without Hesitation, humbly prostrates to implore Forgiveness of Heaven, which proved neither blind to his prompt Humiliation, nor deaf to his fervent Petition: for the Judgment is averted, his Life is spared. Whereas, had he continued proudly erect, regardless of the Advice given him by his Director, he must have been unavoidably shot; and, no doubt, but Soul and Body would have been in a most lamentable State, whilst stained with the damnable Sin.

His Comrades admire the wonderful Escape, and
justly

justly ascribe his Preservation to God's infinite Goodness! It wrought a total Change in the Soldier's Life: and as a small Tribute of Praise and Thanksgiving, he resolves to undertake a painful Pilgrimage to the holy Church of *Loretto*, which he faithfully performed, and where this memorable Fact is recorded.*

Would to God, that they, who are unhappily prone to profane the Lord's most venerable Name, would imitate this Christian Soldier, by humbling themselves to the very Earth, and there in the spirit of true Penitence, say with holy *David:* † *Help us, O God, our Saviour, and for the Glory of thy Name, O Lord, deliver us; and forgive us our Sins for thy Name's Sake.* These, and such-like Acts of Humiliation and Prayer, will prove highly pleasing to Almighty God, and a powerful Means to avert the many exemplary Judgments that daily befal habitual Swearers, Cursers and Blasphemers. How many have had their Mouths contracted? How many have been struck deaf, dumb, or blind? Nay, how many Thousands have been struck dead, for being guilty of blaspheming the Name of the Lord. Sacred History is replete with many Instances thereof, sufficient to strike future Generations with Terror and Amazement ‡.

What Judgment then, can we form of those unhappy Souls, thus suddenly snatched from their sinful Bodies? They justly dread facing an angry God, whose sacred Name they, but a few Minutes before, most impiously profaned. They would give Worlds, if in their Power, to be exempt from appearing before the injured Deity: But the Rigour of God's Justice commands their Attendance at his dreadful

* Segneri, Crist. Istruito, Rag. 10. † Psal. lxxviii. 9.
‡ See Chap. xi.

dreadful Tribunal, to receive a Sentence proportioned to their Crimes. As they are totally unfit for Heaven, where nothing defiled can enter, they shall be hurried into the frightful Dungeon of Hell, there to remain with the accursed Inhabitants of those infernal Regions, so long as there is a God in Heaven to punish them. Remember Christians, in Time, that what has happened to others, may befal you: God's abhorrence of the detestable Crimes, and his Power to punish, are still the same. You have not, nor cannot have any special Protection, unless from a speedy Repentance and Amendment.

In fine, as the Evangelist informs us, our Redeemer *Jesus Christ*, not only raised his Eyes to Heaven, and sighed, but also *touched* the *Tongue* of the dumb Man, before he effected the Cure. Whereby he teaches, that to compleat the Cure of our envenomed Tongues, 'tis not sufficient we shall crave God's Assistance, and repent; but the Lord must touch and sanctify them. It is true, the Lord is not now visibly present to effect the Cure, yet has he been graciously pleased to bequeath himself to you, under the sacramental *Veils* of Bread and Wine, in the most adorable Sacrament of the *Eucharist*, for the Purpose. Receive Him then worthily, receive Him frequently, that by so sacred and powerful a Remedy, all the Diseases of your Souls may be effectually removed, especially those of Cursing, Swearing and Blaspheming. In short, by the Means of Prayer, Repentance, and worthy Communions you will happily obtain the Amendment of your sacrilegious Tongues; and, as the Scripture says, of the dumb Man, you will *speak rightly* [*].

There

---

[*] St. Mark vii. 35.

There are several other Ways of overcoming those Vices: First, by reflecting, that if we are to render an Account, on the Day of Judgment, of every idle Word we say, how much more rigorous shall our Account be of every Oath we have sworn, though of ever so trifling a Nature. Secondly, by reflecting on the many temporal Punishments that have been, and Daily are inflicted on Cursers, Swearers, and Blasphemers: they were formerly, by divine Command, to be stoned to Death: And the Account related by St. *Gregory* * of a Boy, five Years old, being snatched away by Devils, from his Father's Arms, on account of his frequent Swearing, is frightful! A true Fear of the Lord will also remove those Vices: S. *Augustin* thus relates of himself, " † The Time was,
" (says he) when I was much given to Swearing,
" and involved in that dangerous and wicked
" Habit: But I tell you, since the Time I began
" to serve God, and saw the great Evil there was
" in Perjury, I was struck with a Fear of it:
" This Fear bridled the inveterate Habit; being
" bridled, it was restrained; being restrained, it
" languished, and languishing, died; and a good
" Custom succeeded a bad one."

In short, I will tell you a Method, says St. *Chrysostom* ‡, which if observed, you shall overcome the evil Practice. When you find yourselves, your Wives, Children, or Domestics infected with the Vices of Cursing or Swearing, and though often admonished, do not amend; command them to go to Bed supperless: Impose this Penance on the Guilty, and you shall soon reap the happy Fruits of an Amendment.

It

---

* Lib. 4 Dialog. cap. 18.   † Lib. 28. Conf.
‡ Homil. 5. ad Popul. Antioch.

It will also prove conducive to your speedy Amendment, to reflect seriously: That Cursing, Swearing, and Blaspheming is the constant Employment of the *Damned*, who, as they are doomed to unchangeable Torments, without the least Hope of a Mitigation of their Pains, are therefore hurried, out of pure Malice, to the ineffectual Revenge of continually Cursing and Blaspheming the Name of the Lord. St. *John* thus describes to us, Hell, and the State of the Damned: It is an obscure Place, 'tis the Region of Darkness; there *they gnawed their Tongues for Pain: and they Blasphemed the God of Heaven, because of their Pains, and Wounds* *.

Let not then, the Language and Employment of the Damned, be any longer that of a Christian, who hopes for Salvation; but carefully observe the Gospel Maxim, *Swear not at all*, except when the necessary Vindication of Truth obliges you to it. Be mindful also of St. *Paul*'s Advice, not to wish Evil to yourselves or any of God's Creatures: *Bless them that persecute you*, says the Apostle, *bless and curse not* ‡. The same Apostle also cries aloud: *Let all Blasphemy be taken away from you* †. Let all God's Creatures unite to extirpate the dreadful Monster, Blasphemy, big with every other Crime: Let every Heart and Hand be joined to destroy that hellish Fiend; so great an Enemy to God, and so destructive to a Christian Soul. Remember timely, O Blasphemer! *Whom thou hast reproached, and whom thou hast blasphemed, and against whom thou hast exalted thy Voice, and lifted up thy eyes on High? Against the holy One of Israel* §.

In

---

* Revel. xvi. 10, 11. ‡ Rom. xii. 14.
† Ephes. iv. 31. § Isaiah xxxvii. 23.

In short, Tears are more proper to bewail the execrable and damnable Vices, than Words to express them.

A due Attention to the Means prescribed in this Chapter, would prove highly conducive to stay the rapid Progress of the detestable Crimes, and in Time effect an happy Reformation.

Lastly, a most powerful Means to overcome those Vices of Cursing, Swearing and Blaspheming is prescribed; *viz.* To become a Member of the *Sodality* inscribed to the most holy Name of *Jesus*, as also to repeat daily the celebrated Form of Prayer, intitled the *Rosary* of the Name of *Jesus*; as we shall see in the following Chapters. Meanwhile, "let us bridle our Tongues," says St. *Chrysostom*[*], "no great Labour will attend it, nor
"will much Time be necessary to accomplish it:
"'tis sufficient to be willing, and the Work will
"be readily effected. This Matter depends
"wholly on Custom ..... endeavour then, by
"Fasting and Prayer to remove the pernicious
"Habit. There is nothing greater, than to be-
"come Teachers of the World: It will be no
"small Matter, to hear it every where said:
"That there is not one in this City, who swears.
"If this be done, you will not only obtain the
"Reward of your good Works, but what I have
"been," says the Saint, "to you (the Means of
"your Conversion) you shall be to the whole
"World: Others shall follow your Example."

CHAP. XIV.
The Origin of the Sodality inscribed to the most holy Name of JESUS.

CRIMES, so heinous as those of profane Swearing, Cursing or Blaspheming must have

[*] Homil. 8. in Act. Apost.

have unavoidably provoked, long since, God's Wrath and Indignation to fall upon the guilty Heads of those impious Miscreants, who presume to take unwarrantable freedoms with the most holy Names of the *Deity*, were it not, that the Multitude of God's tender Mercies restrains his avenging Justice; nay, and even engages his infinite Wisdom to suggest, from Time to Time, such sweet and efficacious Means as must disarm his Justice, reclaim Sinners, and cause his Mercy to shine upon them.

The celebrated *Sodality*, sacred to the most holy Name of *Jesus*, is one of those powerful Means suggested by God's infinite Wisdom, and his unspeakable Goodness revealed it in the 13th Century, when the abominable Vices of Cursing, Swearing and Blaspheming raged to so great a Degree, that on the 20th of *September*, in the Year 1274, the blessed Pope *Gregory* X. * addressed a *Bull* to the Master General of the Order of Preachers, which begins, *Nuper in Concilio Lugdunensi*, &c. † wherein, after briefly setting forth the Praises of the adorable Name, *Jesus*, he earnestly intreats and requires the said Master General and his Brethren, that so often as they should preach the Word of God to the Faithful, they should be mindful to enforce the profound Respect and Veneration so justly due to that all-saving Name.

The Cause of issuing this *Bull*, was, not only to revive and establish the Love of *Jesus* in the Hearts of the Faithful, but also to banish from their Mouths the detestable Vices of Blasphemy, Cursing

---

* Pope *Gregory* X. by Reason of his singular Piety, and the Miracles he wrought, was declared a *Beatus* or Saint, by Pope *Benedict* XIV.

† Bullarium Ord. Præd. Tom. i. p. 524.

Cursing and profane Swearing, so contrary to the Respect due to God's most adorable *Name*.

The Sovereign Pontiff gives the important Commission, in this solemn Manner, to the Order of Preachers, instituted, as he knew it was, for the glorious Work of propagating the Gospel, throughout the *whole Globe of the Earth*: He therefore wisely judged them, from their Learning Zeal and Eloquence, to be most proper Instruments to re-establish the Honour and Love due to God's most amiable Name, and reform those impious Abuses, which were seminated by the malignant Tongues of Cursers, Swearers and Blasphemers, to the great Disgrace of Christianity.

Nor was the holy Pontiff disappointed in his pious Views: for so soon as the Master General, *John* of *Vercelli*, had received the aforesaid *Bull*, he writes a circular Letter full of Piety*, warmly exhorting his Subjects, in all Parts of the World, to exert themselves in the Execution of the supreme Pontiff's pious Intention, so agreeable to the Tenor of the Gospel, and Advantage of Souls.

In Consequence of this Commission, which the Order of Preachers had received, and as chearfully embraced, they were heard, in almost every Part of the Globe, announcing the Danger and Enormity of the damnable Vices, Blasphemy, Cursing, and profane Swearing, and most strenuously enforcing the profound Respect due to the all-glorious Name of *Jesus*, representing in the most lively Manner to their Hearers, how much Mankind are indebted to the Name of the Lord, for their Redemption, Sanctification and Salvation.—That through it, the Sinner is to hope for Mercy and Forgiveness; the just Man, the Grace of Perseverance and future Glory—That the Name

---

* Bullarium, ibid.

Name of *Jesus* is the Source of every Blessing, whether Spiritual or Temporal, that we have or may expect—That it is a *Name* most holy and terrible: Abundantly sweet to the pious Christian, and formidable to the profane Swearer or Blasphemer—A Name, adored by Angels, and feared by Devils—A Name, in short, which is *above every Name,* at which every Knee should bend of those that are in *Heaven,* on *Earth,* or in *Hell!*

With these and such like Instructions, conveyed to the Faithful with Unction and Constancy, a singular Devotion and Respect for the most sacred Name was introduced among the Faithful, and the execrable Vices of Blasphemy, Cursing and profane Swearing most remarkably decreased, to the great Joy of Heaven and Earth.

To perpetuate this happy Change, the Sons of St. *Dominick* resolved, that an Altar should be erected in all their Churches, dedicated solely to the most holy and august Name of *Jesus,* which the Faithful devoutly frequented, and where, on bended Knees, they offered the Sacrifice of Praise and Thanksgiving to the most holy Name of God: saying with St. *Paul,* * *Let us offer up the Sacrifice of Praise always to God, that is, the Fruit of Lips confessing his Name.* Thus were the first Foundations laid for the sacred *Sodality,* by the Brethren of the holy Order of Preachers, *alias,* of St. *Dominick,* which was afterwards propagated and established by them, to the unspeakable Glory of God's most venerable Name, and signal Benefit of the Christian World.

In this State the Devotion continued until the Year 1432†, at which Time the Kingdom of *Portugal* was visited by a most dreadful Plague, which

---

* Heb. xiii. 15.
† Ravicini, Roseto Prodig. Append. Tom i. 402.

which swept away such Multitudes, that the Kingdom appeared almost depopulated, particularly the City of *Lisbon*, its Capital, seemed only a Receptacle for the Dead. The few that survived, imputing these Chastisements to the just Judgments of Heaven, for the Sins they had committed, particularly those of Cursing, Swearing, and Blaspheming, earnestly sought Forgiveness and firmly purposed Amendment. The Children of St. *Dominick* were singularly active in promoting so desirable a Reformation, and had recourse to the powerful Means of fasting, praying, and preaching, thereby to offer a sacred Violence to Heaven, and become the happy Instruments of appeasing God's Wrath, and moving the People to an unfeigned Repentance.

Among the many engaged in the important Cause, *Andrew Diaz**, of the Order of Preachers, who (being for some Time Bishop of *Megara*, an antient City of *Greece*, in the Province of *Achaia*) renouncing the pastoral Care, retired to his Convent at *Lisbon*, where he soon had an Opportunity of signalizing himself to the unspeakable Joy of the Inhabitants of *Lisbon*, and indeed of all *Europe*, who reasonably dreaded the spreading Infection.

This venerable Prelate, seeing the Distresses of the People, and perceiving, that Heaven seemed deaf to their Lamentations and Intreaties, fired with an holy Zeal, ascends the Pulpit, and most pressingly exhorts them to make their humble addresses to the merciful Name of *Jesus*, reminding them with great Energy, that there is no *other Name under Heaven given to Men, whereby they must be saved* †.

The

---

* Ibid. p. 403. † Acts iv. 12.

The People flocked in Multitudes to his Sermons, particularly those infected with the Plague: And as every Individual was desirous of his Preservation and Safety, so you might behold all and every one calling with great Fervency, on *Jesus*, with their Mouths; revering him with their Hearts; and, on bended Knees adoring his most merciful *Name*. What was the Consequence of this happy Reformation? It caused the Plague to cease on a sudden: the corrupt Morals being banished their Souls, the destructive Contagion that attacked their Bodies, ceased also: Their joyful Acclamations seemed to reach the Skies, and their grateful Acknowledgements were sent up to the Throne of God: Nay, universal Joy and Thanksgiving were diffused through all Europe, on Occasion of this happy and important Event.

The zealous Prelate perceiving the happy Fruits of his Mission, resolved, that a perpetual Remembrance should be kept of God's special Goodness: and to this End, he caused a beautiful Altar to be erected, and Processions made, in Honour of God's most adorable Name, to remind the Faithful of this signal stroke of the divine Clemency. And, to engage future Generations to praise the all-gracious Name of *Jesus*, he founded a *Sodality* or *Confraternity* sacred to that most holy Name, *Jesus*, wherein the Names of all those were to be inscribed, who resolved in future, to praise the most holy Name of God, and to prevent, to the utmost of their Power, the Profanation of it, whether in themselves or others, by observing such Rules, as he wisely prescribed to them.

Such an Institution proved highly acceptable to the Inhabitants of *Lisbon:* the Nobility, Gentry, and Others eagerly sought Admittance into the sacred *Sodality*, vying with each other, who should
first

first inlist under the sacred Banner, and most distinguish himself in promoting a Work, so pleasing to God, and advantageous to Mankind.

Thus did this worthy Son of St. *Dominick* found the celebrated *Sodality* or *Confraternity* sacred to the most holy Name of *Jesus*, to the greater Honour of that most adorable Name, and Welfare of the Christian Religion.

It may be proper here to acquaint the pious Reader, that what is to be understood by the " *Sodality* of the most holy Name of Jesus," is an Assembly of devout Persons, who purpose to give Praise to the Name of *Jesus*, by a Repetition of the *Rosary* inscribed to that sacred Name, and an Observance of those pious Works prescribed to the Members of the *Sodality:* such as frequenting the Sacraments, on the *second* Sunday of every Month; preventing to the utmost of their Power, in themselves and others, the Abuse of God's most sacred Name, &c. And to this End, cause their Names to be inscribed in a Book, appointed for the salutary Purpose, whereby they become, as by spiritual Bonds, united, though in the most remote Parts of the Earth, in one illustrious Society, praising the Name of the Lord; and, by a spiritual Communication, partaking of each other's good Works, though wrought in the most distant Parts of the Globe.

Such a Sodality, Society, or Confraternity must doubtless tend to the greater Honour of God's most adorable Name, and singular Advantage of Souls: for though we are all Members of the same mystical Body of Christ; one Flock under one supreme Pastor, and consequently partakers with one another, of the common Prayers, Fastings and other Works of Piety, in the great Communion of
Saints:

Saints: " Yet," says our learned *Clarkeson* *," " in particular Devotions and Acts of Supererogation, to which we are not in Duty bound, there both may be, and really is a stricter Communication and Alliance, more particular Fellowships and Societies, under the universal Conduct and Œconomy of the Church, among those who aspire after more eminent Degrees of an holy Life, who desire to live more to the Glory of God, and the Improvement of their Souls, in a regular Course of Devotion: For as in temporal Kingdoms, under the same universal Government, we see erected different Academies of the Learned, Societies of Merchants, Sodalities of Mechanics, &c. to the great Improvement of Arts and Sciences: so, in like Manner, under the same general Communion of the Church, we find devout Persons, husbanding the Time, which others throw away upon the idle Impertinences of Life, flowing into particular Societies, inrolling themselves, like Soldiers, under one Banner, and obliging themselves, to certain Rules, wisely adapted to the Nature of the Institution; to their like Proficiency in the great Art of an holy Life, in the Science of the Saints, and Way of Virtue."

It was to this laudable End, that the venerable Prelate, *Andrew Diaz*, already mentioned, exhorted the Faithful to enter into an holy Association or Sodality, to praise the Name of the Lord, by frequently repeating to them the Words of our Blessed Redeemer, † *If two of you shall agree together upon Earth, about any one Thing they shall ask, it shall be granted them of my Father, who is in Heaven.*

* Introduction to the Rosary of the B. Virgin, c. 4.
† Matth. xviii. 19, 20.

Heaven. For where two or three are gathered together in my Name, there am I in the midst of them. After such Encouragement given by the Son of God himself, what Christian, who means to forward the great Work of Salvation, can be so great an Enemy to himself, as to neglect inrolling himself in so holy a Society, evidently calculated to praise the Name of the Lord, and promote the important Work of Salvation?

If any one should ask, why the *Sodality* and *Rosary* are inscribed to the most holy Name of *Jesus*, preferably to any other Name, under which the God-head is worshipped? it can be readily accounted for: First, because we have the strongest Reasons to adore the Divine Being under that most merciful Name, *viz.* It reminds us, that the Son of the living God has deigned to cloath himself with our Mortality, to satisfy for our Sins: That he has lived with us: That he suffered and died for us: That he opened the Gates of the City of God for our Admittance, &c. Besides, as the angelic Doctor remarks, "the Name, *Jesus*, is signified in all the other "Names foretold by the Prophets," as when *Isaiah*, speaking of *Jesus Christ*, says: *His Name shall be called, Wonderful, Counsellor, God, the Mighty, the Father of the World to come, the Prince of Peace**. In all these, the Name *Jesus* is signified, as St. *Thomas* plainly proves †.

So that by praising the Name *Jesus*, all the Names of the Deity are celebrated and glorified. With the greatest Propriety then, the Catholic Church, and with it the *Sodality* and *Rosary*, venerate and adore the second Person of the most adorable Trinity, made Man, particularly under the most amiable and august Name of *Jesus:* because, as
the

---

* Isaiah ix. 6.   † 3. p. q. 37. a. 2. ad 1.

the Apostle St *Paul* says: It is *a Name which is above every Name: That in the Name of* Jesus *every Knee should bend, of those who are in Heaven, on Earth, and in Hell* *.

CHAP. XV.
The Progress of the Sodality in Spain, &c.

IF the sacred Sodality proved so efficacious, as totally to banish the Plague from the Kingdom of *Portugal*, it proved no less powerful in the removal of a yet more dangerous Contagion, which infected entire Kingdoms, especially those of *Spain* ‡. The Contagion I allude to, is the damnable Custom of Cursing, Swearing and Blaspheming, which so universally raged among Men in the 16th Century, whereby the adorable Name of God was treated with Contempt, and called upon in support of Lies, and Acts of Injustice: By their rash or false Oaths, they profaned the Name of the Lord: By their Imprecations, they uncharitably called upon God to curse his Creatures; and by their Blasphemies, insulted God in his own Person. By thus robbing God of the Respect and Worship due to him, they became infected with a Contagion, which must have inevitably given Death to their unhappy Souls, if unrepented for, and plunged them into the Lake of endless Misery and Torments.

Every true Servant of God became alarmed at these heinous Offences given to the infinite Majesty, and trembled at the dreadful Consequences that await such Impieties: They beheld the horrid Scene with Sorrow and Amazement! They exerted every Effort to extirpate the detestable Vices, particularly the Children of St. *Dominick*, who were destined by him, and singularly appointed by the Sovereign Pontiffs, to eradicate those Vices,

* Philip. ii. 9, 10. ‡ Roseto Prodig Append. p. 463.

and re-establish the Glory of God's most sacred Name.

Hence, we might behold those Ministers of the Gospel, with indefatigable Zeal, inveighing against the damnable Vices; especially, our pious and learned *Didacus de Victoria*, Preacher to the Emperor *Charles* V. who flourished about the Year 1540.* This celebrated Man signalized himself most remarkably, by propagating the heavenly Institution, and forming such *additional* Rules, whereby great Glory accrued, and daily accrues, to the most holy Name of God.

Notwithstanding the great Abilities and repeated Efforts of this Evangelical Preacher, so habitual were those Vices, that though Cursers, Swearers and Blasphemers were convinced of the enormity of their Crimes, and roused to a Detestation of them at Church, by his learned Instructions and pathetic Admonitions; yet, when retired to their respective Homes, they relapsed; and, like a Dog to his Vomit, again began to spit forth the Language of Devils.

Didacus,

---

* Pope *Pius* IV. in his Bull, *Salvatoris & Domini*, &c. stiles *Diducus de Victoria* Author of this celebrated *Sodality*; because, he exerted himself in a most singular Manner, not only by recommending the heavenly Devotion, in the most persuasive Language, from the Chair of Truth, but by forming such additional Rules, as effectually tended to perfect and establish the sacred Devotion in the Kingdoms of *Spain*. And though *Didacus de Victoria* be allowed to be the Founder of it in *Spain*, it follows not from thence, that it was not established long before in other Places, by the Brethren of the holy Order of Preachers, as *Bremond* observes, Tract. de Consensu Bull. pag. 442.

Didacus, and his Brethren Preachers, finding the vast Difficulty attending the Removal of those habitual Vices; and, that without a special Assistance from Heaven, it appeared almost impossible to eradicate them, had recourse to Prayer, fervently beseeching the God of Mercy, to suggest some powerful Means to stem the Torrent of Impiety, which threatened Destruction to the whole World.

God, who is ever ready to hear the humble Petitions of his faithful Servants, was graciously pleased to inspire the blessed *John Micon** of the Order of Preachers, celebrated for his Sanctity, Learning and Preaching, to institute a Form of Prayer, totally calculated to praise the Name of God, and remind the Faithful of the unspeakable Blessings, through it, conferred upon them; to the End, that the Faithful, whether at home or abroad, should not want a Remedy for the Cure of their infected Tongues.

This celebrated Form of Prayer, instituted by *John Micon*†, is called the *Rosary* of the most holy Name of *Jesus*, which proved a most powerful Remedy: For, whilst the Hearts of the Faithful were inflamed, from the Pulpit, with the love of God's most adorable Name, and roused to a detestation of the damnable Vices; at their Return to their respective Abodes, they had recourse to a Repetition of

---

* He wrought many Miracles, and received St. *Lewis Bertrand* into the Order of Preachers, in the Year 1544. So that *John Micon*, was not a Disciple of St. *Lewis Bertrand*, as some Authors mention, but St. *Lewis* was a Disciple of his. *Tournon* Hist. Hom. Illus. tom. iv. pag. 488.

† Append. Thesaur. Gratiarum S Smi. Ros. B. V. pag. 248.

of the sacred *Rosary*, which served as a silent Preacher, and a most powerful Form of Prayer, as we shall see in the following Chapter.

Let it suffice to remark here, that the Faithful, from hearing the Praises of, and Respect due to the most holy Name of God in *Church*, and from a devout and constant Recital of the *Rosary* of *Jesus* at *home*, a speedy Reformation took place; their obdurate Hearts became softened and inflamed with the Love of God: They began to entertain a due Sense of their inexpressible Obligations to his All-sacred Name; they conceived an utter Abhorrence to the execrable Vices, and a firm Resolution, in future, to praise his holy Name. O, what a blessed Reformation! Blasphemies, Oaths and Imprecations are no longer to be heard among them; on the contrary, the very Streets and Highways, echoed with Prayers and Ejaculations, addressed to the most holy Name of the Lord. Blessed Change, the happy Fruits of this heavenly Devotion.

What a glorious Sight! to see and hear them encouraging each other to praise the Name of the Lord, in the Words of the royal Psalmist: *Join with me to magnify our Lord, and let us all together celebrate his holy Name: Because I have sought our Lord and he heard me, he has rescued me out of all my Afflictions.** Or to hear them returning their grateful Thanks to *Jesus*, for the innumerable Blessings received from him, through the Merits of his all-gracious Name, in the following Words: *What shall I render to the Lord, for all the Things he has rendered to me? I will take the Chalice of Salvation, and I will call on the Name of the Lord.*†

Or, in short, to hear them addressing an Universal Prayer to the Honour of the most sacred Name

of

---

* Psal. xxxiii. 4. 5.   † Psal. cxv. 3, 4.

of God, in the following Words of *Ecclesiasticus*,* must inspire the most obdurate Hearts with the most profound Veneration, and replenish them with Sentiments of Gratitude and Thanksgiving. *I will give glory to thee, O Lord, my King, and I will praise thee, O God my Saviour. I will give Glory to thy Name: For thou hast been an Helper and Protector to me, and hast preserved my Body from destruction, from the Snare of an unjust Tongue, and from the Lips of them that forge Lies; and in the Sight of them that stood by, thou hast been my Helper. And thou hast delivered me, according to the Multitude of the Mercy of thy Name, from the roaring Lions, that were ready to devour me. Out of the Hands of them that sought my Life, and from the Gates of Affliction, which encompassed me ...... I will praise thy Name continually, and will praise it with Thanksgiving, and my Prayer was heard. And thou hast saved me from Destruction, and hast delivered me from the evil Time. Therefore I will give Thanks, and praise thee, and bless the Name of the Lord.*

The sacred Sodality so excellent in itself, so highly favoured by Almighty God in the Dawn of its Institution, and so advantageous to Mankind, was not to be confined within the Boundaries of *Spain* and *Portugal*, but spread, by the unwearied Labours of the Order of Preachers, with the greatest Rapidity, into the most distant Climes: It has happily reached our Island, and particularly its great Metropolis, *Dublin*, where latterly, the learned *Edmond Burke*, Dr. *Egan*, Dr. *Richardson*,†

among

* Chap. li.

† Dr. *Richardson*, in the Year 1746, published a Prayer-book, intitled, *The Manner of hearing Mass*, &c. and in the same Year published an *Appendix* to it, intitled,

among many others, of the Order of Preachers, zealously exerted themselves, by strenuously recommending to the Faithful the sacred *Rosary* and *Sodality*, whereby numberless Sinners have been happily reclaimed from the hateful and damnable Vices of Cursing, Swearing and Blaspheming; and now give Praise and Glory to the most amiable Name of the Lord—Not to mention the indefatigable Labours of several of our Missionaries, in other Parts of the Kingdom, who have been the Instruments of propagating the heavenly Institution and Devotion, to the greater Glory of God's most adorable Name, and the good of Souls.

From this, and the preceding Chapters, it evidently appears, that as Almighty God had inspired and appointed that illustrious Pillar of the Church, St. *Dominick*, to be the Founder and Preacher of the *Rosary* of *Mary*, Mother of *Jesus*,[*] whereby so many and such signal Blessings have and daily flow on the Catholic World; so the same all-gracious God has been pleased to single out St. *Dominick*'s Children, to be the happy Instruments of instituting and preaching the *Sodality* and *Rosary* sacred to the most holy Name of *Jesus*: And God so amply crowned their Apostolic Labours with such amazing

tled, *An Appendix to the Manner of hearing Mass*, &c. wherein he briefly recites, within the compass of a Sheet, the Conditions, Rules, Indulgences, &c. belonging to the Confraternity or Sodality of the most holy Name of *Jesus*, *alias* of God, &c. He also strenuously and frequently recommended, from the Chair of Truth, the *Rosary* and *Sodality* in his learned and pious Discourses, to the singular Advantage of crowded Audiences, who have reason to revere his Memory.

[*] S. *Pius* V. *Consueverunt*, &c. *Gregorius* XIII. *Monet Apostolus*, &c. *Sixtus* V. *Dum ineffabilia Meritorum*, &c.

zing Succeſs, as made them appear to the World, ſo many Veſſels of Election, bearing the Name of *Jeſus* in Triumph, *before Kings, Gentiles, and the Children of Iſrael.* What wonder then, that theſe Apoſtolic Men, who were choſen and inſpired by God himſelf to inſtitute and cultivate the *Sodality* and *Roſary* of the Name of *Jeſus*, " throughout the univerſal Globe of the Earth*," ſhould be appointed, by his Vicars upon Earth, the ſole Guardians and Stewards of his ſacred Depoſite?

CHAP. XVI.

Of the Roſary *of the Name of* JESUS, *and its Excellency.*

THE *Roſary* of the Name of *Jeſus*, is a moſt holy Form of Prayer, inſtituted, not only to give Praiſe to the adorable Name of *Jeſus*, alias of *God*, but alſo to baniſh the hateful Vices of *Blaſphemy, Curſing,* and *profane Swearing.*

It has been already mentioned, that the celebrated *John Micon*, was the firſt who framed the *Roſary* of *Jeſus*, which he modelled after that of the *Roſary* of the Bleſſed Virgin: For perceiving the happy Conſequences, that have and daily do reſult from the *Roſary* of the Mother of God, which was firſt inſtituted and preached by that bright Luminary of the Church, St. *Dominick*, againſt the Errors and Impieties of the *Albigenſians*, and the Immoralities of the People, with the greateſt ſucceſs†, he

---

* *Benedict* XIV. *Alias Nos*, &c. iſſued 30th. *September*, 1748.

† " By the Roſary of the Mother of God, St. *Dominick* drove out the unclean Spirit, (ſays Pope *Gregory*

he resolved to tread the Steps of his holy Father, in the Institution and Formation of the *Rosary* of *Jesus*; and accordingly forms the Devotion upon the same Plan, dividing it into three Parts, each Part containing profound *Meditations*, sacred *Petitions*, and devout *Prayers*. By its *Meditations*, we are reminded of what *Jesus* has done for us: By its *Petitions*, we are taught how to implore, and actually do implore the divine Clemency to have Mercy on us. And lastly, by its *Prayers* we are briefly reminded of those Mysteries we have been meditating upon, at the same Time fervently praying, in virtue of those Mysteries of our Redemption, Mercy and Grace in this Life, and an happy Eternity in the next. What Form of Prayer can be more acceptable to Heaven, or profitable to us?—A further Explanation of this heavenly Devotion will clearly prove it to be a most powerful Form of Prayer.

As St. *Paul* informs us[*], *That no one can say Lord Jesus,* (worthily) *unless through the Holy Ghost*; hence the Devotion begins with a brief Prayer to the Lord, to open and purify our Lips, that we may worthily announce its Praise, &c. We then proceed to the first Part, of which the Rosary of the Name of *Jesus* is composed, viz. *Meditation.* The impor-

" IX) he destroyed the Lust of the Flesh, as with spi-
" ritual Arrows, he broke in Pieces the stony Hearts
" of the Ungodly: He made Heresy and Error to shake
" and tremble, and the Church of the Faithful to ex-
" ult for Joy." *Fons Sapientiæ* 3 Julii 1235. And S. *Pius*
V. " That the Faithful being inflamed with these Me-
" ditations and Prayers (of the Rosary of the Blessed
" Virgin) they begun to be changed into other Men;
" the darkness of Heresy begun to vanish, and the light
" of the Catholic Faith to shine forth with greater
" Brightness." *Consueverunt.* 27 Sept. 1569.

[*] 1 Cor. xii. 3.

importance of meditating on the Mysteries of *Jesus Christ*, appears from St. *Paul*'s Advice to *Timothy**, when after giving him some important Instructions, he says: *Meditate on these Things, be employed in these Things; that thy Proficiency may appear to all Men.*

What can be more serviceable to a Christian Soul, than to meditate frequently on the most important Mysteries of our Redemption; the Life, Death, Resurrection, &c. of our Lord and Saviour *Jesus Christ?* What can so readily relieve a Christian Soul from the burthensome and unprofitable Thoughts of transitory Beings, than to elevate our Minds to the celestial Regions, to contemplate the Majesty of a God, so immensely great in Himself, and beneficent to us; particularly, in that wonderful Proof of his Love, which he has given us, in not sparing his only Son, that our Sins might be satisfied for, and we become intitled to Mansions in his blessed Kingdom.

So profitable are such Meditations to a Christian Soul, that the Catechism of the Council of *Trent* admonishes the Pastors of the Church, to exhort the Faithful and excite their Penitents daily to revolve in their Minds, something of the Passion of Christ. Hence it is, that the *Rosary* of *Jesus* begins with *Meditation*, to the End, that the important Mysteries of our Redemption, should be frequently remembered and deeply impressed on our Minds, which soaring above all earthly Beings by such divine Contemplations, we might duly dispose ourselves, to converse with God himself, and worthily praise his sacred Name.

What a divine Employment! to meditate on the five following *joyful* Mysteries, in the first Part of the

---

* 1 Tim. iv. 15.

the Rosary of Jesus: The *Incarnation* of our Lord Jesus Christ; his *Nativity*; his *Circumcision*; his being found in the *Temple*; and his *Baptism*. By which Mysteries, we view him preparing for, and giving a Beginning to, the great Work of our Redemption.

In the second Part we contemplate those tragical Scenes, that were acted at the Execution of the important Work of our Redemption, wherein is represented, how much *Jesus* humbled himself and suffered to expiate our Sins, in the following Mysteries: *The washing the Feet of his Disciples; his Prayer and bloody Sweat in the Garden; his being apprehended, as if he had been a Malefactor; his carrying the Cross; and his descent into Hell*.

And in the third Part, we commemorate and meditate upon, his glorious Victory over Death, the Favours conferred on Mankind, and his coming to Judgment, in the following Mysteries of his *Resurrection; Ascension; the Descent of the Holy Ghost; the Coronation of the Blessed Virgin and Saints; and his coming to Judgment.*

These Meditations have been selected from the most sublime Truths, as best adapted and most suitable to every Capacity: Though sublime, they are easy; though plain, they are full of Mysteries. In a Word, the simple or less enlightened Minds shall find the mysterious Truths sufficiently clear and cogent to engage them in the Adoration of God's most amiable Name: Whilst the most acute Understanding shall find wherewith to exercise itself, and at length become absorbed in the Contemplation

* That is, says St. *Thomas*, "into those Regions, where the Souls of the Just were detained," waiting the Arrival of the Son of God, to rise with him, and attend him into the Heavenly *Hierusalem*. 3. p. q. 52. a. 2.

templation of God's unsearchable Ways, and the unspeakable Goodness of his all-sacred *Name*.

The Devouts of the Rosary should be mindful, in the Recital of the Devotion, not only to mention the *Mystery*, but also the *Meditation* which immediately follows: 'Tis an essential Part of the celebrated Devotion, and should not be omitted by those who can read: Agreeable to what St. *Paul* says, *meditate on these Things, be employed in these Things: That thy Proficiency may appear to all Men* *.

The pious *Rosarist*, after premising one of the Mysteries, on which he is to meditate, then breaks forth into *vocal* Prayer, of which its Petitions form a Part: For the Mind being previously disposed by mental Prayer, the Mouth worthily addresses the Lord, by a Repetition of the following Petition, Ten Times: *O Jesus, Son of David, have Mercy on us.* The Decade is terminated by *Glory be to the Father,* &c. and so on for the first Five *Decades* or Tens †.

The second Part is also repeated in the same Manner, with its respective Mysteries, and the following Petition: *O Jesus of Nazareth King of the Jews, have Mercy on us.*

The

---

* 1 Tim. iv. 15.

† Which are usually and regularly repeated by the Assistance of a Pair of Beads, consisting of five *Decades*, or *Tens*, whereby the Faithful (especially those who cannot read, or where there is a Congregation) are brought to recite the sacred Devotion with Harmony and Regularity: For Instance, each Time that you repeat *Jesus, Son of David, have Mercy on us*, you let pass a Mark or Stone; and when arrived at the Eleventh, which is larger than any of the other Ten, you are then silently told to finish the Decade with *Glory be to the Father,* &c.

The third Part is recited in the same Manner, as the former, with its peculiar Mysteries, and the following Petition: *O Jesus, Son of the living God, have Mercy on us.*

From these Petitions we are encouraged to hope the most signal Blessings, as they have already incontestibly proved their Efficacy. If we ask the *blind Men*, mentioned in the Gospel *, what Success they had, when they addressed the Saviour of the World, in these Words: *Lord, Son of David, have Mercy on us:* Or the *Cananean* Woman, who petitioned in the like Words, that her Daughter might be dispossessed of the Devil †. She will inform you, that her Daughter was immediately cured: And the Blind Men will gratefully confess, that they instantly received their Sight. Signal Wonders may indeed be expected from this Petition, because, as the Evangelist St. *John* says, ‡ *Every Spirit that confesseth Jesus Christ to have come in the Flesh, is of God.* They, no Doubt, appertain to God, who make so noble and pious a Confession of the Humanity of *Jesus Christ.*

If you ask St. *Peter*, what was the Consequence of a devout Invocation of *Jesus of Nazareth?* He will assure you, that in Virtue of it, he gave to a Man, who had been a Cripple from his Mother's Womb, the perfect Use of all his Limbs, in these Words: § *In the Name of Jesus Christ of Nazareth, rise up, and walk.*

And let St. *Matthew* recount to you, the singular Reward and Honour conferred on St. *Peter*, for declaring *Jesus Christ, to be the Son of the living God.* He tells you, that the Redeemer was

so

---

* Matth. xx. 30, 31. † Matth. xv. 22.
‡ 1 John iv. 2. § Acts iii. 6.

so pleased with his noble Confession, that he appointed him, Prince of the Apostles, *and the Rock upon which he would build his Church*, with this solemn and absolute Promise: That *the Gates of Hell shall not prevail against it* *: And obtained for him the following Information and Assurance from the Mouth of *Jesus Christ* himself, as St. *Luke* informs us †, *Simon, Simon, behold Satan hath desired earnestly to have you, that he may sift you as Wheat; but I have prayed for thee, that thy Faith fail not, and thou being once converted, confirm thy Brethren.*

No Wonder that the most signal Favours shall be heaped on the Soul, which worthily proclaims *Jesus* to be the *Son of the living God:* For, as the Evangelist St. *John* says: *Whosoever shall confess that Jesus is the Son of God, God abideth in him, and he in God* ‡.

Lastly, each Part of the heavenly Devotion is concluded with a most pious Prayer, which reminds us of the Mysteries we have contemplated, and at the same Time we beseech *Jesus* in Virtue of them, to shower down his Blessings upon us; as may be fully seen in the *Rosary of Jesus*.

I know not any Objection that can be made against this heavenly Form of Prayer, except the frequent Repetition of its *Petitions*. This Objection must appear frivolous and trifling, when we consider, that we cannot too often repeat what is always and unquestionably good, and that a frequent Repetition of the same Words, is warranted by holy Writ: Did not *David* in his 135th Psalm repeat no less than 27 Times, the very same Words: *Because his Mercy is for ever?* Did not the Blind Men, mentioned in the Gospel, receive

their

---

* Matth. xvi. 18.   † xxii. 31, 32.
‡ 1 John iv. 15.

their Sight, by crying out again and again, *Lord, Son of David, have Mercy on us* *? Nor truly, can we poor miserable Sinners, blinded by Passions, too often call upon *Jesus*, the Light of the World, to dispel those thick Clouds that darken our Minds; we cannot too often intreat him to enlighten our Understandings, and have Mercy on us. Nay, did not our divine Master himself, when praying with the greatest Fervour in the Garden of *Olives*, † *pray the third Time, saying the same Words?* Who then, can object to a Repetition of those heavenly Petitions of the Rosary of the Name of *Jesus*, which express so singular a Respect for, and Confidence in, his all-gracious Name? To praise the most amiable and august Name of the Lord, is an indispensible Duty, strongly inculcated by all the inspired Writers, and enforced by the strictest Ties of *Duty, Gratitude, Interest, Necessity*, &c. as has been already set forth. Chap. IV.

And as it is a Duty, equally interesting, to avoid the Profanation of God's most awful Name, so there cannot be a more effectual Means to banish those hateful Vices, contrary to the Respect due to it, than by the constant Practice of the opposite Virtues: For, as Darkness is dispelled by Light; Cold by Heat; Drunkenness by Sobriety; in like Manner, as the most holy and august Name of the Lord is repeatedly profaned and abused by Oaths, Execrations, and Blasphemies; so the atrocious Crimes can never be more effectually removed, than by repeatedly addressing and praising his adorable Name, with that celebrated Form of Prayer, the Rosary of *Jesus* — And as the damnable Custom of Cursing, Swearing and Blaspheming, is

con-

---

* Matth. xx. 30, 31. † Matth. xxvi. 44.

contracted by associating and conversing with Cursers, Swearers, and Blasphemers; so, to overcome the hateful Custom, you must not only decline their Company, but it would prove highly conducive to the Removal of those shocking Vices, to associate with the devout Members of the sacred *Sodality*, who are particularly mindful to praise God's most adorable Name.

They must indeed be abandoned Sinners who can object to the Praises due to the most venerable Name of the Lord, or to a Repetition of them: Their Objections can have Weight only with Libertines and Unbelievers, who regardless of the Respect due to the supreme Being, or the Attention due to the important Concern of Salvation, are ever ready to encourage Impiety and promote Immorality: who are fond to ridicule, condemn and suppress whatever may tend to forward solid Piety and promote a due Respect to the most holy Name of God.

But for a Christian, a Disciple of Jesus Christ, who humbly hopes for Salvation, through the Merits of his most sacred Name, no Employment is more praise-worthy or necessary, than to offer Praise and Thanksgiving to his most adorable Name: Nothing more prudent, than to make Choice of a Form of Prayer, the *Rosary* of the Name of *Jesus*, which is entirely calculated for that glorious End: A Devotion efficacious to Admiration: A Form of Prayer highly extolled by the Church, and strenuously recommended to the Faithful!

Resolve then, to make daily the acceptable Offering, of that most holy and celebrated Devotion of the *Rosary*, and with grateful Hearts say to God: *So will I sing a Psalm to thy Name for ever:*
that

that I may pay my Vows from Day to Day*. Such a divine Employment will cause Heaven to be attentive to the devout Rosarists: Their Petitions will be granted in this Life, and eternal Happiness will assuredly await them in the next. Yes, Christian Reader, their Happiness has been long since foretold by the Royal Psalmist, in these Words: † *Blessed is the Man whose Trust is in the Name of the Lord.*

CHAP. XVII.

Motives to engage us to enter into the sacred Sodality, *and to recite frequently the* Rosary *of the Name of* JESUS.

WHEN we reflect on the Excellency, Sanctity, and Efficacy of the Name of *Jesus*, and how much we are bound to praise it: When we recollect, how effectually the *Rosary* and *Sodality* contribute to the Discharge of that Christian Duty; it will seem needless to expatiate on a Subject so self-evident, or to recommend an Institution, which every Christian should, with open Arms, embrace. A few Motives may, however, be assigned to help weak Minds, and encourage them to the heavenly Undertaking.

The first is, that by being inscribed in the *Sodality*, they become Partakers of the good Works done by the Members of it, in all Parts of the World. What an Happiness! That you, whether asleep or awake; whether Abroad or at Home; whether on Sea or Land; whether in Sickness, unable to assist yourselves, or in Health, perhaps unmindful
of

* Psal. lx. 9.   † Psal. xxxix. 5.

of God, your Conversion, your spiritual and temporal Welfare, &c. are prayed for by your Brethren, the Members of the sacred *Sodality*; who are mutually bound to pray for each other, though in the most distant Parts of the Globe. Add to this, that by being inscribed, you become intitled to share of the Treasures of the Church, (Indulgences, Privileges and Favours) so plentifully granted by the Popes, the Vicars of *Jesus Christ* upon Earth, to all and every of the Brethren duly disposed to receive them.

The second Motive is, that a constant Recital of the *Rosary* of the Name of *Jesus*, will remind us of the principal Mysteries of our Redemption: No Reflection more necessary or important.

Thirdly, the Consideration of your own Interest, should impel you to an Entrance into the one, and to a frequent Repetition of the other: For, what can more effectually move Heaven to shower down its Blessings upon us? *Jesus*, whilst upon Earth, *did not* refuse any Petition duly made in his Name: Is he less exorable now? Or is his holy Name less efficacious? No: for, he is equally ready now to receive our Petitions, and to grant them: Though the Lord has ascended into Heaven, he did not mean to leave us *Orphans*: For he promises to remain with us, *unto the Consummation of Ages*. He has indeed ascended, not to abandon us, but to prepare Mansions for us, in his heavenly Kingdom, where he sits at the right Hand of his Almighty Father, to plead for us: Constantly exhibiting his Wounds, which he still bears on his glorious Body, in perpetual Remembrance of what he has suffered, in Consequence of his all-saving Name, which proclaimed him the Saviour of Mankind; thereby to engage his eternal Father
mer-

mercifully to look down upon those, who shall gratefully praise and glorify it. Nay, *Jesus*, the Wisdom of the eternal Father, assures you, that *If two of you shall agree together on Earth, about any one Thing they shall ask, it shall be granted them of my Father, who is in Heaven. For where two or three are gathered together in my Name, there am I in the midst of them* *.

Can any Thing be more inviting or pressing to enter into an holy Association to praise his adorable Name, than this his kind Declaration? Remember, Christian Reader, 'tis not a weak, mortal Man, whose Powers are confined to very narrow Limits, that gives you this Assurance, or makes the unlimited Promise: But 'tis *Jesus*, Son of the living God himself, whose Power enables him, whose Goodness inclines him, and whose Veracity obliges him to grant the Requests of his faithful Servants, made in his *Name*. *If you ask me any Thing in my Name*, says Jesus Christ, *I will do it* †. Can Words be more expressive of his determined Resolution to grant, unlimited every Blessing humbly and perseverantly asked, through the Merits of his most adorable Name?

In what Light then, are we to consider the devout Clients of the *Rosary?* What Opinion are we to form of the Efficacy of their Prayers? Or to what shall we compare them, when assembled in his *Name*, and on bended Knees, we view and hear them celebrating the Praises of his sacred Name, by a devout Recital of the *Rosary* of *Jesus?* If their Hearts speak the Language of their Mouths, I can compare them to nothing less, than to the Angels and Saints of Paradise, who with one Voice, most harmoniously concelebrate
the

---

* Matth. xviii. 19, 20.   † John xiv. 14.

the Praises of the most adorable Name of their God: for as Blasphemers, Cursers and profane Swearers resemble the Damned by the Vices of Blasphemy, Cursing and Swearing, and their hateful Language proclaims them to be of the Number of the Accursed, so they, on the contrary, who constantly praise the glorious Name of *Jesus*, bear the strongest Resemblance of the Angels and Saints of Paradise: Their angelic Language foretels their future Rewards, and becomes a sure Presage of future Glory. Hence the Royal Prophet thus joyfully expresses himself: *I will sing Praise to thee in the Sight of the Angels: I will Worship towards thy holy Temple, and I will give Glory to thy Name ..... for thou hast magnified thy holy Name above all* *.

Such a Demeanour bespeaks them to be Inhabitants of another Region: The Earth seems transformed into Heaven: Men into Angels or Saints! And to crown all, they are blessed with the Presence of Jesus Christ: *for where two or three are gathered together in my Name*, says he, *there am I in the midst of them* †. O powerful Form of Prayer! which can thus effectually prevail on the Son of the living God, to descend from Heaven, to bless the pious Supplicants with his Presence, and grant their Requests! What an Happiness for the devout Rosarists!

Do not persuade yourselves, that the Recital of the *Rosary* of *Jesus*, will interfere with, or interrupt your worldly Business; nay, on the contrary, it will prove a powerful Means to procure a Blessing on your honest Endeavours: And, if you mean to pray at all, you cannot make Use of a more efficacious, nor scarcely a more brief Form of Prayer: Though brief, it is powerful: though plain, it abounds

---

* Psal. cxxxvii. 2, 3.   † Matth. xviii. 20.

abounds with Mysteries; and may be repeated at Home or Abroad; by Sea or by Land; in the Chapel, or private Chamber, kneeling, standing or walking, yet the most devout Attitude is recommended, as the Name of *Jesus* is so frequently repeated, at which *every Knee should bend.*

It is a Devotion of such a Nature, that not only the Orthodox, but the Heterodox Believers, may recite it, without infringing upon their Principles: The *offensive* Sound of an *Intercessor*, is not so much as hinted at; the Supplication being made immediately to *Jesus Christ* himself, praying him *to have Mercy on us.* Hence, all and every of our separated Brethren, who admit the Use of *vocal* and *mental Prayer*, must approve it. A Repetition of it, therefore, is most earnestly recommended to them—Who can pretend to say, that it may not prove the happy Means of enlightening their Understandings, and disposing their Minds so as, that *the Light of the Gospel may shine unto them*, and engage them in an Unity of Faith with us, firmly believing in *one Lord, one Faith, and one Baptism* *: For, if a devout Invocation of *Lord, Son of David, have mercy on me*, gave Sight to the *Blind*†, why may we not hope the like Blessing for such of our dissenting Brethren, as petition in the same Words, with the like Faith, Humility, and Fervency? For, whatever is asked in his Name, shall be granted, by him, *whose Will is, that all Men be saved, and that they come to the Acknowledgment of Truth* ‡.

But, whilst we are thus encouraged to petition for Favours in the Name of the Lord, with an Assurance of obtaining our Request, we must be ex-

---

* Ephef. iv. 5.   † Matth. xx. 34.
‡ 1 Tim. ii. 4.

extremely careful, that no sordid Interest lurks at the bottom; that what we ask, be not with a View to gratify our Passions, to indulge Pride and Luxury, or any other inordinate End——To such Petitioners *Jesus* will answer; *hitherto you have not asked any Thing in my Name* *.

If then, you petition for any temporal Good, let it be made with an humble Deference to the Will of God: for Instance, if you petition for Riches, let it be accompanied with this Condition, provided the Possession of them would tend to God's Honour, and your eternal Welfare: Let this your Petition be also animated with an Intention, either to pay your Debts, or that you may be enabled to live according to that Sphere of Life, wherein God has been pleased to place you; with a Resolution, to expend any Redundancy in the Relief of your distressed Fellow-creature, &c. If the married Couple pray to Heaven for an Offspring, let it be made with an humble Submission to God's holy Will, and, provided the Child would prove his faithful Servant. *Rachael* importuned for a Child, without Resignation to the Will of God; nay, and declared she would die, if she had not Children: The Lord at length, tired with her Importunities, granted her Request: with the Pangs of Child-bearing she received the Summons of Death: she brought forth a Child, but lived not to see it; *Benoni* or *Benjamin* was scarcely born, when she died. So that *Rachael* was, almost at the same Time, a Mother and a Corpse. This Example is recorded † to teach future Generations, that their most reasonable Requests must be submitted to the Will of Heaven.

In short, let all your Petitions for temporal Blessings be, really and truly, accompanied with this

---

* John xvi. 24. † Gen. xxxv.

this Condition, *viz.* provided, the Enjoyment of them, shall tend to God's Honour and your eternal Welfare. It is then, your Requests will be granted, and your Desires crowned with Success; as *Jesus*, who is ever faithful to his Promise, assures you: *If you ask me any Thing in my Name, I will do it* *. What stronger Inducements can be required to engage you to celebrate the Praises of his most adorable Name, than a solemn and unlimited Promise of granting whatever you ask, provided, it tends to his Honour and your eternal Welfare?

Some Persons are apt to be alarmed, nay and perhaps sometimes despond, when after their repeated Supplications to Heaven, in the Name of the Lord, they think their Petition is not granted; because they obtain not what they request. They should however humbly and chearfully persevere in submitting to the Will of God, and not repine or murmur, though their Requests *seem* to be denied: Because the Lord, at Times *refusing* to gratify your Desires, confers a *Blessing*. For, to what End do you pray to the Lord and petition in his Name? But first, to glorify God; and secondly, to obtain Happiness here, and hereafter.

Hence, any Petition made for a temporal Good, which by being abused, would impede that Happiness, is much better refused, than granted; and will more effectually answer the End of your Prayers; which is, to obtain such temporal Blessings, as will enable you to work your Salvation with Safety: for Instance, you perhaps pray the Lord to grant you an affluent Fortune; he seems deaf to your Supplications, and refuses to grant your Request: Because, he clearly foresees, that
such

---

* John xiv. 14.

such temporal Blessings would be abused: They would cause you to live unmindful of God, and to think only how to gratify frail Nature in all its sinful Desires—Experience proves this to be Daily the Case. Hence, as God's infinite Knowledge informs him, what would really tend to your Welfare, so his wonderful Goodness prevents him granting to his faithful Servants, what short-sighted ignorant Man may esteem a Blessing, which if obtained, would prove a certain Evil. It is however an incontestible Truth, that the Lord will never abandon his faithful Servants; for as the Royal Prophet assures us: *The Lord is become a Refuge for the Poor: A Helper in due Time in Tribulation. And let them trust in Thee who know thy Name: For thou hast not forsaken them that seek Thee, O Lord* *.

We may indeed, with great safety, petition for God's Grace in this Life, and an happy Eternity in the next; because we are warranted so to do, in the following Words: *Whosoever shall invoke the Name of the Lord, shall be saved,* says the Apostle of Nations †. It is not however, to be thought, that a cold or luke-warm Invocation of it, will be attended with that inexpressible Blessing: no; for the Apostle means, says the bright Luminary of the Church, St. *Thomas*, a devout and constant Invocation of it: "Hence," says the holy Doctor, "invoke the Name of the Lord worthily, invoke it perseverantly, and your Salvation will be secure."

If then, worldly Cares shall, at Times, interrupt or distract you; if bad Company attempt to dissuade you; or the Devil, in any shape, by his Wiles endeavour to prevent a constant Recital of the sa-

---

* Psalm ix. 10, 11.   † Rom. x. 13.

cred Devotion of the *Rosary*, by representing, that your Prayers are not heard; that they are unacceptable to God, and so forth; thereby to lead you into a State of Despondency and Distrust in the Mercy and Goodness of *Jesus*: Be on your Guard against such diabolical Suggestions, against the Snares of the infernal Enemy, who is continually going about seeking whom he may devour: Redouble your Addresses to God's most sacred Name, and remember to imitate the Perseverance of the *blind Men* mentioned in the Gospel*, who, being informed that *Jesus* was passing by, prayed him thus, with a loud Voice: *Lord, Son of David, have mercy on us.* Their Companions sought every Opportunity to silence them; they rebuked them, *that they should hold their Peace*; but the more they opposed them, the more they cried aloud; *Lord, Son of David, have mercy on us.* When behold, so pleasing was this Petition, and the frequent Repetion of it, to the Son of God, that as a Reward of both, *Jesus* commands the blind Men to approach him, and instantly restores to them their Sight.

Such are the admirable Proofs of God's amazing Goodness, to animate you, and future Generations, to an Imitation of the blind Men's Perseverance in addressing his most sacred Name, which he promises to crown with a Grant of the desired Blessing: His infinite Goodness inclines him, his Omnipotence enables him, and his Veracity obliges him to grant whatever is asked, worthily and perseverantly, in his Name; provided always, that it tends to his Honour and your own Welfare.

CHAP.

---

* Matth. xx. 30, 31.

CHAP. XVIII.

The Indulgences and Privileges granted to the Members of the Sodality of the most Holy Name of JESUS.

OUR pious Mother, the Church, ever sollicitous to promote the Respect due to God's most venerable Name, and vigilant to engage the Faithful in the Practice of such Works, as most effectually tend thereto, animates her Children to an Entrance into the sacred *Sodality*, and to a frequent Recital of the *Rosary* of *Jesus*, by a solemn Approbation of both*: and generously opens her inexhaustible Treasures, which she plentifully dispenses to such, as shall enter into the sacred *Sodality*, and praise the Name of the most High, by an humble and constant Offering of the *Rosary*, sacred to the most holy Name of *Jesus*.

Convinced of their Excellency to praise the Name of the Lord, and their Efficacy to sanctify a Christian Soul, she exerts every Effort to engage the Faithful in the Practice of such meritorious Works. What *Indulgences* and *Privileges* has she not granted? What *Graces* and *Favours* does she not bestow on the devout Clients, Members of the sacred *Sodality*! But before we enter into a Detail of those *Indulgences*, &c. it appears necessary to premise something with regard to *Indulgences*, thereby

---

* As appears in the several Declarations of Popes; especially *Pius* IV. S. *Pius* V. *Gregory* XIII. *Paul* V. *Innocent* XI. *Benedict* XIII. and lastly *Benedict* XIV. *Ad Execrabile*, &c. 30th of August, 1748. *Et alias Nos*, &c. 30th September, 1748.

to remove some erroneous Opinions, relative to *Indulgences*, conceived by ignorant Catholics, as well as prejudiced Protestants.

Our separated Brethren would fain persuade us to think, that we believe *Indulgences* to be " Pardons granted by the Pope for Sins to come, or Leave obtained, by Money, to commit Sin." The Church assumes no such Power, nay, on the contrary, holds such damnable Doctrine in the utmost Abhorrence. What the Church has declared relative to Indulgences may be known by the following Declaration of the Council of *Trent*: " The most Holy Synod declares, that the Power of granting Indulgences was given by Christ to the Church; that the Church hath made Use of this Power from the earliest Times; that the Practice of them is most wholsome to the Faithful, and approved of by Sacred Councils; that those who affirm, that they are useless, or deny, that there is in the Church a Power of granting them, are excommunicated by the most Holy Synod*."

Hence it is, that as the holy Council of *Trent* has defined, " that the Power of granting Indulgences was given by Christ to his Church," it cannot be supposed, (without Blasphemy) that Christ, who is Sanctity and Goodness itself, could possibly impower the Head of his Church, or any other Person, to grant Leave to commit Sin. The Spouse of Jesus Christ, his Church, neither does, nor can presume such a Power, which would cast indelible Infamy and Reproach on that holy, learned, and illustrious Body, which *Jesus* has solemnly promised to preserve from Errors

against

* Sess. 25.

against Faith, by declaring, that *the Gates of Hell shall not prevail against it* *.

Besides, what the Church means or understands by an *Indulgence*, according to its received Doctrine †, is only a releasing or Remission of such *temporal* Pains or Punishments, as remain to be satisfied for, after the Sin is forgiven in the Sacrament of Penance: granted by the Church out of the superabundant Merits and Satisfactions of Jesus Christ and his Saints, which are the inexhaustible Treasures of the Church.

That a temporal Punishment remains to be satisfied for, after the Guilt of Sin and eternal Punishment due to it, are remitted, appears evidently in the 2d Book of *Kings*, chap. xii. where we read: That after the Prophet *Nathan* had assured *David*, on the Part of God, in these Words: *The Lord hath taken away thy Sin*; notwithstanding the Prophet declares, that *David* must suffer a temporal Punishment, in the Death of his Son, the Fruit of his Adultery: *Nevertheless, because you have given Occasion to the Enemies of the Lord to Blaspheme, for this Thing, the Child that is born of thee, shall surely die.* Hence, the royal Penitent humbly prayed the Lord, Night and Day, in these Words: *Wash me farther from my Iniquity, and Cleanse me from my Sin* ‡. That is, not only from the Crime, and the eternal Punishment, (which were remitted, according to the Prophet *Nathan*) but from the *temporal* Punishments due to it. Nay, is not the Sin of our Proto-parent, *Adam*, though forgiven him, dreadfully punished in himself and his Posterity, even with temporal Death? Thus to remind us Daily, that though the Sin be

* Matth. xvi. 18. † S. Tho. Suppl. q. 25. a. 1.
‡ Psal. l. 4.

forgiven, it does not follow, that the *temporal* Punishment is also remitted.

That Christ has impowered his Church to release us from those *temporal* Punishments which remain due, after our *actual* Sins are forgiven, (which is what we mean by an *Indulgence*) appears from the unlimited Power, wherewith he invested St. *Peter* and his Successors, in the following Words: *Whatsoever thou shalt loose upon Earth, shall be loosed also in Heaven* *. Christ himself † granted a Plenary Indulgence to St. *Mary Magdalen*, the *Samaritan* Woman; and to the penitent Thief, when hanging on the Cross, in these Words: *This Day shalt thou be with me in Paradise* ‡: whereby his Sufferings were declared at an End.

The Church, in its very Infancy, made Use of the Power granted to it by Jesus Christ; witness St. *Paul*, who released the incestuous *Corinthian* from the Penance or temporal Punishments he was to undergo, on Account of the heinous Crime he committed: *I pardoned him for your sake*, (says the Apostle to the Corinthians) *in the Person of Christ* §. As if the Apostle had said, as a certain Interpreter observes‖, " Now as you have
" pardoned him by my Instructions, and have
" received him again into your Communion, I
" also *pardon him* and confirm what you have done
" *for your sake*, as well as for his, and dispense
" with any further Severities of a longer Penance,
" which he deserved, says St. *Chrysostom*. And I
" do this *in the Person of Christ*, by that Power
" and Authority derived from *Christ*, which he
" left

---

* Matth. xvi. 19. † Wigant Exam. iii. de Indulg. Tract. xiv. ‡ Luke xxiii. 43.
§ 2 Cor. ii. 10. ‖ Wetham, Annot. 4.

" left to his Apostles, when he said, Matth. xviii.
" 18. *Whatsoever you shall loose upon Earth, shall be
" loosed in Heaven,* &c. Not only in the Sight of
" Men, says St. *Chrysostom,* but in the Sight of
" God, who hath given us this Power."

Hence it is, that as *Christ* gave to his Apostles and their Successors, a Power, in his Name, to forgive Sins and the eternal Punishment due to them, in these Words: *Whose Sins you shall forgive, they are forgiven them* *: So the Power of forgiving the *temporal* Pains or Punishments is granted, in the following Words: *Whatsoever thou shalt loose on Earth, shall be loosed also in Heaven* †.

Thus does it evidently appear, from Scripture, from the Decisions of general Councils, and the firm Belief of the Fathers and Doctors of the Church, that Christ has invested her with a Power to grant Indulgences, or a Remission of the *temporal* Punishments due to *actual* Sin, already forgiven; and consequently, that those *Indulgences* are not what our Adversaries most unjustly and slanderously report them to be, *viz.* " So many " Licences to commit Sin," *&c.* Nor are *Indulgences* what ignorant *Catholics* take them to be, " so many Remissions of Sins, or the eternal " Punishment due to them :" For, an *Indulgence* supposes Sin, and the eternal Punishment due to it, already forgiven; and can only remit such *temporal* Pains or Punishments as remain to be satisfied for, after the Sin is forgiven in the Sacrament of *Penance.*

The Power of releasing or forgiving those temporal Pains or Punishments was also exercised by the *primitive Bishops,* in Favour of *public Penitents:*

for

* John xx. 23.   † Matth. xvi. 19.

for they often shortened the Time of their Penance, upon the Intercession of the holy *Confessors*, who were in Prison, and had suffered great Torments for the Faith of *Christ*. The Church (invested always with the same Power) has, in succeeding Ages, remitted the *temporal* Punishment, in Imitation of St. *Paul*, and continues now to do the same, when she finds her Children duly disposed by Prayer, Almsdeeds, by frequent and worthy Confessions and Communions, in short, by complying with such Works of Piety and Penance, as she prescribes; she then pressingly invites them to share the Riches of her Treasures, whereby they become enabled to discharge the remaining Debt due to their Sins, left they be obliged to suffer for them in the frightful Prison of *Purgatory*.

Hence, the Church, to induce her Children to an Entrance into the sacred *Sodality*, and to a frequent Repetition of the most holy Devotion of the *Rosary* of the Name of *Jesus*, so pleasing to his infinite Majesty, faithfully promises to enrich them with her spiritual Treasures, which, when applied in 'a *plenary* Manner, and are worthily received by the pious Christian, he becomes enabled to discharge all *temporal* Pains or Punishments, which yet remain to be satisfied for—Sin and the eternal Punishments due to it, being already remitted in the Sacrament of *Penance*.

Thus the pious Rosarists, by properly confessing their Crimes and devoutly receiving the most holy Sacrament of the *Eucharist*, obtain a Remission of their Sins and the eternal Punishment due to them: and by the Benefit reaped from a *plenary* Indulgence, all *temporal* Pains or Punishments are forgiven. So that if a Member of the *Sodality* of the most holy Name of *Jesus*, departs this Life, in that happy State (not having Sin to answer for; temporal or eternal Punishments to suffer) his Soul shall immediately ascend into the Regions of Bliss and Glory, to see and enjoy God for an endless Eternity. What an Happiness for the devout Clients of the *Rosary!*

As there are not only *plenary*, but also particular *Indulgences* of 7 Years, of an 100 Days, of *Quarantines*, &c. granted to the Brethren of the *Sodality*, 'tis proper the Reader should be acquainted with what is to be understood by these several *Indulgences*.

The antient *Canons* assigned severe sacramental Penances, that is, Penances to be injoined by Confessors [*]. For every grievous Sin, *seven* Years of Penance.—An *Indulgence* of seven Years corresponds to, and remits the Penance injoined for seven Years. For other Sins, it appointed *forty* Days Fast on Bread and Water, and other penitential Works: And for the Remission of this, a *Quarantine*, or forty Days Indulgence was applied. For a very atrocious or capital Crime, a *forty* Days rigorous Fast was injoined, and *seven* Years Penitence: For Instance, whosoever was guilty of the Sin of *Perjury*, or induced others to commit it, was obliged to Fast *forty* Days on Bread and Water, and to do Penance for *seven* Years. Such were the Pains or Punishments injoined by the antient penitential Canons of the Church. Which severe Penances the Church was obliged to mitigate, in after Ages, for weighty Reasons; and supplied the Deficiency by the Interposition or Application of *Indulgences*.

A *plenary* Indulgence then, is a gracious Concession of the Church, whereby we may gain a full

---

[*] Wigant de Indulg. Tract. xiv. Ex. iii.

full Remiſſion of all the temporal Pains and Puniſhments, that remain due to *actual* Sin, already forgiven; provided we punctually obſerve what ſhe preſcribes, in order to obtain it. When a *plenary* Indulgence is granted in Form of *Jubilee* (as is granted to the Brethren of the ſacred Sodality of the Name of *Jeſus*) it is attended with many ſingular Graces, Favours, and Privileges: whereas a *particular* Indulgence remits only ſo much of the temporal Puniſhments, as is ſpecified: For Inſtance, an Indulgence of 100 Days remits the temporal Pains or Puniſhments, that were to be ſuffered for 100 Days, *&c.*

The Works injoined by the Church, for gaining an *Indulgence*, muſt be punctually performed, and in the State of Grace, at leaſt the laſt of them, with a pure Intention, and free from every vitiating Circumſtance, which may render them evil in themſelves: For, he who gives Alms out of vain Glory, prays through Hypocriſy, or performs any of the injoined good Works, more to indulge Vanity or his own private Pleaſure, than for Devotion's Sake, merits not the *Indulgence*.

It is to be obſerved, that on Account of the following Clauſe, *being truly penitent, confeſs, receive and viſit the Church or Chapel,* which is uſually inſerted in *Bulls* and *Briefs* for the granting of Indulgences, a Difficulty was propoſed to the late Pope *Clement* XIII; whether, in Conſequence of the before-mentioned Clauſe, an Indulgence can be obtained, without ſacramental Confeſſion, by ſuch Perſons, as are not conſcious of any mortal Sin, ſince their laſt Confeſſion?

The ſovereign Pontiff, to remove Doubts and Anxieties, on the 9th of *December*, 1763, *granted an Indulto* (or Privilege) *to all the Faithful, who are mind-*

mindful, by a frequent Confeſſion of their Sins, to purify their Souls, and are accuſtomed to approach, at leaſt once a Week to the Sacrament of Penance, unleſs lawfully prevented, and are not conſcious of having committed any mortal Sin ſince their laſt Confeſſion, that they may obtain all and every Indulgences, even without actual Confeſſion, which otherwiſe would have been neceſſary, according to the Tenor of a former Decree: without however making any Innovation relative to the Indulgences of the Jubilee, whether ordinary or extraordinary, and others granted in Form of Jubilee, for the obtaining of which, ſacramental Confeſſion, as well as the other injoined Works, is to be performed, at the Time mentioned in the Grant*.

Hence, a Perſon who uſually confeſſes once a Week, if he confeſſes, ſuppoſe on St. *Dominick's* Day, (on which a plenary Indulgence is granted) he is not under the Neceſſity of confeſſing the following *Sunday*, to gain the plenary Indulgence of the *Roſary*, unleſs conſcious of a mortal Sin.

It may be ſaid, what Neceſſity have we for *Indulgences* to remit any temporal Pains or Puniſhments? Have not Sin, and the Puniſhments, whether temporal or eternal, due to it, been ſuperabundantly ſatisfied for, by the Sufferings and Death of *Jeſus Chriſt*, which are of infinite Value? It is moſt certainly true, that the Satisfactions of *Jeſus Chriſt* are of infinite Value, and that by his Sufferings, he has ſuperabundantly ſatisfied for the Sins of the whole World; yet, on our Part, Works of *Penance* are abſolutely neceſſary: Becauſe, Chriſt having purchaſed a ſupreme *Dominion* over us, with the *infinite Price of his Blood*, it cannot be diſputed, but he may lay what Terms or Conditions he pleaſes upon us, as Means, without

---

* Synodus Tuſculana, p. 693.

out which, the Price he has paid down, shall not be applied to us. And therefore, though it be certainly true, that having *satisfied superabundantly* for us, he might have applied that Satisfaction to us, without subjecting us to any *penal Works* or *temporal Sufferings*, after the Guilt of Sin, together with its eternal Punishment, were remitted; yet, it pleased his infinite Wisdom, both for our greater Good, and the Manifestation of his *Justice*, as well as his *Mercy*, to establish Things upon another Footing, by changing (in the Sacrament of Penance) the *eternal Punishment* into a *temporal one*, and obliging us to purchase the *Fruits* and *Application* of his infinite *Satisfaction*, by bringing *forth worthy Fruits of Penance*[*], and submitting humbly and patiently to the Sufferings, he shall think fit to lay upon us. This is what we call *Satisfaction:* which, says the Bishop of *Meaux*[†], is in Effect, "but the Application of "the infinite *Satisfaction* of *Jesus-Christ*."

And, though the Rigour of the antient penitential *Canons* has been mitigated by the Church, yet the Church means not to exempt us from Works of *Penance:* the sacred Scriptures strongly enforce them: *Unless you do Penance,* says *Jesus Christ, you shall all perish*[‡]. If Works of Penance and Mortification were unnecessary, as our Adversaries pretend, the Performance of them would not be required by *Jesus Christ*, under such a severe Penalty. Nay, "it is just and beneficial to our "Salvation," says the Bishop of *Meaux*[§], "that "God in remitting our Sin together with the "eternal Pain which we deserved for it, should "exact of us some temporal Pain to retain us in "our Duties; lest, if we should be too speedily "freed

---

[*] Luke iii. 8.   [†] Exp. Cath. Faith, Sect. viii.
[‡] Luke xiii. 3.   [§] Ibid.

"freed from the Bonds of Justice, we should
"abandon ourselves to a temerarious Confidence,
"abusing the Facility of a Pardon. It is then to
"satisfy this Obligation, we are subjected to some
"painful Works, which we must accomplish in
"the Spirit of Humility and Penance; and it was
"the Necessity of these satisfactory Works which
"obliged the primitive Church to impose, upon
"Penitents those Pains called Canonical. When
"therefore she imposes upon Sinners painful and
"laborious Works, and they undergo them with
"Humility, this is called *Satisfaction*; and when
"regarding the Fervour of the Penitents, or some
"other good Works which she has prescribed
"them, she pardons some part of that Pain which
"is due to them, this is called *Indulgence*." If
she pardons all the temporal Pains and Punishments due, such an Indulgence is called a *plenary*
Indulgence: If only Part, a *particular Indulgence*.

Plenary Indulgences belonging to the Sodality.

DR. *Richardson*, who remarkably exerted himself in propagating the celebrated *Sodality*, particularly in this great Metropolis, to the great Glory of God's most sacred Name, has, in his *Appendix to the Manner of hearing Mass*, given us an *authentic Account* of the Indulgences granted and confirmed to the Members of our sacred *Sodality* by sundry Popes *, which I shall transcribe from him.

I.

On the Day of their being received into this *Sodality*, if they confess, receive and pray according to the Intention of the Church; they have a *plenary* Indulgence.

II.

* Vide Bullar. O. P.

II.

On *New-Year's Day*, on which the Circumcision of our Lord is celebrated, and the Name of *Jesus*, if they confess, receive, and be present at the Offices celebrated in the Chapel of this Society, in the whole or in part, they have a *plenary* Indulgence, in form of *Jubilee*, with ample Privileges thereunto annexed (to be mentioned hereafter) granted by Pope *Pius* IV. in his Bull, beginning, *Injunctum nobis*, dated at St. *Peter's* 13th April, 1564, to be seen in the *Bullarium* printed at Rome, 1740, Tom. 5. p. 95.

III.

Every *second* Sunday of the Month, if they confess, receive and pray, &c. in the Chapel of this Society, they have a *plenary* Indulgence.

IV.

In the Article of Death, if they call devoutly on the Name of *Jesus*, either by Mouth or Heart, recommending their Souls to God, they have a *plenary* Indulgence.

Particular Indulgences belonging to the Sodality.

I.

EVERY *second* Sunday of the Month, if they visit the Altar of the most holy Name of *Jesus*; they will obtain an Indulgence of seven Years, and so many Quarantines.

II.

Every *second* Sunday of the Month, if they hear the Mass, that is offered for all the Brethren, living or dead, they gain an Indulgence of two hundred Days.

III.

All the Members of this Society, at whatever Time they correct, or charitably admonish, those that

that curse or swear profanely, may gain an Indulgence of one hundred Days.

IV.

Whenever they assist at the Mass, divine Offices, or Meetings of this Confraternity, whether public or private, they may gain an Indulgence of one hundred Days.

V.

Whenever they attend the blessed Sacrament, going to the Sick, or, being hindered to go, say the Lord's Prayer, and Hail *Mary*, once for the sick Person, they may gain the Indulgence of one hundred Days.

VI.

Whenever they visit the Sick, they may gain the Indulgence of one hundred Days.

VII.

Whenever they receive the Poor into their Houses or relieve them, they may obtain the Indulgence of one hundred Days.

VIII.

Whenever they make Peace between Enemies, either of themselves or others, they may gain an Indulgence of one hundred Days.

IX.

Whenever they say the Lord's Prayer, and the Hail *Mary* five Times for the Souls of the Dead that belonged to this Sodality, they may have the Indulgence of one hundred Days.

X.

Whenever they draw Sinners to the way of Salvation, or instruct the Ignorant, or do any other Work of Piety or Charity, they may have an Indulgence of one hundred Days.—*Paul* V. *Cum certas*, &c. 31st Octob. 1606. *Benedict* XIV. *Ad Execrabile,*

Execrabile, &c. 30th Aug. 1748, *Et alias Nos*, &c. 30th Sept. 1748.

Note. That no Indulgences are here marked down, only those granted by *Paul* V. who revoked and annulled many Indulgences granted before, in the Year 1606, and determined and settled the Indulgences that each Confraternity is hereafter to enjoy.

Paul V. granted another *plenary* Indulgence to such Members of the Sodality, who having confess'd, received, &c. devoutly assist or are present at the *Procession* made on the *second Sunday* of the Month in the Chapel of this Society. *Pias Christi*, &c. 1612. *Benedict* XIII. *Pretiosus*, &c.

In case of any Impediment intervening, whereby the Brethren of the Sodality are prevented making this Procession, or solemn Supplication, on the second Sunday of the Month; then, on whatever Sunday the Procession is made, the *plenary* Indulgence is transferred to that Sunday, and may be gained by the devout Members that attend. *Paul* V. Const.—*Cum, sicut*—1st April 1613. Confirmed by *Innocent* XI—*Cum dudum*—*Benedict* XIII—*Pretiosus*, &c. *Bremond*, Tract. de Consensu Bullar. pag. 444.

Privileges granted to this Society.

ON *New-Year's Day* the Brethren have a Privilege, that their Vows may be exchanged into other Works of Piety: Except the five Vows ordinarily reserved to the See of *Rome*.

And they have a Privilege, on the same Day, that their Oaths may be relaxed, where there is no Prejudice to a third Person. *Pius* IV. *Salvat. & Domini*, &c.

C H A P.

CHAP. XIX.

The Conditions and Rules of the sacred Sodality.

THE Power of erecting this Sodality or Society, is given by the Apostolic See, to the Order of Preachers, that is, to the Order of St. *Dominick*, and to no other. *Pius* IV. declares *, that *Didacus a Victoria* of the said Order was the Author of this *Sodality*, to remove and prevent Imprecations, Blasphemies and profane Oaths ‖. St. *Pius* V. † declares that it is derived from the said Order of Preachers. St. *Pius* also declares and commands ‡, that the Society of the most holy Name of *Jesus* against profane Cursing and Swearing, can be no where but in the Convents of the Order of Preachers, wherever such Convents are or ever shall be; and that the Functions belonging to this Society, shall not be performed by any, but by the Brethren of that Order. And *Paul* V. who settled the Grants made before §, declares and commands, that the Power of erecting such Sodality, shall belong to the Master General of the Order of Preachers, or to his Vicar General, and to no other Person or Persons whatsoever.

But as some Doubts had been raised in the Year 1748, relative to the Power of erecting this Sodality, &c. being confined to the Order of Preachers only, they have been abundantly cleared, and the Matter effectually determined by the Apostolic Letters of *Benedict* XIV. which begin, *Alias Nos*, &c. issued Sept. 30, 1748, which are at large recorded

---

* Bull. Confirm. *Salvat. & Dni.* Id. April. 1564.
‖ As explained in Chap. XV. † *Decet Roman. Pont.* 21st June, 1571. ‡ Ibid. § *Cum certas unicuique Confrat.* 31st Octob. 1606.

corded in Dr. *Burke's Hibernia Dominicana**, of which the following is an Extract. The Sovereign Pontiff first recites, that he had granted on the 30th of August 1748, to the Bishops of ***** Faculty to erect this Confraternity, &c. but that *Antoninus Bremond*, Master General of the Order of St. *Dominick*, had represented to him *that the ancient and most wholsome Confraternity, under the Invocation of the most Holy Name of* Jesus, *or Name of God, against Blasphemies, Perjuries, and unlawful Oaths, was instituted by the Brethren of the said Order, and by them always cultivated and propagated, throughout the universal Globe of the Earth. Wherefore the Popes of Rome have enriched the said Confraternity with various Graces, Privileges and Indulgences; and earnestly exhorted all Patriarchs, Arch-Bishops, Bishops, and other Ordinaries, to favour, assist and promote said Confraternity, wherever, and whenever it would be necessary, and as often as they would be applied to on the Part of the Brethren of said Society.*

But amongst other Privileges of the same Confraternity, this one is found, that St. *Pius* V. of holy Memory, by his Letters in like form of brief, issued 21st of *June*, 1571, which begin, *Decet*, &c. of his own accord, and through certain knowledge, decreed and resolved that for the Time to come, no new Society or Confraternity of the kind, should be instituted in the Cities, Towns or Places, in which there was no House of the said Order, or in the neighbouring Churches, without the Licence of the Provincial, or of the Conventual Prior of the said Order, in whose District the Church would be situated, in which the said Confraternity were to be erected. Whereas if it were done otherwise, the Brethren so admitted would

not

* Page 177.

not obtain the Indulgences of said Confraternity, nor enjoy the Favours, Graces and Privileges which *should be granted* by the Apostolic See, to the *Brethren lawfully inscribed.* And *he established it so for ever, and he ordained it, and he prohibited with great strictness, and so he willed it and commanded.*

Which Letters Pope *Greg.* XIII. confirmed by his own Letters of the same kind, beginning, *Alias,* issued 11th June 1580. And afterwards Pope *Paul* V. by other Letters of his own, issued the 31st of October, 1606, beginning, *Cum certas,* granted to the Master General of the same Order, and in his Absence to his Vicar, that he might institute and erect the said Confraternities out of the City of *Rome,* in all Places whatever, and might freely and lawfully communicate to them all the above-mentioned Indulgences and spiritual Graces.

Which Faculty Pope *Innocent* XI. also confirmed by his Letters, beginning, *Cum dudum,* issued the 18th of April, 1678, and otherwise, as is more fully contained in the Letters of his aforesaid Predecessors: *The Tenours whereof he wills, by these Presents, to be held as if they were herein expressed*—He *(Benedict* XIV.) then decrees thus :

It is therefore that we, who by our mentioned Letters, *did not mean to bring any Prejudice, or that any Prejudice should accrue to the Privileges granted to the said Order, and Master General thereof, both which we embrace with the Love of a Father,* following the Examples of our Predecessors, do by these Presents, *injoin and command, that in the Erections and Institutions of Confraternities that are to be made in Virtue of our said Letters, under the Invocation of the most Holy Name of* Jesus, *against the*
hateful

hateful Custom of Swearing and Cursing, ye intirely make use of the Concurrence of the Provincial, or of the Priors of the Regular Houses of the said Order, that are in that Kingdom; and *if it should happen to be done otherwise, We decree and declare, that the Brethren of the Confraternities that may be so erected, cannot gain the Indulgences granted for the Brethren in those same Letters of ours, in the same Manner as if our said Letters had not at all come forth, any whatever making for the contrary notwithstanding.* Rome, 30th Sept. 1748.

Thus has the Sovereign Pontiff, *Benedict* XIV. following the Example of his Predecessors, decreed and determined, that the Confraternity, under the Invocation of the most holy Name of *Jesus*, is to be erected in our Churches or Chapels *only*, and not elsewhere, without *intirely making use of the concurrence of the Provincial or Conventual Priors* of the Order of St. *Dominick*, under the Penalty of forfeiting the Indulgences, Graces and Privileges granted to those that are *lawfully* inscribed.

The Rules of the sacred Sodality*.

1. THAT the Names of all those that belong to this Sodality, are to be inscribed in a Book kept for that Purpose, by one of the Order of Preachers, who is authorised to inscribe the said Names.

2. The Members of this Society are to take special Care not to Swear profanely, Curse, or Blaspheme, or in any Manner abuse the Name of the Almighty, either in himself or in his Creatures.

3. If

---

* Bullar. O. P. Tom. vii. pag. 443.

3. If any of them fall into this Crime, they are to inflict on themselves a Penance, and it is recommended to those who are able, to impose on themselves a Penalty of Alms, either by giving immediately to some poor Object, or by laying by, from Time to Time, such small Sum for each Oath, as they can afford, till they choose some Object or Objects in want, whom they may relieve. Those who cannot give Alms, let them perform for each Oath, on their Knees, some Part of the most Holy *Rosary* of the Name of *Jesus*.

4. Those who have Families are reminded to observe the Law of God, in removing and preventing these Vices amongst those who are subject to them, to correct their Children religiously, and to turn away their Servants, if they don't shew speedy Signs of Amendment. It is recommended to them, to prevail on their Families to get their Names inscribed, and to read these Rules to them once a Week.

5. Those who belong to this Society are to hinder and prevent Cursing, Swearing or Blaspheming, not only in those subject to them, but, according to their Influence and Power, in all others—This Rule however, does not bind them to enter into any Contention, but is only to be observed as far as Discretion permits.

6. Every second *Sunday* of the Month, (when it can be performed) the Hymn, *Jesus to us Salvation brings*, &c. (to be found after the Rosary of *Jesus*) is to be sung at the *Procession*, and the Psalm *Praise, O ye Children the Lord:* Repeating several Times the Verse, *May the Name of the Lord be blessed*, &c.

7. There will be also a Mass offered immediately after the Instructions in the Morning, or at Twelve

Twelve o'Clock, on every second *Sunday* of the Month, in the said Chapel, for all those Persons whether living or dead, whose Names are inscribed in this *Sodality*.

8. On the first Day of *January*, on which the most glorious Name of *Jesus* is celebrated, being the principal Feast of this Society, the Brethren are to celebrate the Solemnity by confessing, receiving, and assisting at the Offices, to gain the Indulgence and *Jubilee* of the Day.

9. All the Members of this Society, are to assist at the Anniversary to be celebrated, by the Office of the Dead and Mass, for all the Deceased who belonged to this Society.

Lastly, The Brothers and Sisters of the Rosary of the most holy Name of *Jesus* should be particularly careful, penitently to confess and devoutly receive on the *second* Sunday of every Month, (unless lawfully prevented) that by the Performance of so great and meritorious a Work, in the spirit of true Piety and Devotion, they may effectually give Praise to the Lord, and glorify his most holy Name.

To the Brethren who carefully discharge this Duty, the Sovereign Pontiffs grant a *plenary* Indulgence, as has been already mentioned: requiring at the same Time, that they pray for the Exaltation of our holy Mother the Church, the Extirpation of Heresy, the Peace of Christian Princes, &c. So desirous is she to share of the Prayers and good Works of the Members of the sacred Sodality!

The Members of this Sodality should be mindful to recite every Week, the *entire* Rosary of the Name of *Jesus*, which they may perform at one Time, or by dividing it into three parts, as may best suit their Ease and Convenience.

N. B.

N. B. *No Reward is demanded or expected for Inscription or admission into the sacred Sodality; that so holy a Fellowship, totally founded in Charity, may not be stained with the least Blemish of any temporal View, or Interest whatever.*

CHAP. XX.

An Observance of the Rules of the sacred Sodality, and a daily Recital of the celebrated Devotion of the Rosary of the most holy Name of JESUS, how meritorious.

WHEN we reflect how much the Spirit of Libertinism and Impiety actuates the Generality of Mankind: when we view a glaring Neglect of Religion in some; nay, and often a shameful Contempt of it in others: when we consider their Thoughts totally engaged in the Pursuit of the deceitful Beings and fleeting Pleasures of this transitory Life: when we view them wholly intent on the Gratification of their sinful Appetites, Strangers to Piety and Mortification: and, in short, living as unmindful of God and their eternal Welfare, as if they believed Happiness was to be attained by offending God, or by living unmindful of him; it will not appear surprising, that Works of Piety shall be unwelcome and distasteful to them. Works of Supererogation they cannot at all relish; nor indeed is it easy to obtain from them, an anniversary Compliance with the most important and necessary Duties of Religion. To recommend any Work of Piety, that seems to jarr with their Amusements, or to require a little Restraint

ſtraint or Retirement, ſeems loathſome and frightful!

In ſhort, whatever is propoſed, tending to curb frail Nature, and to bridle its inordinate Deſires, by correcting and ſubjecting them to the Laws of Reaſon and Grace, is, if at all, received with Reluctance by the Generality of Chriſtians; ſo great and lamentable is their Inſenſibility, in regard to the Service of God and their own eternal Welfare!

Yet, Praiſe be to the Name of the Lord, the World is not ſo univerſally depraved, as that ſome pious Souls are not to be found, willing to ſerve God and work their Salvation *with fear and trembling*: who, conſcious of their Sins and Unworthineſs, gladly embrace every pious Work that may tend to appeaſe God's Wrath, excite his Mercy, and avert the terrible Puniſhments that await Sinners, eſpecially in the other Life. Convinced of the inexpreſſible Rewards, which God, in his great Mercy, has prepared for them in the Regions of the Bleſſed, they know they cannot do too much to ſecure it, nor can they ſufficiently thank his infinite Goodneſs, in beſtowing ſuch unmerited Rewards. Hence, theſe pious Souls, ever retaining a grateful Senſe of God's unſpeakable Goodneſs, are not unmindful to offer daily *a ſacrifice of Praiſe* to the Honour and Glory of his moſt ſacred Name.

This is the divine Employment of the worthy Members of the *Sodality*, and Devouts of the *Roſary* of the moſt holy Name of *Jeſus*, whilſt they offer that moſt grateful *Sacrifice of Praiſe always to God,* that is, ſays St. *Paul**, *the Fruit of Lips confeſſing his Name*, by a devout and conſtant Recital of that ſacred Form of Prayer, the *Roſary* of *Jeſus*. This is that Sacrifice of Praiſe, which gives great Glory

---

* Heb. xiii. 15.

ry to God; is highly advantageous to us, and duly difpofes its devout Admirers, to approach the moft facred and important Duties of Religion, worthily.

All the Prophets of the old Law, the Evangelifts and other infpired Writers of the New, loudly proclaim the indifpenfible Neceffity we lie under of praifing the moft adorable Name of the Lord: This is by no Means a Work of *Supererogation*, 'tis a Work of *abfolute* Neceffity: But whether we praife the Name of the Lord by the Performance of one good Work or another, is left to the Option of the Faithful; as may beft fuit their pious Inclination, or may moft contribute to inflame their Souls with the Love of God. But furely, a Form of Prayer, every Word of which breathes a fingular Refpect for, and Devotion to, the moft holy Name of *Jefus*, muft moft effectually anfwer the glorious Purpofe! Such is the moft celebrated Devotion of the *Rofary* of the Name of *Jefus*: Its Excellency and Efficacy have been already inconteftibly proved by the Faithful; as fuch, it continues to be ftrongly recommended to them, by the Sovereign Pontiffs, the Vicars of Jefus Chrift upon Earth.

Will not Prudence then, dictate, that as we are abfolutely *bound* to praife the Name of the Lord, fo we ought to make choice of a Form of Prayer, which is evidently calculated for that laudable End, and appears to be extracted from, and warranted by holy Writ. A Devotion that comes handed to us by our pious Mother, the Church, as a moft powerful Form of Prayer, to give Praife and Thankfgiving to the moft holy Name of God, and to obtain Happiness for us, both here and hereafter.

To perpetuate this *Sacrifice of Praise* to the Name of the Lord, wholsome Laws and Rules have been framed, as has been already mentioned, Chap. XIX. which should be observed, with Punctuality, by these who have the Happiness to be inscribed in the *Sodality*, lest the heavenly Institution should fall into Disuse: for Laws and Rules regularly observed, tend to unite and preserve spiritual, as well as civil Societies, in a flourishing Condition: and as the Rupture of an Artery discomposes the whole Body, and is frequently productive of a total Dissolution of the human Frame; in like Manner, a Breach or Neglect of the Laws and Rules of the sacred Sodality, may produce an Omission of the many good Works prescribed, particularly a Repetition of the *Rosary* of the Name of *Jesus*, which, in the end, may bring it into a total Disuse.

Hence, all those who are actually enrolled, or are determined to become Members of the sacred Sodality of the most holy Name of *Jesus*, should resolve, by the Grace of God, to live up to its Rules and Laws, so wisely adapted to the End of its Institution, and so easy to be observed in every State of Life.

It must, however, be remarked, that the Observance of them does not bind under any Sin whatsoever: for the Obligation is of so sweet and gentle a Nature, as not to subject the Members of it, to any theological Fault or venial Sin whatever, unless where they recommend what is already enforced by the Law of God. This Notice will suffice to remove any Scruples that may arise in the timorous Consciences of many, who dread entering

ing into the sacred Society, lest by the Omission of any of its Rules or the Transgression of its Laws, they should incur the Guilt of Sin.

Though the Members of the sacred *Sodality* are not bound, under Sin, to the Observance of its Rules, yet a wilful Omission or Neglect of what they prescribe, will prove hurtful to them: because, thereby they deprive themselves of the Indulgences and other spiritual Graces granted to the observant Members, and render themselves unworthy of a Participation of the Prayers and good Works performed, by this Society, in all Parts of the World, which is undoubtedly a considerable Loss.

Some may indeed think little of those Advantages and Blessings, reaped from the Prayers of others, but let them think as they may, certain it is, that St. *Paul* derived great Advantages from them: he obtained many Graces from God through the Intercession of others [*]. If then, St. *Paul* thought so much of the Prayers of others, shall we look upon them with Indifference! No: such a Thought would at once imply, that we mean to deprive ourselves of the Benefits and singular Advantages which we might derive, by being inscribed in the Sodality, from the Merits and good Works of such holy Multitudes, though in the most distant Climes, joining with us, by a spiritual Communication, to celebrate the Praises of the most holy Name of *Jesus*.

Besides depriving ourselves of the Blessings attending an exact Observance of the Laws of the *Sodality*, and a devout Recital of the *Rosary* of *Jesus*, (by a Non-observance of the one, or an Omission of the other) there is another Motive that strongly urges the Necessity of a strict Observance

[*] 2 Cor. i. 11.

vance of both, which is, that they most effectually tend to preserve and perpetuate an Institution, which manifestly promotes the profound Respect and Veneration due to God's most adorable Name: and also to extirpate the hateful Vices of Blasphemy, Cursing, and profane Swearing. Who is it, that at one View, does not see the great Utility and Necessity of this heavenly Institution? How meritorious then, the Observance of the Rules of the sacred Sodality! How pleasing to Heaven, a devout and daily Recital of the Rosary of the Name of *Jesus!* Who can refuse to join the Royal Psalmist, whilst breathing forth the Sentiments and ardent Wishes of his Soul, in the following Words: *Let all the Earth adore thee, O God, and sing to thee; let it say a Psalm to thy Name* *.

If an Infinity of Favours conferred on Mankind, proves insufficient to engage them in the important Work of praising God's most adorable Name, and to disengage them from the heinous Vices, so contrary to the Veneration due to it, at least, let the Terrors of Judgment affright Sinners into a Sense of their Duty.

If we, for a Moment, consider the impenitent Curser, Swearer or Blasphemer, lying upon his Death-bed, struggling with the grim Tyrant, unwilling to be gone; his Oaths, Execrations, or Blasphemies staring him in the Face: not knowing whither he is going, but justly fearing the worst, hardly presuming to lift up his Eyes to the offended Majesty on high, much less to invoke his Mercy or expect Forgiveness.

In this dreadful Situation, Death, his Executioner, *lays the Ax to the Root*, the Sinner falls to rise

* Psalm lxv. 3.

rise no more, except to appear before *Jesus*, the Judge of the Living and the Dead. How great shall his Confusion and Consternation be, when the Son of the living God shall, with an Awful and Majestic Voice, tell him, * *I am Jesus whom thou dost persecute.* I am that *Jesus* whom you grievously offended by your vile Oaths, Imprecations, and Blasphemies! It is I, who shed the last Drop of my Blood to wash away your Sins, and died upon a Cross to purchase for you everlasting Life! 'Tis I, O Sinner, who am now to judge those shameful Irreverences and shocking Blasphemies you have been guilty off, contrary to every Tie of Duty and Gratitude! What Reparation did you endeavour to make, for having abused my Goodness and profaned my Name, in Virtue whereof I have brought to you a plentiful Redemption, and rescued you from the Jaws of eternal Death? What Return have you attempted to make? Have you repented sincerely for the many shameful Irreverences offered to my sacred Name? Have you humbly and penitently called upon my Name for Mercy? Have you endeavoured to glorify my Name, or to repair the Injuries offered to it by your abominable Oaths, Imprecations, and Blasphemies? No! regardless of Me, you obstinately persevered in your Wickedness, and notwithstanding my frequent Calls to Repentance, you died in your Sins! What can you, O profane Swearer, Curser, and Blasphemer say in your Defence? What can you expect from my avenging Justice?

Unable to excuse themselves, or deny the Charge, the trembling Criminals will, at once, read their Doom and eternal Reprobation. When

* Acts ix. 5.

upon Earth, they spoke the Language of Devils, and continued in the damnable Practice, till Death silenced their impious Tongues, and closed their sacrilegious Mouths. No other place is fit for their Reception, but that of Hell; nor any other Company, but that of the Damned, for an endless Eternity. Dreadful Situation!

Endeavour then, to guard timely against this impending Danger, by an immediate and unfeigned Repentance: You will find the *Sodality* and *Rosary*, sacred to the most holy Name of *Jesus*, a most powerful Means to reclaim you, and to avert those exemplary Judgments that threaten you. Nay, whether you be a Sinner or a just Man, an Entrance into the *Sodality*, and a frequent Repetition of the *Rosary*, will prove highly conducive to your eternal Welfare; to the Sinner, as an efficacious *Remedy*; to the just Man, as a sure *Preservative*.

It is needless to seek, in Foreign Climes, Instances of the great Good which the *Sodality* and *Rosary* have been productive of, whilst we have so many glaring Proofs at home, particularly in this our great *Metropolis*. The City of *Dublin* can certify, what prodigious Crowds resort to the Chapel of St. *Dominick* *, on the second *Sunday* of every Month; on every Evening during *Lent*, &c. but more especially on the first Day of the *new* Year, on which the principal Solemnity of the sacred Institution is celebrated, what a Multitude of Penitents approach the Sacraments, humbly confessing their Sins, and devoutly receiving the most holy Sacrament of the *Eucharist!*

They begin the *new* Year with praising the most holy Name of *Jesus*, resolving to make every
Repa-

* Commonly called, Bridge-street Chapel.

Reparation in their Power, for having profaned, or in any shape mal-treated the holy Name of God, during the Course of the preceding Year. What an edifying, what a glorious Sight! to behold Multitudes of Sinners, who were unhappily addicted to the damnable Vices of Blasphemy, Cursing, and profane Swearing, crowding to the Tribunal of Confession, penitently confessing their Crimes, and firmly resolving to reclaim and reform.

Nay, many who were shamefully *ignorant* of the Number of Sacraments, are now become devout *Frequenters* of them; from being horrid *Swearers* and *Blasphemers*, they are become humble *Adorers*; and from being Sons of *Wrath*, are become the Children of *God*, and are now happily preserved from a Relapse into the odious Crimes, by a constant Practice of the pious Works enjoined by the sacred Sodality: whilst others, who have escaped the Contagion of those Vices, by an early Application to the sacred Form of Prayer, and a steady Observance of the Rules of the Sodality, have been effectually secured from the mortal Infection. What an happy Change; what a blessed Security, wrought and obtained by Means of the *Sodality* and *Rosary* sacred to the most holy Name of *Jesus!*

How then, can any Christian, whether Sinner or Saint, hesitate a Moment to associate with such faithful Servants of the Lord? Sinners are encouraged thereto, by the many glaring Proofs of the Good it has been productive off; and the many Instances of the Efficacy of the sacred Devotion, the many Conversions wrought by it, and its Power to draw down the Mercy of God upon Sinners, should strongly animate them with an humble and firm

firm Confidence of sharing of the Multitude of God's Mercies, provided they tread the Steps of the devout *Rosarists*. The good Christian will also find his Account in the Observance of those pious Works: for, you ought to *labour the more*, says the Prince of Apostles*, *that by good Works, you may make sure your Vocation and Election.*

A Man must indeed be lukewarm in the Service of God, and shamefully negligent of his eternal Welfare, who shall require to be pressed to partake of those invaluable Blessings, or to taste of those Torrents of Delight, which God has graciously prepared for those who love, praise and adore his most holy and ineffable Name. " When there-
" fore, (says S. *Charles Borromæus*, upon a similar
" occasion †) an Exercise of so great Piety is pro-
" posed to us, with an Occasion of obtaining so
" many heavenly Treasures....I exhort you all not
" to delay, but to give in your Names as soon as
" possible, into the Confraternity of the *Rosary*,
" animated by the Example of so many noble,
" pious and learned Men....to the Honour of
" God, ... and the Joy of the Catholic Church."

In short, Christian Reader, by being enrolled in the Sodality, by a strict Observance of its *Laws*, and by a devout and constant Recital of the *Rosary* of the most holy Name of *Jesus*, you will doubtless give great Glory to God, and reap inexpressible Rewards for yourselves: you will assuredly obtain every real Blessing you ask in his Name, and your grateful Remembrance of his sacred *Name*, will be crowned by the Grace of our *Lord Jesus Christ*
in

---

* 2 Pet. i. 10.   † In his Pastoral Letter 25th *March*, 1584. wherein he most strenuously recommends, and strictly commands the Recital of the Rosary of the B. Virgin in the Seminary, Nunneries, &c.

in this Life, and by an Eternity of Glory in the next. You have his faithful Promise for it: *Every one that calleth upon my Name*, says he, *I have created him for my Glory* *.

Let us therefore, says S. Paul, offer the sacrifice of Praise always to God, that is, the Fruit of Lips confessing his Name* †. To praise God's adorable Name is a most acceptable Sacrifice: 'tis the Language, 'tis the Employment of the Angels and Saints of Paradise. By accustoming ourselves to glorify the Name of *Jesus*, with Heart or Mouth, upon Earth, it will be quite familiar to us, when we happily arrive at the Regions of Bliss and Glory. Nay, in the Agony of Death, when the World with all its transitory Beings and momentary Pleasures, are bidding us an eternal Farewel, a devout Invocation of the most holy Name of *Jesus*, shall administer to the devout *Rosarist*, unutterable Comfort.

Nay, such shall be the ardent Wishes of the devout Rosarists, enamoured with the most august and amiable Name of *Jesus*, that they shall warmly petition for a Dissolution of the human Frame, for a Separation of the Soul from its tottering Mansion: that being delivered fom the oppressive Load of the Flesh, they may behold him Face to Face, glorify his all-sacred Name more fervently, and receive the unspeakable Rewards faithfully promised to those who have worthily praised it upon Earth. The Language of the Royal Psalmist will be that of those pious Souls to their *Jesus*, when, with the Heart or Mouth, they shall thus address him: *Bring my Soul out of Prison, that I may praise thy Name: the Just wait for me, until thou reward me* ‡. Oh, what unspeakable Comfort do these

* Isaiah xliii. 7.   † Heb. xiii. 15.   ‡ Psal. cxli. 8.

these Words convey to the Soul blessed with Resignation to the Will of God, and a Confidence in the Merits of his all-saving Name!

The devout Rosarist, thus disposed to quit his earthly Mansion, will not be unmindful to entreat *Jesus* who expired upon a Cross for his Salvation, to have Mercy on his departing Soul; and, with an humble Confidence in the Multitude of his tender Mercies, will beseech him thus, in the Words of St. *Stephen* Proto-martyr, *Lord Jesus, receive my Spirit* *.

The *Lord Jesus*, ever mindful of his Promises † to his faithful Servants, will not delay to grant their Requests: He will address them, as he did these trusty Servants mentioned in the Gospel‡: *Well done, thou good and faithful Servant, enter into the Joy of thy Lord.* The Soul will most chearfully obey this joyful Summons and wing its Way to the blissful Regions, where, like St. *Stephen*, you, O happy Soul, shall *see the Heavens open*, you shall be blessed with the Sight of *the Glory of God, and* Jesus *standing at the right Hand of God* §, inviting you to the perpetual Enjoyment of that endless Happiness prepared for you in his blessed Kingdom, where you shall incessantly and most harmoniously sing the Praises of his all-gracious and ineffable Name, with the blessed Choristers of the Celestial Regions for an endless Eternity! Happy State!

In short, the Rosary of the most holy Name of *Jesus* is a summary or brief Account of the Life, Sufferings, Death, Resurrection and Ascension of
Jesus

---

* Acts vii. 58. † Such as—*Every one that calleth upon my Name, I have created him for my Glory*—*you ask me any Thing in my Name, I will do it*—*Whoever shall invoke the Name of the Lord shall be saved.* ‡ Matth. xxv. 21. § Acts vii. 55.

Jesus Christ, and the glorious Triumphs attending these mysterious Truths, together with the Execution of the great Design he had in View, by assuming our Mortality, which was, to satisfy for our Sins, to enable us to work our Salvation, and to crown our good Deeds with eternal Bliss and Glory. All which is commemorated in the sacred Devotion. Besides, by a Repetition of the holy *Rosary*, we make an acceptable Return of Praise and Thanksgiving to his most sacred Name, for the unspeakable Favours and Blessings conferred upon us.

What Form of Prayer more acceptable to Heaven, what Employment more necessary or more useful to a Christian Soul, than a constant Recital of the Rosary inscribed to the most holy Name of *Jesus*? Do not the Ties of Duty, Gratitude, Interest and Necessity strongly enforce it? Let every Christian then, who hopes to enjoy an happy Eternity, form the following Resolution and endeavour to adhere strictly to it: *So will I sing a Psalm to thy Name for ever: that I may pay my Vows from Day to Day* *, by a devout and humble Offering of the Rosary of the Name of *Jesus*. And how justly! Since there is no *other Name under Heaven given to Men, whereby we must be saved*†.

If, O Christian Soul, 'tis through the Merits of Christ's most adorable Name, and by worthily praising it, we are to be saved, how can we possibly refuse or neglect to address him with that powerful Form of Prayer, the *Rosary*, sacred to his most holy Name, *Jesus*, as it cannot fail to prove most acceptable to him, and efficacious, to Admiration, for us. In short, let every Individual, who hopes to be blessed with the Sight and Enjoyment of God in

his

---

* Psal. lx. 9. † Acts iv. 12.

his Glory, say with the Royal Prophet[*]: *I will praise the Name of God with a Canticle.* I will praise thy Name, O *Jesus*, with that Canticle, that heavenly Form of Prayer, sacred to thy most august Name, that I may make some small Return for thy unparalleled Favours, and merit a Continuance of them; and that I may effectually partake of that plentiful Redemption, which thou hast mercifully brought to us, in Vertue of thy ineffable and all-saving Name.

It is through the Merits of thy glorious and all-saving Name, O *Jesus*, that we humbly hope to accomplish the great Work of our Salvation. Yea, *Save us, O Lord, our God: ...... that we may give Thanks to thy holy Name, and may glory in thy Praise. Blessed be the God of Israel from everlasting to everlasting: and let all the People say: So be it. So be it.*[‡]

---

[*] Psal. lxviii. 31.   [‡] Psal. cv. 47, 48.

THE

THE METHOD

Of Saying the

ROSARY

Of the Most Holy NAME of

JESUS,

AND THE

ROSARY

OF THE

BLESSED VIRGIN:

ACCORDING

To the FORMS prescribed By the Sovereign Pontiffs CLEMENT VIII, and St. PIUS V.

Praise ye the Lord, for the Lord is good: Sing ye to his Name, for it is sweet. Psalm cxxxiv. 3.

Hail Mary full of Grace: Our Lord is with Thee: Behold from henceforth all Generations shall call me Blessed. Luke i. 28, 48.

THE Rosaries of the most Holy Name of JESUS, and his Blessed Mother, are here carefully set down from the most approved Authors. —The Liberties taken by Printers and Booksellers to curtail from, or add to them, agreeable to their Caprice, is injurious to the sacred Devotions: Many shameful Omissions and unnecessary Additions have crept into the various Editions of both Rosaries, which may be corrected by a due Attention to them, as they are here set forth.

A PRAYER

Recommended to be repeated before the

ROSARY OF *JESUS*,

By Dr. LAWRENCE RICHARDSON.*

O THOU the Son and the Image of the Almighty Father, anointed Saviour of Mankind. O Thou who art †. O Jehovah. O Emanuel. O Adonai. O Thou the holy one. O Thou the dreadful one. O Thou the wonderful. O Thou our God. O Thou the strong one. O Thou the Prince of Peace. O Thou the Father of the future Age. We adore thee in all thy Names—But thou hast humbled thyself being made obedient unto Death, even the Death of the Cross. For which God hath exalted Thee and given Thee a Name above all Names, that in the Name of *Jesus* every Knee bend of those that are in

---

* In his Appendix to *The Manner of Hearing Mass*.
† That is, who hast thy Being independently. Exod. iii. 14.

in Heaven, on Earth, and in Hell. I offer Thee my Thanks for uniting me in this Holy Society. O grant me to partake of those Benefits which were obtained by the Merits of the glorious Order of St. *Dominick*. I purpose for ever to honour Thee in all thy sacred Names, and never to profane them. I purpose to hinder and prevent so great a Crime in others, to the best of my Ability. Inspire me with Reverence and Zeal to fulfil this Purpose. I implore Thee in Vertue of the Mysteries of thy most holy Rosary. O Thou the Son of *David*, miraculously made Man and born from the Womb of a Virgin. O Thou the King of the *Jews* who bore for me a most bitter Passion. O Thou the Son of the Living God, risen from Death, and the Judge of the Living and the Dead. Grant to me, and to all our Society to perform this great Devotion in the Spirit of thy Church, that we may duly celebrate thy mysterious Grandeurs and obtain Grace and Merit in this Life, and Happiness in the next, through Thee, who with the Father and Holy Ghost, livest and reignest one God for all Eternity. *Amen*.

THE ROSARY

Of the Most Holy NAME of

JESUS.

✠

In the Name of the Father, and of the Son, and of the Holy Ghost. *Amen.*

Vers. THOU, O Lord, wilt open my Lips.

Resp. And my Tongue shall announce thy Praise.

Vers. Incline unto my Aid, O God.

Resp. O Lord make haste to help me.

Glory be to the Father, and to the Son, and to the Holy Ghost.

As it was in the Beginning, is now, and will be for ever. *Amen. Alleluia* *.

* Which is said throughout the whole Year, except between *Septagessima Sunday* and *Thursday* in Holy Week; in which Time is said: *Praise be to Thee, O Lord, King of eternal Glory.*

The Five Mysteries of the First Part *.

I.

The Incarnation of our Lord Jesus Christ.

The Meditation.

THE Son of God assumes human Flesh, out of the pure Blood of the blessed *Mary*, ever Virgin, and is made Man in her Womb.

O Jesus, Son of *David*, have Mercy on us.

To be repeated ten times, and to conclude with,

Glory be to the Father, &c.

II. The

---

* They who do not say the whole Rosary at one Time, but divide it into three Parts, for three different Days, are to take Notice, that the first Part of the Rosary of *Jesus* is to be said on *Mondays* and *Thursdays* throughout the Year, on the *Sundays* in *Advent* and after *Epiphany* until *Lent*.

The second Part on *Tuesdays* and *Fridays*, throughout the Year, and the *Sundays* in *Lent*.

The third Part to be said on *Wednesdays* and *Saturdays*, throughout the Year; and on the *Sundays* after *Easter*, until *Advent*.

II.
The Birth of our Lord Jesus Christ.

The Meditation.

THE Saviour of the World is born for our Redemption: His Mother remaining a Virgin.

O Jesus, Son of *David*, have Mercy on us.
Ten Times.
Glory, &c.

III.
The Circumcision of our Lord Jesus Christ.

The Meditation.

OUR Saviour being eight Days old, begins to suffer for our Sins, and his Blood already flows for us. He is circumcised according to the Law, as if he had been himself a Sinner.

O Jesus, Son of *David*, have Mercy on us.
Ten Times.
Glory, &c.

IV. Our

IV.

Our Lord Jesus Christ is found in the Temple.

The Meditation.

OUR Saviour being twelve Years old, shews himself more than mortal, by his Knowledge and Wisdom, teaching the Teachers of the *Jews*.

O Jesus, Son of *David*, have Mercy on us.
Ten Times.

Glory, &c.

V.

The Baptism of our Lord Jesus Christ.

The Meditation.

THE Saviour of the World is baptised by St. *John*. The eternal Father declares him to be his Son.

O Jesus, Son of *David*, have Mercy on us.
Ten Times.

Glory, &c.

Let us pray.

O Jesus, whose Name is above all Names, that in the Name of Jesus, every Knee may bend of those that are in Heaven, on Earth or in Hell. Who at the Time appointed by the eternal Wisdom, assumed human Flesh in the Womb of the blessed *Mary* ever Virgin, and thus became the Son of *David*. Whose Birth gladdened Men and Angels. Who began so early to suffer for us, and to shed on our Account, that Blood that washeth away the Sins of the World. Whose immortal Wisdom appeared at the Age of twelve Years. To whose Baptism all Heaven was attentive, grant to us to celebrate those Mysteries to thy Honour, and our own Salvation. Who, with the Father, and Holy Ghost, livest and reignest, one God, for all Eternity. *Amen*.

The Five Mysteries of the Second Part.

I.

Our Saviour washeth his Disciples Feet.

The Meditation.

OUR Saviour to shew us an Example of Humility, and how much we ought to serve each other, descendeth so low, as to wash the Feet of his Disciples, tho' he is the God whom Heaven and Earth adore.

O Jesus

O Jesus of *Nazareth*, King of the *Jews*, have Mercy on us.   *Ten Times.*
Glory, &c.

II.

The Prayer of our Lord Jesus Christ in the Garden.

The Meditation.

OUR Saviour knowing his Passion to be now at Hand, is so affected with the Thoughts of it, and so oppressed by the Load of our Sins, that he prays to his Almighty Father, that the bitter Cup might pass away from him.

O Jesus of *Nazareth*, King of the *Jews*, have Mercy on us.   *Ten Times.*
Glory, &c.

III.

Our Saviour is apprehended.

The Meditation.

OUR Saviour, as if he had been no more than mortal Man, yields to the Power of Men, and permits himself for our Redemption, to be apprehended, as if he were a Malefactor.

O Jesus

O Jesus of *Nazareth*, King of the *Jews*, have Mercy on us. *Ten Times.*

Glory, &c.

IV.

Our Saviour carries his Cross.

The Meditation.

OUR Saviour being torn with Scourges, and pierced with Thorns, to expiate our Sins, is obliged to carry the Cross, on which he is to die, and moves on, labouring in Sorrow towards the Place of his Execution.

O Jesus of *Nazareth*, King of the *Jews*, have Mercy on us. *Ten Times.*

Glory, &c.

V.

The Descent of our Saviour into Hell.

The Meditation.

THE Soul of our Saviour being separated by Death from the Body, descends to that Place where the Saints were expecting his Redemption.

O Jesus of *Nazareth*, King of the *Jews*, have Mercy on us. *Ten Times.*

Glory, &c.

Let us pray.

O Jesus, whose Name is above all Names, that in the Name of Jesus, every Knee may bend, of those that are in Heaven, on Earth, and in Hell. Whose mysterious Humiliations and Sorrows appointed for thee, on account of our Sins, appeared in thy washing of the Feet of thy Servants and Creatures: in thy Distress and Prayer, and bloody Sweat: in thy being secured and brought before Courts as a Criminal: in thy bearing the Load of the Cross: and in the Separation of thy Soul from the Body, and its Descent to the Regions below, grant to us to celebrate these Mysteries, to thy Honour, and our own Salvation. Who, with the Father, and the Holy Ghost, livest and reignest, one God, for all Eternity. *Amen.*

The Five Mysteries of the Third Part.

I.

The Resurrection of our Lord Jesus Christ.

The Meditation.

THE Soul of our Lord Jesus Christ, which had been separated from the Body, is reunited to it by a Miracle of the Almighty

Almighty Power, and that Body which had been dead, rises to die no more.

O Jesus, Son of the living God, have Mercy on us. *Ten Times.*

Glory, &c.

II.

The Ascension of our Lord Jesus Christ.

The Meditation.

THE Body of our Lord Jesus Christ ascends into the high Heaven, where the Saviour of Mankind sits at the right Hand of God, the Almighty Father.

O Jesus, Son of the living God, have Mercy on us. *Ten Times.*

Glory, &c.

III.

Our Lord Jesus Christ sends down the Holy Ghost.

The Meditation.

OUR Saviour now seated at the right Hand of God, his Almighty Father, sends down the Holy Ghost, to inspire and animate his Disciples, that they may be qualified to publish to Mankind his Cross and his Glory.

O Jesus, Son of the living God, have Mercy on us. *Ten Times.*
Glory, &c.

IV.

Our Lord Jesus Christ crowning the blessed Virgin and Saints.

The Meditation.

OUR Saviour having by his Passion, Resurrection, and Ascension, opened the Way for the Sons of *Adam* to the Heaven which they had lost by Sin, bestows to his Mother and his Saints, a Crown of immortal Glory.

O Jesus, Son of the living God, have Mercy on us. *Ten Times.*
Glory, &c.

V.

Our Lord Jesus Christ coming to Judgment.

The Meditation.

OUR Saviour will come in Power and Majesty, to judge the Living and the Dead, and to return to every one according to his Works.

O Jesus, Son of the living God, have Mercy on us. *Ten Times.*
Glory, &c.

Let

Let us pray.

O *Jesus*, whose Name is above all Names, that in the Name of *Jesus*, every Knee may bend of those that are in Heaven, on Earth, and in Hell: whose Body that was murdered by Mankind, the Almighty raised from Death, glorious and immortal: who by thy Ascension, triumphed over Death, and held Captivity captive: who according to thy Promise, sent down the Spirit that proceedeth from the Father, and the Son, the Comforter and the Enlivener: who stretching forth the Bounty of thy Almighty Hand, shed upon the chosen Children of *Adam*, that Glory that neither Eye hath seen, nor Ear hath heard, nor hath it entered into the Heart of Man, and who will come forth in Power and Majesty, to judge the Living and the Dead, before whose Throne all Mortals will appear; grant to us to celebrate those Mysteries, to thy Honour, and our own Salvation, who with the Father and Holy Ghost, livest and reignest, one God, for all Eternity. *Amen.*

N. B. *The repeating of the above Prayers or Meditations, is not absolutely necessary. Those who cannot read or meditate on the Mysteries, let them say the* Creed *before-hand, in this Rosary and in that of the blessed Virgin.*

THE LITANY

OF THE

Most Holy Name of

JESUS.

LORD, have Mercy on us.
Christ, have Mercy on us.
Jesus, hear us.
Jesus, graciously hear us.
God the Father of Heaven,
God the Son, Redeemer of the World,
God the Holy Ghost,
Holy Trinity, one God,
Jesus Splendor of the Father,
Jesus Brightness of eternal Light,
Jesus King of Glory,
Jesus Sun of Justice,
Jesus Son of the Virgin *Mary*,

} Have Mercy on us.

Admirable Jesus,
Jesus the strong God,
Jesus Father of the future Age,
Jesus Angel of the great Council,
Jesus most powerful,
Jesus most obedient,
Jesus most patient,
Jesus meek and humble of Heart,
Jesus Lover of Chastity,
Jesus our Love,
Jesus Pattern of Virtues,
Jesus zealous Lover of Souls,
Jesus our God,
Jesus our Refuge,
Jesus Father of the Poor,
Jesus Treasure of the Faithful,
Jesus the good Shepherd,
Jesus the true Light,
Jesus eternal Wisdom,
Jesus infinite Goodness,
Jesus our Way and Life,
Jesus Joy of Angels,
Jesus Master of the Apostles,
Jesus Teacher of the Evangelists,
Jesus the Fortitude of Martyrs,
Jesus the Light of Confessors,
Jesus the Purity of Virgins,
Jesus the Crown of all Saints,
Jesus Son of *David*,
Jesus of *Nazareth*, King of the *Jews*,
Jesus Son of the living God,

} Have Mercy on us.

Lamb

Lamb of God, who takeſt away the Sins of the World,
>Spare us, O Jeſus.

Lamb of God, who takeſt away the Sins of the World,
>Hear us, O Jeſus.

Lamb of God, who takeſt away the Sins of the World,
>Have Mercy on us, O Jeſus.

V. Bleſſed be the Name of the Lord,
R. From now unto all Eternity.

Let us pray.

O God who haſt made the moſt glorious Name of Jeſus Chriſt thy Son our Lord, moſt lovely to thy Faithful, by the great and affecting Sweetneſs of it, and at the ſame Time dreadful to malignant Spirits; grant propitiouſly that all, who venerate it on Earth, may obtain the Sweetneſs of Conſolation for the preſent, and afterwards the Joy of Happineſs without End, through our Lord Jeſus Chriſt thy Son, who liveth and reigneth with thee, in the Unity of the Holy Ghoſt, through all Eternity. *Amen.*

N. B.

Pope *Sixtus* V. grants an Indulgence of three hundred Days to every one who devoutly says the above Litany. *Constitutione Reddituri.*

☞ *It is recommended, that the Faithful shall say the foregoing Litany so often as they repeat the Rosary of the Name of* Jesus, *and especially on the* second *Sunday of the Month, a Day particularly sacred to the Praises of his most adorable Name.*

The Pfalm and Hymn, to be fung at the Proceffion, made on the fecond Sunday of the Month, are here fet down, in Latin

Psal. CXII.

LAUDATE pueri Dominum: laudate nomen Domini.

Sit nomen Domini benedictum: ex hoc nunc, & ufque in fæculum.

A folis ortu ufque ad occafum: laudabile nomen Domini.

Excelfus fuper omnes gentes Dominus: & fuper cœlos gloria ejus.

Quis ficut Dominus Deus nofter, qui in altis habitat: & humilia refpicit in cœlo, & in terra?

Sufcitans a terra inopem, & de ftercore erigens pauperem.

Ut collocet eum cum principibus, cum principibus populi fui.

Qui habitare facit fterilem in domo, matrem filiorum lætantem.

Gloria Patri, &c.

Hymnus.

JESU noftra redemptio,
Amor, & defiderium:
Deus creator omnium,
Homo in fine temporum.

Quæ te vicit clementia;
Ut ferres noftra crimina,
Crudelem mortem patiens,
Ut nos a morte tolleres?

Inferni

and *English*, for the Convenience and Satisfaction of those who attend, or are present at it.

Psalm CXIII.

PRAISE, O ye Children, the Lord: praise the Name of the Lord.

Blessed be the Name of the Lord: from now unto all Eternity.

From the rising to the setting of the Sun: the Name of the Lord is worthy to be praised.

The Lord is high above all Nations: and his Glory is above the Heavens.

Who is like unto the Lord our God who dwelleth on high: and looketh upon humble Things in Heaven and on Earth?

Lifting up from the Earth the needy one: and raising the poor one from the Dung.

That he may place him amongst Princes: amongst the Princes of his People.

Who maketh the barren one dwell in the House: the joyful Mother of Sons.

Glory be to the Father, &c.

The Hymn.

JESUS to us Salvation brings,
 The God Creator of all Things:
The Object of our Love and Hope,
Compleats his full Design and Scope.

What Clemency in thee prevail'd,
To bear our Crimes which long we wail'd:
A cruel Death thou did'st endure,
That Souls from Death thou might'st secure?

L 5   *Into*

Inferni clauſtra penetrans,
Tuos captivos redimens,
Victor triumpho nobili,
Ad dextram Patris reſidens.

Ipſa te cogat pietas,
Ut mala noſtra ſuperes:
Parcendo, & voti compotes
Nos tuo vultu ſaties.

Gloria tibi Domine,
Qui natus es de Virgine;
Cum Patre et Sancto Spiritu,
In ſempiterna ſæcula. *Amen*.

At Eaſter time, inſtead of the laſt

Quæſumus auctor omnium
In hoc Paſchali gaudio,
Ab omni mortis impetu
Tuum defende populum.

Gloria tibi Domine,
Qui ſurrexiſti a mortuis;
Cum Patre & Sancto Spiritu,
In ſempiterna ſæcula. *Amen*.

The Hymn, *Pange Lingua* (compoſed by St. *Thomas* of *Aquin*, *Opuſcul.* 57.) ſung at the *Benediction*; as it is found tranſ-

HYMNUS.

PANGE lingua glorioſi
 Corporis myſterium,
Sanguiniſque pretioſi,
Quem in mundi pretium

Fructus

Into the Deep thou did'st descend,
That captive Souls should thence ascend:
Then glorious triumphant shone,
Sitting on thy Father's Throne.

May Pity still thy Breast possess,
Our many Evils to redress:
Grant, through thy Mercy, we may see
Thy sacred Face eternally.

To thee be Glory and Praises sung,
Jesu, who from a Virgin sprung:
The like to God the Father be,
And Paraclete eternally. Amen.

Strophe, *the two following are sung.*

We pray thee, Author of all Things,
Whose Paschal Feast glad Tidings brings:
From every Ill of Death defend,
That so our Lives may safely end.

Lord! who from the Dead hast risen,
Be Glory, Praise and Honour given:
The like to God the Father be,
And Holy Ghost eternally. Amen.

lated in our *Lady's Primer*, in honour of the most holy *Sacrament*.

HYMN.

SING, O my Tongue, adore and praise
The Depth of God's mysterious Ways:
How Christ, the Gentiles King, bestow'd
His Flesh conceal'd in human Food;

And

Fructus ventris generosi
Rex effudit gentium.

Nobis datus, nobis natus
Ex intacta Virgine,
Et in mundo conversatus,
Sparso verbi semine,
Sui moras incolatus
Miro clausit ordine.

In supremæ nocte cœnæ
Recumbens cum fratribus,
Observata lege plenè
Cibis in legalibus :
Cibum turbæ duodenæ
Se dat suis manibus.

Verbum caro, panem verum
Verbo carnem efficit :
Fitque sanguis Christi merum,
Et si sensus deficit,
Ad firmandum cor sincerum
Sola fides sufficit.

Tantum ergo Sacramentum
Veneremur cernui :
Et antiquum documentum
Novo cedat ritui :
Præstet fides supplementum
Sensuum defectui.

Genitori, Genitoque,
Laus, & Jubilatio,
Salus, Honor, Virtus quoque,
Sit & Benedictio ;
Procedenti ab utroque
Compar sit laudatio. *Amen.*

Vers.

*And left Mankind the Blood, that paid
The Ransom of the Souls he made.*

*Born from above, and born for Man,
From Virgin's Womb his Life began:
He liv'd on Earth, and preach'd, to sow
The Seeds of heavenly Truth below;
Then seal'd his Mission, from above,
With strange Effects of Power and Love.*

*'Twas on that Ev'ning, when the last
And most mysterious Supper past;
When Christ with his Disciples sat
To close the Law with legal Meat;
And with his Hands himself bestow'd
The Christian's Food, and Lamb of God.*

*The Word made Flesh for Love of Man,
With Words, of Bread, made Flesh again;
Turn'd Wine to Blood, unseen by Sense,
By Virtue of Omnipotence;
And here the Faithful rest secure,
Whilst God can vouch, and Faith ensure.*

*To this mysterious Table now
Our Knees, our Hearts, and Sense we bow:
Let ancient Rites resign their Place
To nobler Elements of Grace;
And Faith for all Defects supply,
Whilst Sense is lost in Mystery.*

*To God the Father, born of none,
To Christ his co-eternal Son,
And Holy Ghost, whose equal Rays
From both proceed, one equal Praise;
One Honour, Jubilee, and Fame,
For ever bless thy glorious Name.* Amen.

Vers.

Verſ. Panem de cœlo præſtitiſti eis.

Reſp. Omne delectamentum in ſe habentem.

ORATIO.

DEUS, qui nobis ſub Sacramento mirabili, Paſſionis tuæ memoriam reliquiſti: tribue quæſumus, ita nos corporis & ſanguinis tui ſacra myſteria venerari; ut redemptionis tuæ fructum in nobis jugiter ſentiamus. Qui vivis & regnas, &c.

Verf. *Thou haft given them Bread from Heaven.*

Refp. *Filled with all Delight.*

The Prayer.

O God, *who in this wonderful Sacrament, haft left us a perpetual Remembrance of thy Paſſion: Grant us, we beſeech thee, ſo to reverence the ſacred Myſteries of thy Body and Blood, that in our Souls we may be always ſenſible of the Fruit of thy Redemption. Who liveſt and reigneſt, &c.*

THE ROSARY

OF THE

BLESSED VIRGIN.

✠

In the Name of the Father, and of the Son, and of the Holy Ghost. *Amen.*

Verſ. HAIL *Mary*, full of Grace, our Lord is with thee.
Reſp. Bleſſed art thou amongſt Women, and bleſſed is the Fruit of thy Womb, Jeſus.
Verſ. Thou, O Lord, wilt open my Lips:
Reſp. And my Tongue ſhall announce thy Praiſe.
Verſ. Incline unto my Aid, O God:
Reſp. O Lord, make Haſte to help me.
Glory be to the Father, and to the Son, and to the Holy Ghoſt.

As

As it was in the Beginning, is now, and ever shall be. *Amen.*

Alleluia.

Except from Septuagessima to Easter, then say; Praise be to Thee, O Lord, King of eternal Glory.

The FIRST PART.
The five Joyful Mysteries *.

THE FIRST MYSTERY.
The Annunciation.

THE MEDITATION.

LET us contemplate in this Mystery, how the Angel *Gabriel* saluted our blessed Lady, with the Title of, Full of Grace; and declared unto her the Incarnation of our Lord and Saviour Jesus Christ.

Then say; Our Father, &c. *once.* Hail Mary, &c. *ten Times.*

OUR Father who art in Heaven. Hallowed be thy Name. Thy Kingdom come.

---

* The five Mysteries of the first Part, called *Joyful*, to be said on all *Mondays* and *Thursdays*; the *Sundays* of *Advent*, and after *Epiphany*, till *Lent*.

come. Thy will be done on Earth, as it is in Heaven. Give us this Day our daily Bread. And forgive us our Trespasses, as we forgive them that trespass against us. And lead us not into Temptation, but deliver us from Evil. *Amen*.

HAIL *Mary* full of Grace, our Lord is with thee; blessed art thou amongst Women, and blessed is the Fruit of thy Womb, JESUS. Holy *Mary*, Mother of God, pray for us Sinners, now, and in the Hour of our Death. *Amen.*

When the Hail Mary *is repeated a tenth Time, the* Decade *finishes with*, Glory be to the Father, &c. *then follows the Prayer* *.

Let us pray.

O Holy *Mary*, Queen of Virgins, by the most high Mystery of the Incarnation of thy beloved Son, our Lord Jesus Christ, by which our Salvation was so happily begun: obtain for us by thy Intercession, Light to know this so great a Benefit, which he hath bestowed upon us; vouchsafing in it to make himself our Brother, and thee, his own most beloved Mother, our Mother also. *Amen.*

II. *The*

---

* Which Method is to be observed in beginning and saying each Part of the Rosary.

II.
The Visitation.

LET us contemplate in this Mystery, how the blessed Virgin *Mary* understanding from the Angel, that her Cousin St. *Elizabeth* had conceived, went with Haste into the Mountains of *Judea*, to visit her, and remained with her three Months.

Our Father, &c.

Let us pray.

O Holy Virgin, most spotless Mirror of Humility; by that exceeding Charity, which moved thee to visit thy holy Cousin St. *Elizabeth*, obtain for us by thy Intercession, that our Hearts may be so visited by thy most holy Son, that being free from all Sin, we may praise him, and give him Thanks for ever. *Amen.*

III.
The Birth of our Lord Jesus Christ, in Bethlehem.

LET us contemplate in this Mystery, how the blessed Virgin *Mary*, when the Time of her Delivery was come, brought forth our Redeemer, Christ Jesus, at Midnight, and laid him in a Manger, because there was no Room for him in the Inns at *Bethlehem*.

Our Father, &c. *Let*

Let us pray.

O Most pure Mother of God, by thy virginal and most joyful Delivery, in which thou gavest unto the World, thy only Son our Saviour, we beseech thee, obtain for us, by thy Intercession, Grace to lead such pure and holy Lives in this World, that we may worthily sing, without ceasing, both Day and Night, the Mercies of thy Son, and his Benefits to us by thee. *Amen.*

IV.

The Oblation of our blessed Lord in the Temple.

LET us contemplate in this Mystery, how the most blessed Virgin *Mary*, on the Day of her Purification, presented the Child Jesus in the Temple, where holy *Simeon*, giving Thanks to God, with great Devotion, received him into his Arms.

Our Father, &c.

Let us pray.

O Holy Virgin, most admirable Mistress and Pattern of Obedience, who didst present in the Temple, the Lord of the Temple, obtain for us of thy beloved Son, that with holy *Simeon* and devout *Anne*, we may praise and glorify him for ever. *Amen.*

V.

The finding of the Child Jesus in the Temple.

LET us contemplate in this Mystery, how the blessed Virgin *Mary*, having lost without any Fault of hers, her beloved Son in *Jerusalem*, she sought him for the space of three Days, and at length found him the fourth Day in the Temple, in the midst of the Doctors, disputing with them, being of the Age of twelve Years.

Our Father, &c.

Let us pray.

MOST blessed Virgin, more than Martyr in thy Sufferings, and yet the Comfort of such as are afflicted, by that unspeakable Joy, wherewith thy Soul was ravished in finding thy beloved Son in the Temple, in the midst of the Doctors, disputing with them; obtain of him for us, so to seek him, and to find him in the holy Catholic Church, that we may never be separated from him. *Amen.*

Salve Regina.

HAIL holy Queen, Mother of Mercy, our Life, our Sweetness and our Hope; to thee do we cry, poor banished Sons of *Eve*; to thee do we send up our Sighs,

Sighs, mourning and weeping in this Valley of Tears. Turn then, most gracious Advocate, thy Eyes of Mercy towards us, and after this our Exile ended, shew unto us the blessed Fruit of thy Womb, Jesus. O clement, O pious, O sweet Virgin *Mary*.

Vers. Pray for us, holy Mother of God.

Resp. That we may be made worthy of the Promises of Christ.

Let us pray.

O God, whose only begotten Son, by his Life, Death and Resurrection, has purchased for us the Rewards of eternal Life; grant, we beseech thee, that meditating upon those Mysteries, in the most holy Rosary of the blessed Virgin *Mary*, we may imitate what they contain, and obtain what they promise, through the same Christ our Lord. *Amen.*

☞ This Prayer was formed, for the Rosary of the Blessed Virgin, by the express Order of Pope *Benedict* XIII. and by him approved as most suitable to the sacred Devotion, and more expressive of its Design. It is, therefore, now universally adopted and read in Catholic Countries, as well in Celebrating the Solemnity of the *Rosary*, as in the Recital of the *Devotion*. Hence, in Conformity to the Sovereign Pontiff's pious Intention and the general Practice of the Church, it is here substituted in place of the former Prayer, *Hear, O merciful God, &c.*

The

The SECOND PART.
The five Dolorous Mysteries*.

I.

The Prayer and bloody Sweat of our blessed Saviour in the Garden.

LET us contemplate in this Mystery, how our Lord Jesus Christ was so afflicted for us in the Garden of *Gethsemani*, that his Body was bathed in a bloody Sweat, which ran trickling down in great Drops to the Ground.

Our Father, &c.
Hail *Mary*, &c. } as before.
Glory, &c.

Let us pray.

MOST holy Virgin more than Martyr, by that ardent Prayer, which thy only and most beloved Son poured forth unto his Father in the Garden, vouchsafe to intercede for us, that our Passions being reduced to the Obedience of Reason, we may always, and in all things, conform and subject ourselves to the Will of God. *Amen.*

II. *The*

---

* These five Mysteries of the second Part, called *Dol.rous* or *Sorrowful*, to be said on *Tuesdays* and *Fridays* throughout the Year, and *Sundays* in *Lent*.

II.

The Scourging of our blessed Lord at the Pillar.

LET us contemplate in this Mystery, how our Lord Jesus Christ was most cruelly scourged in *Pilate*'s House, the Number of Stripes they gave him being above five Thousand.

[As it was revealed to St. *Bridget*.]
Our Father, &c.

Let us pray.

O Mother of God, overflowing Fountain of Patience, by those Stripes thy only and most beloved Son vouchsafed to suffer for us; obtain of him for us Grace, that we may know how to mortify our rebellious Senses, and cut off all Occasions of Sinning, with that Sword of Grief and Compassion, which pierced thy most tender Soul. *Amen.*

III.

The Crowning of our blessed Saviour with Thorns.

LET us contemplate in this Mystery, how those cruel Ministers of Satan platted a Crown of sharp Thorns, and most cruelly

cruelly pressed it on the most sacred Head of our Lord Jesus Christ.

Our Father, &c.

Let us pray.

O Mother of our eternal Prince, and King of Glory, by those sharp Thorns wherewith his most holy Head was pierced, we beseech thee, that by thy Intercession, we may be delivered here from all Motions of Pride, and in the Day of Judgment from that Confusion which our Sins deserve. *Amen.*

IV.

Jesus carrying the Cross.

LET us contemplate in this Mystery, how our Lord Jesus Christ, being sentenced to die, bore with the most amazing Patience the Cross which was laid upon him for his greater Torment and Ignominy.

Our Father, &c.

Let us pray.

O Holy Virgin, Example of Patience, by the most painful carrying of the Cross in which thy Son our Lord Jesus Christ bore the heavy Weight of our Sins, obtain of him for us, by thy Intercession, Courage

rage and Strength to follow his Steps, and bear our Cross after him to the End of our Lives. *Amen.*

V.

The Crucifixion of our Lord Jesus Christ.

LET us contemplate in this Mystery, how our Lord and Saviour Jesus Christ, being come to *Mount Calvary*, was stript of his Cloaths, and his Hands and Feet most cruelly nailed to the Cross, in the Presence of his most afflicted Mother.

Our Father, &c.

Let us pray.

O Holy *Mary*, Mother of God, as the Body of thy beloved Son was for us extended on the Cross, so may our Desires be daily more and more stretched out in his Service, and our Hearts wounded with Compassion of his most bitter Passion: And thou, O most blessed Virgin, graciously vouchsafe to help us to accomplish the Work of our Salvation, by thy powerful Intercession. *Amen.*

Hail holy Queen, &c. with the *Verse* and *Prayer*, as before.

The THIRD PART.
The Five Glorious Mysteries *.

I.
The Resurrection of Christ from the Dead.

LET us contemplate in this Mystery, how our Lord Jesus Christ, triumphing gloriously over Death, rose again the third Day immortal and impassible.

Our Father, &c.
Hail *Mary*, &c. } as before.
Glory, &c.

Let us pray.

O Glorious Virgin *Mary*, by that unspeakable Joy thou receivedst in the Resurrection of thy only Son, we beseech thee, obtain of him for us, that our Hearts may never go astray after the false Joys of this World, but may be ever and wholly in the Pursuit of the only true and solid Joys of Heaven. *Amen.*

II.
The Ascension of Christ into Heaven.

LET us contemplate in this Mystery, how our Lord Jesus Christ, forty Days after

---

* These Mysteries are assigned for *Wednesdays* and *Saturdays* through the Year, and *Sundays* from *Easter* until *Advent*.

after his Resurrection, ascended into Heaven, attended by Angels, in the Sight of his most holy Mother, his holy Apostles and Disciples, to the great Admiration of them all.

Our Father, &c.

Let us pray.

O Mother of God, Comfort of the Afflicted, as thy beloved Son, when he ascended into Heaven, lifted up his Hands, and blessed his Apostles: So vouchsafe, most holy Mother, to lift up thy pure Hands to him for us, that we may enjoy the Benefit of his Blessing, and thine here on Earth, and hereafter in Heaven. *Amen.*

III.

The Coming of the Holy Ghost to the Disciples.

LET us contemplate in this Mystery, how our Lord Jesus Christ, being seated at the right Hand of God, sent, as he had promised, the Holy Ghost upon the Apostles, who, after he was ascended, returning to *Jerusalem*, continued in Prayer and Supplication with the blessed Virgin *Mary*, expecting the Performance of his Promise.

Our Father, &c.

Let us pray.

O Sacred Virgin, Tabernacle of the Holy Ghost, we beseech thee, obtain by thy Intercession, that this most sweet Comforter, whom thy beloved Son sent down upon his Apostles, filling them thereby with spiritual Joy, may teach us in this World, the true Way of Salvation, and make us walk in the Paths of Virtue and good Works.

IV.

The Assumption of the blessed Virgin Mary into Heaven.

LET us contemplate in this Mystery, how the glorious Virgin, twelve Years after the Resurrection of her Son, passed out of this World unto him, and was by him assumed into Heaven, accompanied by the holy Angels.

Our Father, &c.

Let us pray.

O Most prudent Virgin, who entering into the Heavenly Palace, didst fill the holy Angels with Joy, and Man with Hope; vouchsafe to intercede for us in the Hour of Death, that free from the Illusions and Temptations of the Devil, we may joyfully and

and successfully pass out of this temporal State, to enjoy the Happiness of eternal Life. *Amen.*

V.

The Coronation of the most blessed Virgin Mary *in Heaven.*

LET us contemplate in this Mystery, how the glorious Virgin *Mary* was with great Jubilee and Exultation of the whole Court of Heaven, and particular Glory of all the Saints, crowned by her Son, with the brightest Diadem of Glory.

Our Father, &c.

Let us pray.

O Glorious Queen of all the Heavenly Citizens, we beseech thee, accept this *Rosary*, which as a Crown of Roses we offer at thy Feet; and grant most gracious Lady, that by thy Intercession, our Souls may be inflamed with so ardent a Desire of seeing thee so gloriously crowned, that it may never die in us, until it shall be changed into the happy Fruition of thy blessed Sight. *Amen.*

Hail holy Queen, &c. with the *Verse* and *Prayer,* as before.

NOTE.

Those who are in the Society or Confraternity of the Rosary of the Blessed Virgin, may have a plenary Indulgence,

The Day they are received.

Any one Time of this Life that they please to pitch upon.

At the Hour of their Death.

Every first Sunday *of the Month.*

Every Day of the fifteen Mysteries.

And for saying the Rosary, for one Hour, once in the Year.

Besides several other Indulgences.

Note, *The great Solemnity of this Devotion, is on the first* Sunday *of* October, *called* Rosary Sunday.

☞ Whoever doubts, and is willing to satisfy himself with regard to the Excellency and Efficacy of this Devotion, let him read the pious Work intitled, *An Introduction to the celebrated Devotion of the most holy Rosary of the Blessed Virgin, &c.* by the Rev. *John Clarkeson*, of the holy Order of Preachers.

THE

THE LITANY OF OUR BLESSED LADY.

ANTHEM.

WE fly under thy Patronage, O sacred Mother of God, despise not our Prayers in our Necessities, but deliver us from all Dangers, O ever glorious and blessed Virgin.

Lord, have Mercy on us.
Christ, have Mercy on us.
Lord, have Mercy on us.
Christ hear us.
Christ graciously hear us.
God the Father of Heaven, have Mercy on us.
God the Son, Redeemer of the World, have Mercy on us.
God the Holy Ghost, have Mercy on us.
Holy Trinity, one God, have Mercy on us.

Holy *Mary*,
Holy Mother of God,
Holy Virgin of Virgins,
Mother of Christ,
Mother of divine Grace,
Most pure Mother,
Most chaste Mother,
Inviolated Mother,
Unspotted Mother,
Amiable Mother,
Admirable Mother,
Mother of our Creator,
Mother of our Saviour,
Most prudent Virgin,
Virgin to be venerated,
Virgin to be praised,
Powerful Virgin,
Clement Virgin,
Faithful Virgin,
Mirror of Justice,
Seat of Wisdom,
Cause of our Joy,
Spiritual Vessel,
Honourable Vessel,
Rare Vessel of Devotion,
Mystical Rose,
Tower of *David*,
Tower of Ivory,
Golden House,
Ark of the Covenant,
Gate of Heaven,

} Pray for us.

Morning

Morning Star,
Health of the Sick,
Refuge of Sinners,
Comfortress of the Afflicted,
Help of Christians,
Queen of Angels,
Queen of Patriarchs,
Queen of Prophets,
Queen of Apostles,
Queen of Martyrs,
Queen of Confessors,
Queen of Virgins,
Queen of all Saints,
Queen of the most sacred Rosary,
} Pray for us.

Lamb of God, who takest away the Sins of the World,
    Spare us, O Lord.

Lamb of God, who takest away the Sins of the World,
    Graciously hear us, O Lord.

Lamb of God, who takest away the Sins of the World,
    Have Mercy on us.

ANTHEM.

ANTHEM.

WE fly under thy Patronage, O sacred Mother of God: Despise not our Prayers in our Necessities, but deliver us from all Dangers, O ever glorious and blessed Virgin.

ANGELUS DOMINI.

Vers. THE Angel of the Lord declared unto *Mary*.

Resp. And she conceived by the Holy Ghost. Hail *Mary*, &c.

Vers. Behold the Hand-maid of the Lord.

Resp. Be it unto me according to thy Word. Hail *Mary*, &c.

Vers. And the Word was made Flesh.

Resp. And dwelt amongst us. Hail *Mary*, &c.

Vers. Pray for us, holy Mother of God.

Resp. That we may be made worthy of the Promises of Christ.

Let us pray.

POUR forth we beseech thee, O Lord, thy Grace into our Hearts, that we, who by the Message of an Angel have Knowledge

ledge of the Incarnation of thy Son, by his Crofs and Paffion, may be brought to the Glory of his Refurrection. Through the fame Chrift our Lord. *R. Amen.*

V. May the divine Affiftance remain always with us. *R. Amen.*
V. And may the Souls of the Faithful, through the Mercy of God, reft in Peace. *R. Amen.*

May the Bleffing of the Father, and of the Son, and of the Holy Ghoft, defcend upon us, and remain always with us. *Amen.*

The Canticle *Magnificat*, sung at the Procession made on the *first* Sunday of the

S. LUC. 1.

MAGNIFICAT anima mea Dominum.

Et exultavit spiritus meus, in Deo salutari meo.

Quia respexit humilitatem ancillæ suæ: ecce enim, ex hoc beatam me dicent omnes generationes.

Quia fecit mihi magna, qui potens est: & sanctum nomen ejus.

Et misericordia ejus a progenie in progenies, timentibus eum.

Fecit potentiam in brachio suo: dispersit superbos mente cordis sui.

Deposuit potentes de sede: & exaltavit humiles.

Esurientes implevit bonis: & divites dimisit inanes.

Suscepit *Israel* puerum suum: recordatus misericordiæ suæ;

Sicut locutus est ad Patres nostros: *Abraham*, & semini ejus in secula.

Gloria Patri, &c.

Month, by the Brethren of the Rosary of the Blessed Virgin, in *Latin* and *English*.

S. LUKE 1.

*M*Y *Soul doth magnify the Lord.*

And my Spirit hath rejoiced in God my Saviour.

Because he hath looked upon the Humility of his Handmaid: for behold, from henceforth all Generations shall call me Blessed.

Because he that is the Mighty, hath done great things to me: and holy is his Name.

And his Mercy on them that fear him, from Generation to Generation.

He hath shewn Might in his Arm: he hath dispersed the Proud in the Imagination of their Heart.

He hath deposed the Powerful from the Throne, and those of an humble Condition he hath exalted.

He hath filled the Hungry with good Things: and the Rich he hath sent away empty.

He hath favoured his Servant Israel, being mindful of his Mercy;

As he spoke to our Fore-fathers, Abraham, and to his Seed for ever.

Glory be to the Father, &c.

At

At the Request of some pious Persons who attend at Complin, *which is sung on the Evenings of Sundays and principal Feasts in our Chapel, the following* Hymns, Antiphons, *&c. peculiar to our Chapel, are*

HYMNUS.

TE lucis ante terminum,
   Rerum Creator poscimus
Ut solita clementia,
Sis præsul ad custodiam.

Procul recedant somnia
Et noctium phantasmata;
Hostemque nostrum comprime,
Ne polluantur corpora.

Præsta Pater Omnipotens,
Per Jesum Christum Dominum,
Qui tecum in perpetuum
Regnat cum Sancto Spiritu. *Amen.*

In Solemnitatibus B. Mariæ Virginis.

Maria Mater Gratiæ,
Mater Misericordiæ;
Tu nos ab hoste protege,
Et hora mortis suscipe.

Gloria, tibi Domine,
Qui natus es de Virgine;
Cum Patre, & Sancto Spiritu
In sempiterna sæcula. *Amen.*

set down in Latin *and* English.——*As the* Psalms *of* Complin *are to be found in most Prayer-books, they are here omitted for Brevity's sake.—The following Hymn is generally sung through the Year.*

AN HYMN.

*O God, before the Close of Day,
We beg thy usual Mercies may
Direct us with thy purer Light,
Through all the Dangers of the Night.*

*Suppress our Foes infernal Arts,
Lest sensual Dreams defile our Hearts
With vain deluding Thoughts, that creep
On heedless Minds disarm'd with Sleep.*

*Grant, Mighty Father, what we pray
Through Jesus Christ, without Delay,
Who with the Holy Ghost and thee
Reigns God for all Eternity.* Amen.

On the Feasts of the Blessed Virgin, instead of the last Verse, the two following are sung.

*Mother of Grace, we thee invoke,
To shield us from old Satan's Yoke;
Mother of Mercy, we humbly crave,
At the last Hour our Souls to save.*

*To thee be Glory and Praises sung,
Jesu, who from a Virgin sprung;
The like to God the Father be,
And Holy Ghost eternally.* Amen.

The following Hymn is sung at *Complin*, from the first Sunday in *Lent*, until Wednesday in Holy Week.

HYMNUS.

CHRISTE, qui lux es, & dies,
Noctis tenebras detegis,
Lucifque lumen crederis,
Lumen beatum prædicans.

Precamur, sancte Domine,
Defende nos in hac nocte:
Sit nobis in te requies,
Quietam noctem tribue.

Ne gravis somnus irruat,
Nec hostis nos subripiat,
Nec caro illi consentiens,
Nos tibi reos statuat.

Oculi somnum capiant,
Cor ad te semper vigilet:
Dextera tua protegat
Famulos, qui te diligunt.

Defensor noster aspice,
Insidiantes reprime:
Guberna tuos famulos,
Quos Sanguine mercatus es.

Memento, nostri Domine,
In gravi isto corpore:
Qui es defensor animæ,
Adesto nobis Domine.

THE

HYMN.

O Christ, who art our Day and Light,
   Dispel the Darkness of the Night:
The Light of Light we thee proclaim,
Thou, sacred Light, shalt be our Theme!

We pray, O Lord, that with thy Might,
Thou wilt protect us all this Night:
Let our Repose be fixed in thee,
Undisturbed, from Dangers free.

Lest heavy Sleep shou'd us oppress,
Or Satan us by Stealth possess,
To him let Nature ne'er consent,
Nor guilty Souls to thee present.

Whilst Sleep our wearied Limbs doth ease,
Our Hearts may never cease to praise:
May thy strong Arm protect us all,
Who love and on thee loudly call.

Divine Protector, us behold,
Disperse all those of Satan's Fold:
Direct thy Servants all to thee,
Whom with thy Blood thou did'st set free.

Remember us, O Lord, we pray,
Laden with this Body of Clay:
Hasten to us, we humbly crave,
O holy Lord! our Souls to save.

Præsta Pater Omnipotens,
Per Jesum Christum Dominum :
Qui tecum in perpetuum,
Regnat cum Sancto Spiritu. *Amen.*

Antiph.

SALVE Regina, Mater Misericordiæ, vita, dulcedo, & spes nostra salve. Ad te clamamus exules filii *Hevæ.* Ad te suspiramus gementes & flentes in hac lacrymarum valle. Eja ergo advocata nostra, illos tuos misericordes oculos ad nos converte. Et Jesum benedictum fructum ventris tui nobis post hoc exilium ostende. O clemens, O pia, O dulcis Virgo *Maria.*

V. Dignare me laudare te, Virgo sacrata.
R. Da mihi virtutem contra Hostes tuos.

Oremus.

CONCEDE nos famulos tuos, quæsumus Domine Deus, perpetua mentis, & corporis salute gaudere, & gloriosa beatæ *Mariæ* semper Virginis intercessione, a præsenti liberari tristitia; & æterna perfrui lætitia. Per Christum Dominum nostrum. *Amen.*

Commemoratio S. Crucis.

CRUCEM sanctam subiit, qui infernum confregit : accinctus est potentia, surrexit die tertia.

V. Ado-

Grant, mighty Father, what we pray,
Through Jesus Christ, without Delay:
Who with the Holy Ghost and thee,
Reigns God for all Eternity. Amen.

The Hymn, *Jesu nostra redemptio*, &c. p. 220, is sung during the Time of *Easter* until *Trinity Sunday*.

Antiph.

HAIL holy Queen, Mother of Mercy; our Life, our Sweetness, and our Hope. To thee do we cry, poor banished Sons of Eve. To thee we send up our Sighs, Mournings and Weepings in this Valley of Tears. Turn then, most gracious Advocate, thy Eyes of Mercy towards us; and after this our Exile ended, shew unto us the blessed Fruit of thy Womb, Jesus. O clement, O pious, O sweet Virgin Mary.

V. *Make me worthy to praise thee, O sacred Virgin.*
R. *Give me Power against thy Enemies.*

Let us pray.

O Lord God! grant to us, thy Servants, to enjoy a constant Health of Mind and Body, and that through the glorious Intercession of the blessed Mary ever Virgin, we may be freed from present Sadness, and possess eternal Joys. Through Christ our Lord. Amen.

A Commemoration of the holy Cross.

HE bore the holy Cross, who subdued Hell: He is armed with Power, and arose the third Day.

V. *We*

℣. Adoramus te *Christe*, & benedicimus tibi.
℟. Quia per Crucem tuam redemisti Mundum.

Oremus.

DEUS, qui pro nobis Filium tuum Crucis patibulum subire voluisti, ut inimici a nobis expelleres potestatem, concede nobis famulis tuis, ut Resurrectionis gratiam consequamur. Per eundem Christum Dominum nostrum. *Amen*.

Commemoratio S. *Dominici.*

O Lumen Ecclesiæ, Doctor Veritatis, Rosa Patientiæ, Ebur Castitatis, Aquam Sapientiæ, propinasti gratis: Prædicator gratiæ, nos junge beatis.

℣. Ora pro nobis beate Pater *Dominice*.
℟. Ut digni efficiamur promissionibus Christi.

Oremus.

CONCEDE quæsumus Omnipotens Deus, ut qui peccatorum nostrorum pondere premimur, beati *Dominici* Confessoris tui patris nostri, patrocinio sublevemur. Per Christum Dominum nostrum. *Amen*.

F I N I S.

V. *We adore thee,* O Christ, *and bless thee.*
R. *For by thy Cross thou hast redeemed the World.*

Let us pray.

O God, *who wert willing, for our Sakes, thy Son should bear the Gibbet of the Cross, to free us from the Power of the Enemy; grant to us, thy Servants, that we may obtain the Grace of an happy Resurrection. Through the same Christ our Lord.* Amen.

A Commemoration of St. *Dominick.*

O Light *of the Church, Teacher of Truth, Rose of Patience, Chaste as Ivory, thou hast charitably tendered to us the Waters of Wisdom: Preacher of Grace, join us to the Blessed.*

V. *Pray for us, O blessed Father* Dominick.
R. *That we may be made worthy of the Promises of Christ.*

Let us pray.

GRANT *we beseech thee, O omnipotent God, that we who are oppressed by the Weight of our Sins, may be relieved by the Patronage of the blessed Father* Dominick, *thy Confessor. Through Christ our Lord.* Amen.

THE END.

www.ingramcontent.com/pod-product-compliance
Lightning Source LLC
Chambersburg PA
CBHW031952230426
43672CB00010B/2134